# ANDREA LEADSOM

## SNAKES AND LADDERS

### NAVIGATING THE UPS AND DOWNS OF POLITICS

Biteback Publishing

This paperback edition first published in Great Britain in 2023 by
Biteback Publishing Ltd, London
Copyright © Andrea Leadsom 2022, 2023

ISBN 978-1-78590-795-1

10 9 8 7 6 5 4 3 2 1

A CIP catalogue record for this book is available from the British Library.

Set in Adobe Garamond Pro and Regulator Nova

Printed and bound in Great Britain by
CPI Group (UK) Ltd, Croydon CR0 4YY

FSC
www.fsc.org
MIX
Paper | Supporting
responsible forestry
FSC® C171272

*To my great friend Peter Warner, who was a brilliant man and a loyal friend. He passed away in 2020 – far too young.*

# CONTENTS

# PREFACE

I had just finished a meeting with the Warwick University Politics Society. It was late, very dark and I was tired as I drove the ninety-minute journey home with my new apprentice, Harry. He had come with me to see what it was all about, and he was asking about my three years at Warwick studying Political Science almost forty years earlier, when a highlight was the visit by Margaret Thatcher to open the arts centre, and when a career in politics seemed so exciting. I was reflecting on the enthusiasm of the students we had met that evening and how optimistic they were, as I was all those years ago. 'Your phone is ringing,' said Harry. A name flashed up – Rishi Sunak. I took the call on handsfree, wondering why the Chancellor was calling me, and why so late.

'Hi Andrea,' came Rishi's voice, always cheerful, 'I'm just finalising the Spending Review, and wanted to give you a quick heads-up that I will be announcing a big new funding commitment for your Early Years project.' Amazing and brilliant in equal measure!

'Thank you so much, that's fantastic news. Can I ask what the Budget figure will be?'

'Yes, £300 million for the Start for Life, plus extra funding of £200 million for the Supporting Families programme.' We spoke a little longer then hung up and I completely missed my motorway exit in my incredible joy. Harry felt it too – the extraordinary turn of events that meant I could now fulfil an ambition of more than two decades in transforming the support for babies and their families right across our country.

I take a very non-Marxist view of the history we have all lived through: that is to say, I am convinced it is shaped not by immutable and therefore unchangeable forces but rather by the very personal, sometimes even emotional, motivations of the men and women who enter the political fray and in doing so change the course of our national story. And it seemed to me on that night that everything I had experienced over the previous twelve years in politics had brought me to this point.

Politics can look, from the outside, like a high-stakes game of snakes and ladders, played out by alpha personalities with sharp elbows. And being in the middle of the game can be incredibly frustrating and frequently disappointing. Yet being an elected MP is also an enormous honour, bringing with it an opportunity to change the world for the better, meet some fascinating people and take part in extraordinary events first-hand – more than just a ringside seat in the making of history. The thrill of getting stuck in as life-changing decisions are made in the Commons Chamber or in Cabinet is a privilege not many experience, and I would not swap places with anyone working in a less tempestuous environment.

It is amazing to reflect on how much has been packed into the sharp end of British politics since 2010; these have been extraordinary times with some momentous events. We have seen the testing of our democratic institutions and an unprecedented degree of vitriol enter the political discourse, particularly over the hugely divisive issue of Brexit. When you consider how much has happened – four UK-wide general elections; the coalition government; the referendums on the Alternative Vote, Scottish independence and membership of the EU; and now a global pandemic – it is fair to say we have witnessed what seems like several lifetimes' worth of politics. There could be several PhDs written on the consequences of the Fixed-Term Parliaments Act alone, never mind all the other tumultuous events that have played out during my time in the Commons so far. My own roles inside and outside government – on the Brexit issue, the leadership campaigns, the hung parliament, the run-ins as Leader of the Commons with the Speaker – inspire me to capture the story while it is still fresh in my mind, and give the reader an insight into what it is really like... the snakes as well as the ladders.

As the chapters which follow will show, the highs of being in politics can be very high, and the lows extremely low. If at times it seems as if I am painting politicians in a poor light, or describing a world that no one in their right mind would wish to enter, I would stress that despite all the pitfalls I have still loved every moment. It is an honour to serve your country in this way, and I have never regretted the effort it took to be elected to Parliament. My three children, Freddie, Harry and Cookie, and my husband Ben have not always enjoyed the personal dramas, but they have loved the journey, the intrigue and the achievements.

If there is one message I would like every reader to take away from this account, it is that politics can be transformative. And that if you ever think you are not smart or beautiful or young or ruthless or wealthy enough to become an MP, think again. Parliament is an arena to which anyone can aspire. To the cynical who feel there is no point entering politics because a lone individual can't achieve anything, think again. I know from first-hand experience that if you put your heart and soul into it, you can change the world.

So my motivation in writing this book is not to settle scores or rewrite history – far from it. Instead, I am eager to pull back the curtain and allow those who must live by the rules set by Parliament and government to get something of a glimpse of what takes place behind the scenes. I hope some of my reflections may prove useful for those interested in a career in government; others are a broader critique for every reader to take away, and still more are lessons which have shaped my own thinking about myself and my approach to politics.

# CHAPTER ONE

# PATH TO PARLIAMENT

I don't come from money or privilege and I'm not a member of a political dynasty. No one in my family had ever taken much interest in politics before me. Yet from the age of thirteen, I knew I wanted to be a Member of Parliament. Like many young people of my generation, I was truly frightened by the government's public service information notices about how to survive a nuclear war. With a nuclear attack a serious and ever-present risk in those days, I decided – with support from the teachers at my all-girls grammar school – to become an MP and stop those politicians who it seemed to me were sleepwalking towards a nuclear holocaust. As I like to joke with children in my constituency when I visit their primary schools, so far it's worked!

My own childhood fears about nuclear war have a parallel with today's teens, growing up as they are in a world dominated by fears about climate change. Just like I did four decades ago, I'm sure many lie awake worrying the world could end because of catastrophic mistakes made by adults. I urge them to consider a career in politics, to make a difference. Most of all, I tell them it's never too late to get stuck in. In my own case, it would take more than thirty years before I fulfilled my childhood ambition to become an MP. And when I finally walked into Parliament for the very first time as an MP on 10 May 2010, it felt like I was coming home.

It was an extraordinary time to join the Commons. Mine was the biggest intake since the Second World War – 227 of us – meaning more than a third of the seats in the House were now held by someone new. In lots of ways that was a good thing – while settling into life as an MP is always challenging, I had the comfort of knowing I was not alone. I had become friendly with many fellow Tories during our long slog to first get selected for a seat and then win an election, a process which had taken me almost a decade. Our class of 2010 would prove to be an interesting one, packed with talent, including several who would make it to the Cabinet and some who would become good political friends. But it was clear from day one that you had to find your feet quickly and make your mark if you wanted to stand out.

One reason there had been so many retirements at the 2010 general election was the expenses scandal, which broke the year before and saw a number of MPs heavily criticised for their use of an expenses system that sought to boost salaries through expenses. A number were found to have abused the system at the taxpayers' expense. New Members tried not to judge – how could we without knowing the true pressures and circumstances of an MP's life yet? But many of us had spent years working hard in our prospective seats, so it was frustrating that for many newbies it was as if the sins of the fathers were being visited upon us; there was so much understandable anger about expenses and we were all tarred with the same brush, regardless of whether we had actually been in Parliament at the time. That air of bitterness hung around much of that first term like a bad smell, and it left a deep impression on my intake.

In other ways it was an incredibly exciting time to join the Commons – for the first time since the 1940s, we were entering into a coalition, this time between the Conservatives and Liberal Democrats. Like every MP, and many members of the public, I spent the days after the election glued to the news channels as the coalition talks rumbled on and we waited to learn if we could form a government. By the time David Cameron and Nick Clegg held a press conference in the Downing Street rose garden to announce the coalition deal, our nerves were completely shot. But I was elated by the outcome.

Perhaps because of my upbringing, I've never been a tribal politician. My mum is a natural Tory, a staunch survivor who held down two jobs to keep my sisters and me afloat after my parents split up when I was four. She taught us two life lessons: first, the world doesn't owe you a living, and second, never become dependent on anyone, particularly not a man. Make your own way in life. My father, a successful businessman, is also a lifelong Conservative free enterprise supporter, who encouraged his three daughters to strive in whatever we do. Later on, my stepdad, Geoff, who came into our lives when I was seven, offered an alternative view of politics. He has always been something of an armchair socialist, a warm-hearted man who believes the state should provide, but I would argue (and often do when we get together!) is less clear about who should pay.

My mum and stepdad worked hard in the furniture shop they set up together, and we would thrash out our different political views around the dinner table from a young age. And while I concluded early on that on a basic intellectual level Mum was right, feeling a deep resonance in her belief in the hand up over the handout, I have great admiration for Geoff's opinions. I think this is one reason I have always had friends from different political parties and a level of respect for my political opponents. So going into government alongside the Liberal Democrats held no fear for me.

At this stage, I'd had little contact with David Cameron or his Chancellor, George Osborne, and the rest of the Cameroons. But their project to get our economy back on its feet and to reform both the country and our party felt like a breath of fresh air. David Cameron was my kind of Conservative: socially liberal, but economically more on the right. It was an exciting time to be a Tory: we were modern, forward-looking, ready to shake the cobwebs out of our party and to govern in a way that would prove being a Conservative could be transformational.

On a practical level, I was profoundly grateful to David for one of his early initiatives: the A-list of prospective parliamentary candidates. This was intended to be fifty men and fifty women assessed by Conservative Central Office as being of strong potential, and which local parties were encouraged to pick from when making selections. The scheme was designed to help constituency associations look beyond their perceived idea of what a candidate should look and sound like. It resulted in many more women, ethnic minorities and LGBT people being selected for winnable seats, and for those who made it on to the list there was the added benefit of massively truncating the expensive and exhausting process of finding a seat.

In my case, this journey had proved something of a mission. I had never given up on the teenage dream of becoming an MP, but it wasn't until I had my two sons in the 1990s that I began to turn my ambition into reality. Before then, politics seemed like a distant and daunting prospect. I had joined the Young Conservatives at the freshers' fair at Warwick University (where the stand was manned by a young Tim Loughton, the future Children's Minister, great friend and fellow early years advocate) – but after graduating in Political Science I craved the financial security many people with my early background seek. My sisters and I would always have a fear of poverty, a hangover from the years after my parents' divorce when my mother made our clothes and we ate a lot of tinned pilchards on toast. Those early years contained a great deal of love and plenty of laughs, but now as a new graduate it was important to me to have security, and it seemed the City was the place to start. I never quite abandoned my political ambitions, but they would have to go on the backburner while I held down a series of fascinating and rewarding jobs in banking and finance.

I was working at Barclays when I met Ben, and we married in 1993. He knew of my interest in politics from the start, but in those first years I was very caught up in my banking career, and in starting a family. I had been telling my family for years that I wanted to be the first female Chancellor of the Exchequer, but it seemed unlikely (looking at all those Old Etonians and public school boys in government) that someone like me would ever get there.

I had gone through a difficult time after the birth of my first son, Freddie, with postnatal depression and then two miscarriages. My wellbeing wasn't improved by my then employer's decision to 'persuade' me to return to work when Fred was just nine weeks old, and then to refuse to consider my request to work part-time or in a job share. I like to think things would be very different now, but in 1996 it wasn't clear where I stood legally. I was now the youngest senior executive in Barclays and one of only eight women; our contracts were different to those of other bank staff and didn't specify working hours. My boss insisted my job could not be done other than full-time, and it was only after taking legal advice that I found I had a case for both constructive dismissal and sex discrimination, but, now expecting my second child, I opted to accept a financial settlement via voluntary redundancy. I moved on to pastures new, first as MD of a new start-up hedge fund, and then two years later as part-time senior investment officer of Invesco Perpetual in Henley – at last a fulfilling role that also allowed me time to be a parent.

It was after I had my second son, Harry, that I started to properly plan to become an MP – I just thought: I'm bloody well going to make a difference for my own kids. By now I felt quite zealous about improving the experience of working mums, to ensure other new mothers were spared my ordeal. During the late '90s, I also became chairman of the early years charity Oxford Parent–Infant Project, the start of what would prove to be my most rewarding work and greatest passion in politics.

And so it was that in 2001, when the boys were six and four, I took the first steps in my political career by putting my name down on the Conservative Party's candidates list. I also stood for election as a local councillor in our home of south Oxfordshire to get some practical experience of politics. By the time I fought and won the council seat in 2003, I was five months pregnant with my third child, yet the desire to enter politics stayed with me. Before the 2005 general election, I applied to more than a hundred seats, had my CV shortlisted for interview in about seventeen, got down to the second-round interview in eleven and made the final round in five. For some colleagues, getting selected was easy; for others, like me, it was a huge undertaking and the many rejections were tough.

Before the A-list, there were 500+ people on the candidates list and a minority of them were women. Travelling to interviews and doing my homework on the constituency while juggling work and small children proved an exhausting and expensive process.

I came pretty close to winning Reading West in 2003, just up the road from where we were living – it would have been ideal. However, I was six months pregnant when I applied and eight and a half months by the time I got through to the second round. The night before the final round, I felt the now rather familiar sensation telling me the baby was on the way. As I put the boys to bed that night, I told them: 'Your sister's going to be here in the morning.' And she was: Charlotte (Cookie, as we call her) was born at home at 2.30 a.m. with just a midwife, my husband and my mum (herself a qualified midwife) present.

As I basked in the glow of welcoming our baby girl, Ben offered to take her from me while I got some sleep, and to call Reading West to pull out of the final. We all pondered for a moment.

'Well, is there any real reason not to go ahead with it?' I asked.

My mum laughed. When my youngest brother was born at home, she came downstairs soon after and made us all a curry for supper. We have form for this.

So after a fabulous first day with the growing family, and a few hours' rest, we all set off together for Cookie's first political outing. Looking back, I can't quite believe I did it – but as many mothers will agree, on the day you have a baby you're so elated you could fly, while twenty-four hours later you feel as if you've been knocked over by a bus.

When I stood before the association membership, I proudly announced I had given birth that morning. The looks on their faces! Some of the more elderly among them were clearly wondering if they had misheard, while others were worrying for my sanity. Suffice to say, I was not chosen, and on this occasion I was highly relieved to get back home to the good work–life balance I had established between family, politics, part-time job and charity work.

When I did finally get selected, in February 2005, it was for Knowsley South, the successor to Harold Wilson's old constituency and in the top five safest Labour seats in England. In other words, it was what is known in the jargon as a 'no-hoper'. I was determined to give it my all. That campaign was also a real family affair. I would drive from Oxfordshire to Knowsley on a Thursday and stay until Monday, while Ben picked the older kids up from school and followed with Cookie on the Friday. My association chairman, Gary, was a local bus driver and steward at the nearby Conservative club.

Every Friday we would turn up at Gary's house, where Gary's wife Gill and their two kids would have a takeaway Chinese with Ben and our three while Gary and I went to the Conservative club. The first time I went, I remember being so impressed that Gary had managed to get around 200 people all seated at tables to hear from me (or so I thought). I soon realised that the club was always full of local people and they often had great bands playing live at the weekends – almost a Beatles-style music scene – but most of them were definitely not Conservative supporters. Gary insisted, though, that as it was a Conservative club, I should be allowed to speak to the Friday night customers. As I started my speech that first evening, a woman's voice piped up from the back of the room: 'Will this take long, love? We want to start the bingo.' Those who think politics is about being put on a pedestal, think again!

The campaign in Knowsley was a great learning experience, and it was here that I met a number of Conservative candidates, including Amber Rudd, my political mate right up until the EU referendum – but more on that later.

Gary owned part shares in a vintage double-decker bus, so near to election day we organised a number of the local Conservative candidates in Merseyside to take part in a tour of the area with him driving his bus, decked out in Vote Conservative posters for the occasion. I let Fred and Harry, then eight and six, sit in the luggage racks with megaphones, periodically shouting 'Vote Conservative' out of the window. It was all pretty good-natured, and we got some friendly abuse, until we found ourselves driving past Goodison Park, home to Everton Football Club, just as the crowd was leaving after a home team loss. Gary had to put his foot down.

A Conservative was not about to win Knowsley South, but I got a good swing and some valuable campaigning credentials. With time as a district councillor also under my belt, I now had the experience to make it on to the A-list once it was introduced. Even better, in June 2006 I was selected early for South Northamptonshire, where my family has roots going back generations. It would be four years before I finally fought the campaign to win this new seat – a chance to learn the ropes from the much-loved retiring local MP, Tim Boswell, move into a new home in the heart of the constituency, and get the kids into a local school. I kept working part-time at Invesco Perpetual in Henley and concentrated on doing everything I could locally to win as many votes as possible.

Over the following months, I saw many talented people from the candidate circuit successfully land seats. There was Priti Patel, smart and punchy; Amber, a friend from Merseyside; Liz Truss, whom I would work closely with in Theresa May's Cabinet; and Thérèse Coffey, to become famed for her karaoke nights in Parliament. My family got to know Chris Heaton-Harris's family when he won the neighbouring Daventry constituency; he would become a close friend in politics, and our eldest kids later became flatmates after university. It was an exciting time, as one by one these good people were picked for winnable seats.

Moving to South Northamptonshire really was coming home. My father came from a local farming family, my mum grew up in a village in my constituency and my parents married in a nearby church. Perhaps what finally won over the local members to select me, however, was the story of my great-uncle Ron, who worked at Haynes & Cann (the now closed big military boot factory in Northampton) during the war and helped design the famous Second World War Escape Boot. It was a pilot's leather boot with sheepskin leggings containing silk maps; you could remove the leggings to reveal an Oxford brogue with a compass in the heel, and the laces concealed a flexible saw. Pilots shot down behind enemy lines would have a chance of finding their way home thanks to those RAF flying boots. Today, one of these memorable pieces of footwear is on display in the Northampton Museum and Art Gallery.

I recount this tale of the journey to becoming an MP because all too often great candidates fall by the wayside – it takes too long, it's too expensive and exhausting, it takes too great a toll on families. All valid reasons and particularly, I'm sorry to say, for women – but take heart. Those who really want to do it, in my experience, will make it despite the hurdles that still exist. Frankly, I would like to see a return to the A-list, but there are also some tactical ways to secure a safe seat. By chance I stood first for a seat where there was no likelihood of winning, yet that put me in a good place for selection in a winnable seat. In hindsight this turned out incredibly well from a family and work perspective, because the first seat was only a four-month time commitment, with no need to relocate, and then the second seat was somewhere Ben and I wanted to make our permanent home and we could do so in the belief that I had a good chance of winning the election whenever it came.

From day one I have loved representing South Northants. From marching against unwelcome development outside Northampton to fighting against the proposed HS2 project, to campaigning for a relief road around Towcester, a new medical centre in Brackley and a whole raft of other issues. Visiting schools and businesses, promoting the Silverstone Circuit and our own high-tech engineering sector, holding advice surgeries to directly help individuals and families. The job of constituency MP has proved constantly varied, fascinating and rewarding. And when it comes to helping individual constituents at the regular advice surgery, MPs apparently have almost magical powers. So many times I have picked up a problem – health, benefits, visas, mental health, planning, you name it – and my polite letter on my constituent's behalf written on a House of

Commons letterhead has worked like waving a magic wand. Suddenly the problem is given proper attention and is miraculously resolved. This must surely be the best bit of an MP's job – literally making the world a better place for those who come seeking your help.

My first election night, in 2010, was superb. My campaign team and almost the entire extended family spent the day visiting polling stations and driving around the constituency with megaphones shouting Vote Conservative. It has become our thing; we love a bit of megaphoning on election day. The count took place from 10 p.m. in the gym at the local leisure centre, and (as is always the case for some inexplicable reason) mine was among the last results to come in, at around 6 a.m. Each candidate is permitted a number of guests at the count, whose formal role is to watch all those who are emptying ballot boxes and counting out the votes. Piles of votes for each candidate form very quickly, and the watchers get quite intensely involved making sure votes are not being accidentally added to the wrong pile.

After a few hours, we moved to the leisure centre café to watch the results coming in on the television. My boys, then aged twelve and fourteen, had come with their sleeping bags. They were allowed strong coffee with sugar and several Mars Bars each to keep them awake – true decadence.

By the time I took to the stage to learn my own fate, it was clear that the Conservatives would be the biggest party, but also that we would not have a majority – Labour's seemingly endless government was defeated, but what would happen now was very unclear. Although this new seat had a predicted majority of about 10,000, no candidate ever feels confident, and I was beyond nervous. So the size of my majority – 20,478 – was quite an incredible moment, an amazing feeling. The prospect of entering Parliament had been theoretical for so long; now it was time to stop the chat and get on with the action. Ben and the kids were just as excited as me. My husband is definitely up for adventure, and we all felt this was a new chapter. It was going to be a blast.

Standing on the stage with Ben and the boys grinning, I had no idea what I was getting into – and nor did they. As I would find out a few days later when I arrived at Parliament, becoming an MP is like no other job. For starters, I went from the two days a week I was by now working in the private sector to earning less than half the salary but working the extraordinarily long hours of a backbencher. For the first few weeks, the whats and the wheres and the hows fill your days: what's a delegated legislation committee? Where's the Grand Committee Room? How do you table an amendment? The experience was equal parts fascinating and pressurised, and I soon felt the reality of the whips' joke that MPs spend years fighting to win a seat to get into the House of Commons – and then expend huge energy trying to get 'slipped' to get away from Parliament for the day. Whether for a constituency event, a family crisis or an overseas delegation, every minute away from Parliament has to be approved.

We new MPs were stationed in shared committee rooms on the top floor of the old Palace, because MPs who have retired or lost their seats are given a few weeks to move out of their offices. So I was allocated a hot desk in Committee Room 17, sharing two printers and a workspace with eight other newbies. We each had a locker outside the room that was soon stuffed full with hundreds of letters from constituents – long-running disputes, congratulations, invitations. All needed an answer and the buck stopped with us. Those were long and tiring days, but incredibly exhilarating.

If becoming an MP was a shock to the system for me, it was perhaps even more so for the kids. We moved into the flat we had bought in Westminster, and Cookie (then aged six) started at day school in London while the boys went to boarding school. Our Northants nanny Philippa (Filo, as we call her) stayed at the flat with us Monday to Wednesday to look after Cookie. We soon developed a routine. Ben or I would take Charlotte to school, Filo would pick her up, and some days would bring her in to Parliament, where we could meet for a quick hot chocolate after school in the Pugin Room, the grand tea room for MPs and peers. The staff there took a shine to Cookie, and there was one particular waitress from Northern Ireland with whom she would love to chat.

Another friend Cookie made in the House of Commons was a very different Northern Ireland character, the Reverend Ian Paisley, feisty one-time leader of the Democratic Unionist Party. There is a strange, rather dismal room in Parliament near Central Lobby called the Family Room. It's not exactly kid-friendly, decked out as it is, like the rest of the Palace of Westminster, in grand wallpaper and heavy curtains. But it has a TV and a rocking chair up one end, and toys and building blocks and dolls houses and books for the kids at the other. Cookie would run into the Family Room, switch all the lights on, and often the Rev. Ian Paisley would be sat in the rocking chair snoozing with the TV on. He never minded – they would sit together and chat. By the time of his death in 2014 they had a great little friendship.

The boys found those first years tough, particularly Harry. While Fred was already at boarding school, Harry had to switch from day school to weekly boarding, which he disliked. Soon Ben, while still meeting the full-on demands of a growing fintech business in London, began to commute from Northamptonshire from the middle of each week to take him out of school because he was homesick.

Being a mum and an MP is not an easy balance, but it is manageable. I got adept at reading Charlotte a bedtime story with my trainers on and BlackBerry in hand, so if a vote was called, I would see the 'Division' text from the whips, then leg it down several flights of stairs (the ancient lift was far too slow) and run up the street and into the Lobby in time to vote. With practice, I got it down to six and a half minutes (you get eight minutes before the Lobby doors are slammed in your face) and I always made it in time – sometimes by the skin of my teeth.

While the kids have complained at times that the years have been orientated around their mum, they also say they have loved the experience. They've taken part in some amazing events and been very much part of the journey. And for all the sacrifices, I never once doubted that becoming an MP was the right thing for both me and my family. For anyone considering this job, it does give you the chance to be a good role model, to your own children as well as those you meet in the constituency. And it is never too late to follow your calling. While I dreamt of being an MP at thirteen, I waited until I was forty-six to get there. So I tell school pupils I meet: if you want something hard enough, it doesn't matter if life gets in the way for a time, you can get there in the end – your dreams are not just dreams, they can become reality, and there are many people along the way who can help you achieve them.

# CHAPTER TWO

# BABIES, BANKS
# AND BRUSSELS

The message was passed to me as I prepared to speak in a debate on a topic dear to my heart: a backbench motion calling for a referendum on Britain's membership of the European Union, which I was keen on but which the coalition government at this point opposed. The Chancellor wanted to talk to me. This was not a common occurrence for an MP who at this point had been in Parliament for just eighteen months. Feeling slightly nervous, I left the main Chamber and went behind the Speaker's Chair to take the call in the library corridor. George Osborne began with flattery: 'Well, Andrea. I just wanted to let you know we think very highly of you, we're very pleased with how you've been getting on, and we really want you to support the government on this vote.'

Time was not on my side. 'I'm really sorry, Chancellor,' I said with huge embarrassment, and some urgency, eager to get back to the debate before I was called to speak. 'I can't. I simply can't. I came into politics determined to give people a say over our membership of the EU. And also, I'm really sorry, but I'm going to have to go now because I am about to be called to speak.' And with that I rang off.

I returned to my seat in the second row of green benches and one of my colleagues leaned over to ask what Osborne and I had discussed. 'I just told him that I couldn't support the government,' I replied.

That was the first time I rebelled against a three-line whip. The whipping system is designed to make sure the government (or opposition) can keep their MPs supporting their party agenda. A three-line whip means you MUST vote with your party – going against it means being sacked if you are a minister or hold a job as a trade envoy or other prime ministerial appointment. So it isn't something to be done lightly.

Back in my parliamentary office, I was later told, calls began coming in from journalists requesting interviews. Luke Graystone, my assistant, was at first chuffed for me; my speech must have made a real impression. Then he checked Twitter. Somehow my polite conversation with Osborne was being written up as Leadsom tells the Chancellor to 'fuck off'. For the record, I would not tell anyone, let alone the Chancellor, to do that – and I did not say it to George!

But while George knew the truth of that encounter, it didn't help matters when we had a second brush the following year. I was now a member of the Treasury Select Committee, where I had made something of a splash during a grilling of Bob Diamond, who had just resigned as chief executive of Barclays Bank over the Libor-rigging scandal. This had led to numerous interview requests, including one from Radio 4's *The World*

*Tonight.* As I rushed between studios, Amber Rudd, herself pretty media-savvy, warned: 'Don't do too much. Be careful.' I should have heeded the advice. When the Radio 4 presenter asked whether Osborne should apologise for suggesting Ed Balls (then shadow Chancellor) had encouraged the Bank of England to invite the banks to fabricate their daily Libor submissions – something which had been shown not to be true – I found myself agreeing. I failed to recognise the bear trap for what it was and generated some appalling headlines the next day as a result. I went to see him in his office and apologised to him profusely.

As he rightly told me, 'This should have been a story about the last Labour government's failure to regulate the banking system ahead of the 2008 financial crisis, but you've made it into a soap opera about me.' I had to agree. Not my finest hour, and for any student of politics it's a lesson in how alert you have to be whether live on air, on social media or on a careless pre-record. So much political damage can occur from a few careless words.

George was right to be annoyed but was gracious enough in accepting my apology. Unfortunately, however, as a result of these two incidents, a rumour gained currency that the Chancellor couldn't stand me and had vowed never to let me near the Treasury. The following year, I rebelled for a second time, on a Paving Bill to approve HS2, the high-speed railway connecting London to the north of England, which I had always implacably opposed on value for money grounds – but also because the line was due to go right through South Northamptonshire. By now, while I was of course ambitious for a role in government, I was realistic about how far I was likely to go.

\* \* \*

Promotion to the ministerial ranks is the carrot by which so much is achieved in politics. The promise of it, or the threat of never attaining it, is a devastatingly powerful tool for the whips and the Prime Minister of the day. Sadly, the tantalising prospect of promotion also creates jealousy and a strong sense that there is no meritocracy in politics: your preferment or otherwise is viewed too often as a result of voting as you are told to, or because you're part of the right clique. In some ways, real contentment as an MP is found more often by those who have built a satisfying role for themselves outside government. Those who make it to the Cabinet face the spectre of being sacked at the peak of their performance, and those in the ranks of junior ministers are rarely satisfied with their lot, longing to reach the next rung on the ladder.

For now, I was personally content with forging my career on the back benches. On entering Parliament, I had three priorities, on which I was totally focused. They were what I called my 'three Bs': babies, banks and Brussels. In those early days, as I did my best to navigate Parliament's twisting corridors which always reminded me of Hogwarts (how come the top of this staircase ends in a broom cupboard? I could swear yesterday it was the door to the committee corridor), I thought hard about how I could make my mark in all three areas. Today, my strongest piece of advice to any new backbencher is to take a focused approach. Don't get distracted by the hundreds of different campaigns and lobbyists, but instead focus on achieving the real change for which you came here.

Even the focus on just three Bs was a challenge because there are so many ways to advance a specific interest. My first B, 'babies', reflected my passion for ensuring every baby has the best start for life. So I chaired the All-Party Parliamentary Group (APPG) for Sure Start Children's Centres, set up an APPG for Conception to Age Two, created the cross-party manifesto for the 1,001 critical days, and launched a national charity to help new families. Pretty much a full-time job in itself!

I devoted part of my maiden speech to my second 'B' – banks. After the customary tribute to my new constituency, I spoke about what I saw as the continuing threat to the global economy of unfinished regulatory reform of banks. That speech was the first and thankfully only time in the Chamber that I felt my legs shaking. After that, the Commons always felt like home, but there was something about the magnitude of being in that incredible place and delivering my first ever speech that brought home the huge honour of being elected an MP.

One way I knew would help me influence bank reform was winning election to the Treasury Select Committee. Committee elections were one of David Cameron's excellent yet under-appreciated innovations. In the past, appointments to select committees were determined by party whips as a reward for those in favour. That meant that until 2010 it was barely heard of for an unknown backbencher to serve on a select committee, particularly a high-profile one such as the Treasury Committee. But there was a benefit to coming in with such a large intake. Not only were there gaps in the committees' membership, but the class of 2010 worked together to make sure some of us were able to fill some of the empty chairs, holding hustings and then voting en bloc once we had our shortlist (I noted with interest that the 2019 intake, also large, did the same). With over twenty-five years in finance, I sought membership of the Treasury Select Committee, and I was thrilled to get a place.

Chaired by the Chichester MP Andrew Tyrie, the Treasury Committee was fascinating from the start. I enjoyed sparring with fellow Tories Jesse Norman and Mark Garnier and also appreciated getting to know opposition MPs on the committee, particularly Stewart Hosie of the SNP and Labour's Pat McFadden. Early on, we had a ten-day trip to China to look at international money flows. It turned out to be one of the most interesting trips I've done, because it helped us to understand the way national and local finance work in China, the extremes of wealth in the country, and the vast scale of it. I remember when we visited the biggest indoor market in the world, selling an extraordinary range of ultra-cheap goods. I set off with Pat to try to find his toddler a toy car, except we found you could only buy them in hundreds.

From uncovering abuse of the public finance initiative under the last Labour government to saving the paper cheque book from being scrapped by the banks, we held some great inquiries.

And then there was Libor. The scandal had been bubbling under for a while, with rumours that the banks had been rigging Libor – the London Inter-Bank Offered Rate. During the financial crisis, it emerged that some banks were putting in false submissions to the Bank of England on the level at which they could borrow/lend overnight. Traders were making millions, if not multiple millions, at the expense of the taxpayer and the Bank of England. It was despicable behaviour by banks whose recklessness had already brought the world into a deep recession.

Having spent my first year in banking in the treasury department of BZW, Barclays' investment arm, I knew how Libor worked, with people calling out across their desks, all shouting what their position was and what their book looked like. I knew how easy it would be to manipulate Libor. Bob Diamond, Barclays CEO, was appearing before the committee to face questions, and listening to him argue that it was just a few isolated incidents, all I could think was: *That's utter rubbish.*

When it was my turn to question him, I challenged him to explain the numbers. We had clear evidence that Libor manipulation had happened not once or twice by one or two people but hundreds of times. It wasn't isolated cases. He had nothing credible to say and resigned soon after. The upshot of that inquiry was that the overnight benchmark was radically changed, but the one big regret over the Libor-rigging scandal is that more people were not held personally accountable. Not long afterwards, when I was City Minister, we made sure that fines imposed on banks for rigging Libor went to good causes, including Armed Forces charities, which was a bit of a silver lining.

My first few years in Parliament, however, were dominated by my third 'B': Brussels. At that time, I was far from a dyed-in-the-wool Leaver. I was much more interested in reforming the EU than quitting it, and I was optimistic we would be able to do so. I even gave a speech around that time to the Hansard Society in which my central theme was that the EU was behaving like the Roman Empire at the end of its days, believing it would always lead the world, in spite of over-regulation, slowness to agree free trade and a declining share of global prosperity. Fundamental reform rather than leaving the EU was the answer.

Given my strength of feeling, I teamed up with two other Eurosceptic MPs, George Eustice and Chris Heaton-Harris, to found the Fresh Start Project, with the aim of reforming the EU while remaining a member. For the launch, we invited all our Conservative colleagues to a meeting; an astonishingly high number turned up, with several ministers saying they would have come along too had they been permitted. The Fresh Start Project produced a comprehensive body of work, culminating in a document we called Options for Change, which offered a traffic light system for reform: green for light-touch change, amber for change which involved some effort on the part of the UK and the EU, and red for initiatives requiring changes in EU directives.

Throughout, we worked with the Open Europe think tank to ensure our proposals were sound and comprehensive. As momentum built, I co-founded the All-Party Parliamentary Group on EU Reform, which engaged in a series of visits to EU states, finding that right across Europe there were politicians of different persuasions who were interested in making the EU more responsive to its citizens.

It was clear to me that getting stuck into those issues and making some real, tangible progress in each of them was the right way to enjoy being a backbencher. It felt like I had thrown a six on the dice and was properly starting to play the game. But that's not to say life in the Commons was always plain sailing.

\*    \*    \*

The trickiest, and in many ways most pressured, votes an MP is required to take part in are those around military action and around matters of conscience. In 2013, I found myself in one of the more difficult dilemmas of my time in politics when David Cameron recalled Parliament from the summer recess asking us to authorise a military attack on the Syrian regime, following the clear evidence that President Bashar al-Assad had used chemical weapons on his own people. What to do? If we voted against, Syrians could be subjected to further agonising deaths at the hands of their own government; if we voted in favour, innocent people could die. For me, the imperative of preventing future attacks on innocent men, women and children was the priority, so I supported military action that would be limited to targeting military assets. Although the vote was whipped, the government lost on that occasion. There are those who argue that it was this failure to act that encouraged some of the more recent aggression we have seen from dictators and terrorists.

In 2015, the House was asked to vote to allow assisted dying for the terminally ill. This vote, like most votes on matters of conscience, was not whipped. Such votes can be the hardest to resolve because there are strong arguments on all sides. As politicians, many of us prioritise national interest followed by constituency interest followed by party interest – in that order. Usually for me, following the party whip, with the notable exceptions of HS2 and the early EU referendum debate, has been in line with that prioritisation. This vote to permit assisted dying was defeated by a huge majority. My personal view on this was clearly informed by a constituent with motor neurone disease who told me that, in spite of having only a tiny bit of movement left to her, she loved reading and had no desire to die until her time was up. Her fear was that assisted dying could give some in her extended family an opportunity to put pressure on her to consider her life effectively over, and that in her love for them, she might feel somehow obliged to end her own life because by doing so she would be taking away their ongoing responsibilities to her and she would also enable them to inherit her considerable wealth. I think the current legislation, whereby assisted dying is illegal but the law will always take account of the particular circumstances (and whether prosecution would be in the public interest), offers the right balance, so I have always voted against the legalisation of assisted dying.

And in 2013, legislation to legalise same-sex marriage was introduced. Another whipped vote, and this one was passed with a huge majority, but not without a great deal of concern from many of my constituents. My view is that the love of same-sex couples is every bit as important as the love of opposite-sex couples. What we were being asked to vote on, however, were the matters of legal and religious marriage ceremonies. The issues were complicated by the fact that civil partnership was already available for same-sex but not for opposite-sex couples. Many constituents wrote expressing their concern that religious marriage was being undermined, and others expressed the view that it was unfair that civil partnerships were not being equalised at the same time. Given my view on the wider principle, I decided to vote both Aye (for the sake of equality) and No (to object to what I felt was poorly crafted legislation). This is the only time I have ever voted both Aye and No, not wishing to abstain but trying to represent the deeply held views on all sides. Now, almost a decade later, it is clear that allowing same-sex couples to express their love in an equal way was the right thing to do – but it also illustrates the complexity of some of the choices facing Members of Parliament.

# CHAPTER THREE

# MINISTER

The call every backbencher dreams of receiving came in early April 2014, just shy of four years after my election as an MP. I was on my way into the Chamber when my phone rang and a brisk voice announced herself as the No. 10 switchboard. She asked if I would hold for the Prime Minister. The corridors around the Chamber have an infuriatingly poor signal.

'Yes, of course,' I said, and headed for the Lady Members' Room – a fancy name for what is actually the ladies' loo, complete with ironing board, and the nearest spot I could think of with decent phone reception.

When David Cameron came on the line and said he would like me to become City Minister, serving under George Osborne at the Treasury, I was astonished and delighted in that order. I was aware that a game of ministerial musical chairs was underway due to the resignation of Maria Miller, Culture Secretary, over expenses. But even when Sajid Javid was promoted to the Cabinet to replace Maria, it didn't occur to me I might fill his now empty spot at the Treasury. After all, if the press was to be believed, I was the last person Osborne would want working alongside him. But I couldn't very well say that when the Prime Minister was offering me my dream job. So I thanked him gratefully, accepted the offer and phoned my husband to tell him.

Whether he knew it or not, David Cameron had given me the perfect job: Economic Secretary, otherwise known as City Minister, with responsibility for financial services. Before entering Parliament I had been in finance for more than twenty-five years in a number of different roles – in treasury, structured finance, institutional banking, a new hedge fund start-up, and finally corporate governance. In my final months at Invesco Perpetual, the financial crisis was underway; I saw at first hand both the best and the worst of the financial system, and I had confidence that in this new ministerial role I could make real, practical improvements.

Before starting any new ministerial job, there is first an appointment with Propriety and Ethics, where new ministers are asked about any possible conflicts of interest. It is a slightly nerve-racking occasion when you have a family as huge as mine, because you worry you might not remember what everyone is up to at all times! I have altogether eight parents (including stepparents and parents-in-law) and just the one husband, but between us we have six siblings, each of whom is married, plus their adult children. So twenty-four working adults whose relevant interests must be recorded and updated.

The other real shock was to find that my charitable interests as chairman of the parent–infant charity PIP UK, my trusteeship of other PIPs and my chairmanship of the All-Party Groups on Early Years and EU Reform all had to come to an instant end. Tim Loughton amazingly stepped in straight away with the early years work, and with years of experience as Children's Minister both in shadow and in government he successfully led each of those organisations for several years. And Chris Heaton-Harris took on the EU Reform APPG as well as continuing our shared work on the Fresh Start Project; all of his years as an MEP and as a campaigner for EU reform meant he was incredibly effective. I've always been of the view that no one is irreplaceable, regardless of their specialism or skillset. Tim and Chris certainly proved that!

On my first weekend in the job, I sat in the garden at home enjoying an unusually early heatwave and ploughing my way through my first red box. Nothing can describe the feeling of being met for the first time by a government driver with one of these iconic items on the back seat. After a few weeks, the inconvenience of a lead-lined briefcase that opens at the 'wrong' end, with an old-fashioned key that rarely works the first time, takes over. Then the red box is reduced to becoming an Instagram sensation, something to photograph your daughter sitting in, and a decoration for the office. Government papers move to a utilitarian lockable wheeled suitcase.

But on that first Saturday, realising I probably had ten hours of policy submissions to work through, each requiring a response by Monday morning, I cheered myself up by ordering some large fake plants for the office. They proved strikingly realistic and made the place a little less gloomy – until the day one of the kind cleaning staff watered them, leaving big puddles on the desk and floor.

I would now spend much of my day (and evening) at the Treasury, and far less time in the Commons. It was a wrench being so distant from my parliamentary team, but they would maintain an important line to the constituency as I entered a new chapter in which the macro concerns of the department contrasted sharply with the day-to-day issues of South Northamptonshire. So during the week I was making decisions which affected millions of people, then returning to the constituency at the weekend to help deliver food boxes to the elderly or to answer questions from primary school children.

Here at the Treasury, in place of my now longstanding parliamentary team, I was surrounded by civil servants, who are quite different in nature. I came into contact for the first time with the private office group of (usually young) officials there to support me in every way possible. So if I wanted a policy briefing, a meeting with bank chiefs or even a cup of tea, all I had to do was call and someone would come in and sort it out. They were incredibly helpful and kind – but I soon came to realise that politicians and civil servants occupied very different worlds. Although they were ostensibly there to support me, civil servants in fact have their own management structure, appraisals and reporting lines. As a minister, you might find out your private secretary was moving to a new post only when an interview for a new one suddenly popped up in your diary. With my long years in business management, it was strange to realise I would never be on their team, that in fact they had their own, separate team. It took a while before the private office would share the normal office chit-chat – one of the team had just got engaged or moved house or was having a birthday. And while I was friendly enough with my new ministerial colleagues – including Danny Alexander, then Lib Dem Chief Secretary, David Gauke and Priti Patel – we were all so busy we saw little of each other.

And then there was George Osborne himself. My appointment as City Minister may have been accompanied by headlines suggesting David Cameron had forced me on George, but the truth was he couldn't have been better to work with. As a junior minister, I didn't spend a great deal of time with him, but on the occasions we were together he was always very friendly and supportive. One thing that genuinely amused me, though, was the rather relaxed manner of one of his special advisers, Thea Rogers. From time to time, ministers, advisers and a few senior officials would be summoned to the grand Chancellor's office to discuss something important like a Budget or spending round. For me, these were serious, even daunting, occasions. However, Thea would sometimes turn up in casual clothing, sit down cross-legged on a chair and get stuck into her lunch. (Since those days, Thea and George have got engaged and have a young son together.)

Thea and George's other special adviser, Ramesh 'Mesh' Chhabra were two of the good guys among the spads I would come to know during my ministerial career; kind, helpful and good at their jobs. Mesh in particular was invaluable when inevitable press attacks came. Mesh's sound (but very difficult to heed) advice not to pour fuel on the fire by responding to media accusations would stay with me over the years.

If negative press attention was the downside of being a minister, there were plenty of upsides. Having loved being a backbencher, I soon became hooked on ministerial life, with the ability it brought to make a tangible difference in some key policy areas. It was a new and massive learning curve.

As is standard for a new minister, on the day I arrived I was given a brief that covered the entire portfolio, and soon after I was asked which areas I was most interested in focusing on. My response was taken to the relevant policy teams, who then drew up a list of options for action. I'm told it's an exciting moment for a policy official when a new minister expresses an interest in their area, and they can be relied on to work flat-out to deliver. In my case, I was clear about where I wanted to make a difference: bank reform, financial exclusion and social justice and influencing EU policy towards banks.

A few weeks into the job, I met the heads of all the major banks one by one, to make clear my anger on behalf of the taxpayer at what the poor risk management in the banking sector had done to the economy. While I had met many of the CEOs during my time on the Treasury Select Committee, these sessions would have a fresh perspective as the minister in charge of the City. The first few meetings went well, and next on my list was António Horta-Osório, the much-admired chief executive of Lloyds. António had joined the bank after the crash, so bore no responsibility for the misdeeds of his predecessors, and our encounter would therefore be friendlier than some.

About ten minutes before the meeting, my personal phone rang. It was Ben. Alarm bells began immediately at his first words: 'Everything's fine.' Then he said: 'Fred's OK.' My eldest son Freddie had just finished his A-levels and was off on a cheap-as-chips holiday with his schoolmates on a Greek island.

I panicked, of course. 'What's happened? Where is he, is he in hospital?'

Ben relayed the news calmly: 'He's been beaten up outside a nightclub. He's fine, but he has a broken nose.'

My beautiful boy with a broken nose! I swung into action, tracking down Fred's medical insurance details and trying to find a way to fly him home right away. When I got through to him on the phone, he sounded very odd thanks to the broken nose, but he insisted he would go home the next day with the other lads as planned. As I hung up, my private secretary crept into the room to say she couldn't help overhearing, and to ask if there was anything she could do. Would I like to cancel Mr Horta-Osório? I pulled myself together: 'No, no, I'm fine.'

The meeting began well enough, as we made small talk about the recent Lloyds–HBOS merger. Then António asked: 'And how are you, Andrea? How is your first month going?' I found myself confessing that I was rather distracted by what had happened to Fred, tears welling up. I was mortified: whenever the media suggest a female politician was 'crying', the social media response is usually terrible. António, on the other hand, could not have been more understanding. He has a daughter of about Freddie's age, and we spent the next half-hour discussing not bad debts, mortgage rates or even bond yields but instead the perils of parenting teenagers. After that first meeting, we have often seen each other at events over the years and always have a laugh about the time I (almost) cried on his shoulder.

A few months into my time at the Treasury, I had the chance to claw back more than £1 billion for the taxpayer. Thousands of Brits had lost their savings following the collapse of Icesave, the online Icelandic bank which it seemed half the country, including my mum and stepfather, had piled into because it offered extremely good interest rates for personal savers. During the financial crisis, the UK government had decided to make good to all those small investors their losses in Icesave, and we had advised the Icelandic government, the ultimate owner of Icesave, that as a result they now owed us around £2 billion. I heard the Icelandic Finance Minister Bjarni Benediktsson was in London, so I invited him out for a drink. Benediktsson turned out to be another very friendly (and famously rather handsome) man.

We met at the Blue Boar, a fashionable drinking hole in Westminster. As one Icelandic blogger later described it, 'He had been expecting a friendly fireside chat – what he got was a full-on handbagging.' It was all very good natured, but I made quite clear to Bjarni that I was determined to get our money back. He seemed a little embarrassed, but I'm delighted to say that £1.4 billion rolled in with perfect timing for Christmas, like Father Christmas arriving from the North Pole.

From working closely with charities and the banks to launch basic, free-from-charges bank accounts for the million Britons who were previously denied an account due to a poor financial history to supporting Somali and other diaspora communities to be able to keep sending payments home to support family members, there was some great work done on financial inclusion.

And I learned a hard lesson about coalition politics when negotiating with post offices to replace 'the last bank in town' by agreeing with them to provide retail banking services at post office counters. Vince Cable, the Lib Dem Business Secretary, decided to announce the scheme as his own. I long ago concluded that politicians should focus on winning the battles, not winning the medals – there is a saying that 'success has many parents, and failure is an orphan'. Well, in politics this is definitely true.

\*　　\*　　\*

Working on the 2014 Budget was an enjoyable if relentless slog, and the resulting document represented the culmination of many months of work. It began with a schedule of ideas for both saving and spending money, which we worked through and discussed from every possible angle to avoid a repeat of occasional horror shows such as the 'pasty tax'. Among the measures unveiled that Budget Day, we were able to announce a new personal savings allowance, taking 95 per cent of people out of savings tax altogether; the Help to Buy ISA; and pensions freedoms to allow those who were entering retirement to take a lump sum from their pension.

The day itself is a big media event. We lined up for the traditional Budget Day photograph in 11 Downing Street and then marched out in single file to a huge crowd of photographers for George to hold up the famous red box. The women – Priti Patel and myself – were strategically placed along the line-up of men. We then jumped into a convoy of ministerial cars to drive over to the Commons. My bubble was punctured somewhat when I realised I wouldn't actually get to sit alongside George on the front bench because he would be surrounded by the Cabinet. But it was a fantastic day and felt like something of a turning point for the government and the country. After five years of cost-cutting following the financial crisis, it felt like we were turning a corner.

Around this time, I was asked to represent the Prime Minister as keynote speaker at the Dubai International Finance Summit. The call asking me to take Cameron's place came with just two days' notice. I had a very full diary myself, but of course the answer was: 'Yes, I'd be delighted.' I worked a full day then went to the airport, where six private secretaries were waiting for me. It seemed ridiculous, but it was something I learned as a minister: you genuinely need that many people to cover all aspects of the trip, from policy and media to logistics. We flew overnight and got a few hours' sleep on the plane before landing early the following morning. I was due to be the first speaker and there wasn't time to go anywhere to change and freshen up, so we went straight to the venue, a big international hotel. Unfortunately, the spa, where the logistics team had planned for me to change and shower, was closed. Instead, I was offered the ladies' changing room in the hotel gym – very much open to the public. This is where the private secretary's general duty to not accidentally 'lose the minister' took on a farcical dimension as my excellent female private secretary stood guard outside the shower while making sure I kept a bit of personal privacy!

The next forty-five minutes were a flurry of activity. I emerged washed and brushed and ran the gauntlet of preparations: was I dressed appropriately? Did I know the protocols of how to address everyone? Was I happy with my speech? Did the mic work? At events like this, a minister's role is that of a 'show pony' to be managed and pushed along by the 'handlers' to deliver the Prime Minister's message without putting a foot wrong or creating a diplomatic incident. Of course it all went smoothly, and afterwards I was invited to sit down to hear the others, at which point my biggest challenge was, frankly, staying awake after a long night on a plane.

Suddenly, my ears pricked up. The Prime Minister of Luxembourg, Xavier Bettel, was speaking. The year before, David Cameron had given his pledge to hold a referendum on our membership of the EU; Bettel was basically saying: 'Bring it on.' If the UK leaves, Luxembourg will take on the role of greatest financial centre in the world. In my tired state, I remember thinking: *Luxembourg? There are over a million people in financial services in the UK; could they all even fit into Luxembourg? The queue for morning coffee would go down the street!*

My brother and his wife live in Dubai and had just moved into a trendy new high-rise flat. Although I had a full schedule of events, I was determined to squeeze in a quick visit. When the conference was over, we set off for downtown Dubai. Arriving at their apartment building, I got into the lift and pressed the button for the thirty-sixth floor, and a couple of private secretaries jumped in alongside me. When my brother opened the door, he gave me a big hug then looked at the private secretaries with bemusement. 'Um, would you like to join us?' he asked politely. They agreed to wait in the car but would come back up to escort me down when the time came to leave. Sure enough, forty-five minutes later, after a glass of wine and fabulous hummus, the private secretaries rode up in the lift and took me downstairs again. It was strange but always very reassuring to be so well looked after by the private office. On every trip, the minister is seen to their hotel room, accompanied on almost every visit, and then escorted all the way back to their own home.

As I would find throughout my ministerial career, there were definitely two sides to foreign travel. It was always full-on and tiring, and it was sometimes hard being away from the family, particularly when Charlotte was still young. On the other hand, representing Britain abroad is a huge honour.

My thirteen months at the Treasury were a superb start to a ministerial career. I loved the job and would have been quite content to stay there for many years. People talk about politicians being desperate to climb the greasy pole; that is not always the case in my experience. Some jobs just feel right, and the City role was a great fit. I did achieve a lot in that year and a bit, but I would have loved the opportunity to do more. It was a big lesson learned: you can't afford to hang about when you become a minister. Your shelf life is invariably short.

This was the start of six years in government, being something of a slave to the red box, when every day of the week was a juggling act to manage the competing demands of constituency, ministerial portfolio and family. I would spend many a Saturday afternoon on the touchline at school, trying not to miss a big moment, while reading through some of the weekend submissions. Cooking and eating Sunday lunch – a must each week – was topped and tailed by hours of policy and constituency work. Holidays were accompanied by a pile of reading and decisions to make, continuous emails and, often, emergency returns to Westminster.

But there are no regrets. The chance to change things for the better – to make a difference – is something that many people aspire to in their career. For anyone looking for a really rewarding job, I would always recommend a career in Parliament.

# CHAPTER FOUR

# AN UNEXPECTED PROMOTION

The helicopter module rose into the air on its hydraulic arm and I took a deep breath before plunging upside down into the water below. As I scrambled for my air canister, I knew I had just three minutes to unbuckle my seatbelt and push the window out with my elbow to free myself before making it back to the surface. Later, dripping wet and exhilarated from the adrenaline rush, I posed for a photograph on top of a life raft alongside my equally intrepid private secretaries and couldn't help reflecting how much had changed in the space of a year. The rarefied boardroom meetings and intense number-crunching that had characterised my time as City Minister seemed a long way away.

My escapade with the helicopter crash simulation was a safety requirement needed to visit an oil rig off the coast of Scotland, an important trip given that North Sea oil and gas were a key part of my new portfolio as Minister of State in the Department of Energy and Climate Change.

It was a promotion, albeit at first, without wishing to sound ungrateful, a not entirely welcome one. I had felt a real wrench at leaving my fascinating post in the Treasury, but DECC was certainly making up for it, providing as it did a whole new policy area to get my teeth into, as well as extraordinary visits such as this one.

The day after obtaining my certificate, I was in a dry suit in a real helicopter being flown an hour offshore to visit the rig in the North Sea. As we flew, I looked at the endless sea and wondered how much of my training I would actually have the composure to remember if we did go down. My companion was an interesting person – a lifelong oil man. He often accompanied VIPs to a rig and said the only person ever permitted to do so without prior safety practice was David Cameron, who I can imagine would have relished being deposited upside down into a swimming pool at high speed but who didn't have the time to take the course. He told me he spent the entire helicopter ride worrying that they would go down and that his three minutes of air could be taken up trying to rescue the Prime Minister.

When we finally landed on one of the supply ships carrying provisions to the rig, it felt a long way from the shore. I climbed up the metal ladder which rose from the sea, battling vertigo all the way. It struck me how isolated the life of an oil rig worker is; no wonder they need long breaks between shifts. Unbidden images of the 1988 Piper Alpha disaster, in which 167 people died when the oil rig exploded and sank, floated through my mind. As soon as I was safely up on the platform, I felt a lot better, and the rest of the day proved fascinating. The technological advances of the past few decades are awe-inspiring, particularly the new techniques which have been developed to ensure as much oil and gas as possible can be extracted before abandoning a well. Environmental protections are also now highly developed, as is the decommissioning process, so the whole operation is much kinder to the environment. By the time we flew the hour back again to shore, I was filled with admiration for the solitary, highly skilled men and women who toil in such challenging conditions to provide us with those vital resources.

\*　　\*　　\*

It was David Cameron who gave me the news that I was no longer a junior minister at the Treasury but now a Minister of State at DECC. I got the call summoning me to No. 10 a couple of days after our impressive result in the 2015 general election. It was a great feeling to no longer be in coalition and to have a majority government at last. With ministerial positions opening up thanks to the departure of the Liberal Democrats, more of the 2010 intake were able to take their first steps on the ministerial ladder.

I'm sorry to say this did create a few tensions, however, between some of those who got ministerial jobs and others who felt stuck on the back benches. Politics is a brutal business – while many MPs keep their views on promotions to themselves and carry on to forge brilliant careers on select committees, as government trade envoys or lobbying for major policy changes, there are definitely some who struggle with feelings of being overlooked. The truth is that there is no real meritocracy in politics. You don't apply for a ministerial job, undertaking job interviews and proving your relevant experience; instead, you get the summons, and you never really know why. That, in my view, is why the game is more snakes and ladders than chess. It's a roll of the dice – finding your face fits or that you recently did something pleasing to the government that co-incides with a reshuffle – it's as simple as that. There is a big role for the whips in assessing an MP's Chamber performance, loyalty to the government and willingness to defend unpopular policies, but beyond that, every appointment is pretty much at the behest of the PM, advised by his or her close team in Downing Street. So to say reshuffles are controversial is an understatement.

But back in May 2015, I had no expectation that I would be on the move. To my mind, I was doing a good job as City Minister, by now firing on all cylinders; there didn't seem any reason to move me on. In fact, I was always surprised to find myself caught up in a reshuffle. With the exception of my job as Leader of the Commons, I never stayed in any post for much more than a year, and the same was true of many colleagues. This constant movement of ministers is definitely a downside of our form of government. When reshuffled you literally drop everything you're doing (you don't even get the chance to pack your bags – they're sent on by your private office) and off you go to your new department. There's no formal handover as you would be expected to have in business or even the civil service.

So when the call came from No. 10 to go and see David Cameron, I was surprised. It seemed a positive sign that I wasn't being summoned to the Prime Minister's Commons office, traditionally used to deliver bad news so the defenestrated can make a miserable departure away from the cameras' gaze. It didn't occur to me that I wouldn't be returning to the Treasury; I even allowed myself to wonder if I might be named the new Chief Secretary, given the Lib Dem Danny Alexander was no longer in the frame. As I walked up Downing Street to No. 10, I felt on top of the world. For the first time in my five years in Parliament, the Conservatives finally had a majority, I knew I had done well at the Treasury and now it seemed I was in line for a promotion.

But instead of offering me the role I was hoping for, David said: 'I'm pleased with your work in the Treasury, and so I'm promoting you to Minister of State in DECC.' For a moment I was so stunned I wondered if he had mixed me up with someone else.

'Oh, I thought you were going to leave me at the Treasury,' I managed to say, but clearly he did have the right person so I accepted the promotion with gratitude. 'My goodness, that's fantastic.'

Throughout the rest of our conversation, all I could think was: *Energy?* Of all the departments across Whitehall, this was the one I least expected to find myself in. It's another idiosyncratic facet of British government: if you've been a brain surgeon before becoming an MP, you'll probably end up in the Department of Transport; if you're a planning expert, you'll end up a Health Minister.

In a way, this makes sense: it's the role of civil servants to be the policy experts, while ministers must assimilate the brief, form views quickly and set the direction or choose between competing options. To this day, however, I am not sure this is a good thing. The way the civil service works does not lend itself to achieving deep policy expertise. It has a very hierarchical structure on the whole, and junior civil servants move around swiftly, usually on promotion, and favoured departments such as the Treasury and the Foreign Office are highly desired locations. This doesn't help build up expertise and risks significant policy mistakes when combined with the speed of ministerial moves.

\* \* \*

After new photos, and a fresh visit to Propriety and Ethics, I was whisked off to DECC, a grand building just off Whitehall which had been recently modernised so it was all glass walls and open-plan offices inside. It felt more comfortable and friendly than the imposing Treasury building. Also, unlike the Treasury, where I was several corridors and floors away from the Chancellor, my office was close to the new Secretary of State – who happened to be my old friend Amber Rudd.

This was another surprise to absorb. Amber had been the most junior minister at DECC before the election and suddenly she was in the Cabinet, a huge jump. It showed how much the PM thought of her, but it also made sense to me, given she already had some knowledge of energy policy – the department having been dominated by the Liberal Democrats during the coalition years. It certainly showed the benefit of being in the right place at the right time. I must admit to mixed emotions at the realisation that I would be working under someone from my own intake. On the other hand, this wasn't some villainous rival; it was my friend Amber, and I felt it would be good fun working together.

And so it proved: Amber and I were a good team, along with Nick Bourne, our minister in the Lords. On making me Minister of State, David Cameron took a ministerial portfolio away from DECC, meaning I was doing the work of previously two Commons ministers. Amber was great to work with, very open to sharing policy views freely and willing to act on recommendations in those areas where Nick or I developed the greater knowledge.

This time around, I knew how the private office worked and we hit the ground running. Around three months into my time at the department, my senior private secretary was moved on and gave me as a farewell gift a framed copy of a directive issued by Winston Churchill to his civil servants during the war. It was all about brevity, effectively saying: *Don't make your memos so wordy; give it to me straight.* My DECC private office were great – no endless policy submissions, but a clear summary of the problem, the possible solutions and the recommendation, with background information annexed. Every minister will always find that the workload is never-ending: if you think about it, the size of Whitehall departments means that the minister will always be the bottleneck. Private office teams wield great power in determining what to bring to your attention, and with what degree of urgency. The policy teams in DECC and I had a good relationship from day one, a process helped when Marc Pooler, a longstanding member of my original parliamentary team, who had subsequently joined the civil service, successfully applied to DECC to join the private office.

Doing the work of two ministers meant life at DECC was frantic. I had gone from a department where there were loads of ministers and plenty of capacity to one in which I was the jack of all trades. Energy must have had one of the largest volumes of statutory instruments of any Whitehall department; the regulations constantly change to deal with anything from the national grid to national security, and as the only Commons minister aside from Amber as the Secretary of State, I had to do countless delegated legislation committees. I was also responsible for responding as minister to what turned out to be a huge number of Westminster Hall and adjournment debates, which by tradition Secretaries of State do not attend, on everything from fuel poverty and the renewable heat incentive to solar subsidies and nuclear power. When it came to departmental oral questions, Amber would take some as Secretary of State, but I would have to cover the brief of the Lords minister as well as the remainder of the Commons portfolio. I also dealt with most of the departmental correspondence – plus we had an Energy Bill to take through both Houses. So it was pretty full on.

Those early days at DECC felt like studying for a degree in energy policy. I spent the weeks before the summer recess having one-on-one policy briefs on everything relating to energy, including a deep dive into the science of climate change and the physical safety of shale gas extraction, otherwise known as fracking. Recess was devoted to reading anything relevant I could get my hands on. Given this was a world I had not been exposed to in the past, I found this new brief deeply absorbing. It was here that I developed a deep passion for energy and climate change that continues to this day and I was able to strongly promote the subject later as Secretary of State for BEIS.

Amber and I took enormous flak over what would be our first big controversy, when it became glaringly obvious that it was necessary to reduce subsidies for renewables. In many ways, renewables were a victim of their own success. Unlike most subsidies, which are borne by the taxpayer via the Treasury, subsidies for renewables were being funded by a levy on energy bills, introduced by George Osborne. This proved a game-changer, and renewables firms were soon benefiting from the economies of scale of new onshore wind farms and solar fields and their profit margins were increasing. The subsidies being paid out were far greater than had been expected and the burden of paying for them was falling equally on every energy billpayer, so there was great concern about the fuel-poor, the elderly and those in uninsulated homes. We had to take urgent action to cut subsidies, a move popular with communities who did not welcome these sometimes huge-scale developments, but which sparked the rage of the developers and those who accused us of being in denial about climate change – an allegation which could not have been further from the truth.

Another major controversy was the decision to give the go-ahead to the development of the Hinkley Point C nuclear power plant in Somerset. We approved a contract for difference mechanism (an energy billpayer subsidy) to incentivise the production of clean electricity from this French-led project. In the run-up to the decision, which I fully supported, I went on a number of visits, including to the Sellafield nuclear plant in Cumbria. It was extraordinary to hear that the enormous volumes of nuclear waste stored there from the early days of the race to nuclear in the 1940s and 1950s were kept in pools and grain stores because there was no expectation, in that time of the threat of nuclear war, that the world would be around long enough to need to dispose of it.

In more recent decades, dealing with the waste in the most professional way possible has been a top government priority, and one that carries a huge taxpayer cost. I was particularly struck by a shining star of a project leader called Dorothy, one of a small number of women working in the industry. While legions of engineers (usually men) had agonised for decades over what to do with this waste, she took a deeply practical perspective. Her approach was: a day when we've not dealt with a bit of radioactive waste is a day wasted. Eventually, it is planned, all Sellafield's nuclear waste will be contained in a geo-disposal unit two miles underground, and in the meantime we can count on the expertise and commitment of people like Dorothy.

*   *   *

The Paris-based International Energy Agency hosted ministers from over thirty nations in November 2015, and as the UK's delegate I attended amid extraordinary security in the wake of the horrifying terrorist attacks that led to the deaths of 137 people in Paris. Each attendee was determined not to be cowed by Islamist extremists, and we created a book of condolence and solidarity with the people of France. That week, I was staying in the UK's beautiful Parisian embassy and woke up to hear what sounded like gunshots. Next day it emerged that, during the night, the French police had raided an apartment in Saint-Denis and killed the terrorist leader and two others. The big political focus for that gathering was the upcoming climate talks to be held the following month in Paris.

And in December 2015, Amber had the honour of going to Paris, along with representatives from nearly 200 other nations, to represent the UK at the Paris Conference of the Parties, that transformative moment at which so many global leaders signed up to an agreement to limit temperature change by tackling greenhouse gas emissions. What an incredible time for her: what politician wouldn't want to be out there saving the world rather than staying home to hold the fort? Everyone at DECC was enormously proud of the UK's role in helping to establish the Paris Climate Accords and of our leadership on some of the finance aspects, achievements which will hopefully outlive us all.

I was profoundly disappointed when the Trump administration withdrew from the Paris Accords in 2017. When I returned to the Energy and Climate Change brief as Secretary of

State (the department having been renamed Business, Energy and Industrial Strategy), I formed a view that going forward, the focus needs to be on not just the decarbonisation efforts of governments but also those of individual states, regions and businesses, which have proved themselves more than capable of taking the lead.

An important moment as DECC Minister was attending the G7 Energy Ministers meeting in Kitakyushu, Japan, in which the packed itinerary included some life experiences I will never forget. On the first evening we were invited to a beautiful, traditional Japanese house where, out in the garden, dancers performed a stunning display in costumes representing the flags of different countries. The lacquered dining table was set for twenty or so ministers and senior officials, and eight courses of the most delicious Japanese food were sent out one by one, none of which I recognised. I resolved to try everything, and by the time dinner ended I was so tired my head was sinking into my plate.

Throughout my career, I have tried to take moments like Kitakyushu to remind myself how fortunate I am to have served as a minister. It is so important to stop, pause for breath, look around the sometimes beautiful, sometimes extraordinary, surroundings, and realise what an opportunity you have to make a positive difference.

All too often, MPs can feel discontented. On the back benches, some are frustrated not to be a minister. For some ministers, that promotion isn't enough – the Cabinet is the real place to make a difference. And of course even in Cabinet it can be frustrating to be overruled by a more senior colleague, or by the Prime Minister. So is the only solution to become Prime Minister? Even then, as all three Prime Ministers I served discovered, you still can't necessarily achieve all the changes you want to see. In many ways, being a politician means a life of frustration. You can never be radical enough; the positive change you desire takes too long. It's almost as though it is only in leaving politics that you can appreciate how influential the role is compared to other walks of life.

This was my big takeaway from my time as Energy Minister. There was another lesson too: when you become a minister, you have only a few short weeks to thoroughly learn your brief and decide what your priorities are going to be. You then have to work flat-out to set in train your ideas within the first three months. There will be some policy ideas that you inherit and want to promote, others with which you disagree, and then there are your own plans. Getting a grip on the job early on is critical to success, because you just don't know how long you'll have in the post. And sure enough, by the summer of 2016 I was off on my travels again.

# CHAPTER FIVE

# BACKING BREXIT

It was late morning on Friday 24 June 2016 and I was fast asleep. Overnight, voters had delivered a shock to the political establishment, voting by 52 per cent to 48 per cent to liberate the United Kingdom from the European Union and free us from the anti-democratic drag on our ability to flourish as a nation state. Having become, to my surprise, one of the key figures on the Leave side, I had spent the night dashing from television studio to radio station and back again. I was live on air when the BBC called the referendum for Leave just as dawn broke – a moment of pure exhilaration at our accomplishment which I will treasure for ever. And I will certainly never forget the look on David Dimbleby's face when he turned to ask me how I felt and I punched the air with glee. His lip definitely curled… or maybe he was just stifling a yawn.

When I finally flopped into bed after my last interview a few hours later, it was with a profound sense of satisfaction at a job well done, exhausted but relieved. The hard work had paid off and I could be confident of a bright future for our country. And then Ben woke me.

'Andrea – it's eleven o'clock. David Cameron resigned three hours ago.' Oh no.

The Prime Minister's departure had never been part of the plan – in fact, the idea that he might walk away had not really been a risk uppermost in my mind until the final few days leading up to the referendum. I was very aware that a vote to leave the EU had the potential to cause both political and economic instability if it was coupled with the departure of the Prime Minister and a lengthy contest to replace him. Yet David Cameron had pledged to remain in office no matter the outcome; why would he walk away? It was Iain Duncan Smith, with the insight that came from having been leader himself, who warned that Cameron might not be able to stomach what would be a devastating personal rejection.

I had spent those last couple of days doing my best to help shore up the PM, repeating in every interview that a vote to leave in no way meant Cameron should resign. In the final days of the campaign, a number of Vote Leave colleagues and I wrote a letter to the Prime Minister, to be sent in the eventuality that we won, setting out the reasons he should remain in office, a letter which had duly been sent overnight. It was to no avail.

I switched on the television and watched in disbelief: the talking heads had already abandoned serious discussion of the historic referendum result and had moved on to gossip about who the next leader would be. And my name was among those in the frame to replace the Prime Minister. As I watched, the joy I had felt at the referendum result seeped away like air from a deflating balloon. I couldn't help reflecting on how much had changed in the three years since I visited David Cameron at No. 10 to suggest to him how to avoid this exact outcome.

Back in November 2012, I was still on the back benches and focusing much of my energy on running the Fresh Start Project. We had been granted an audience with David Cameron to discuss our document, 'Mandate for Reform', which set out clear ways the EU could reform for the benefit of all. It was good of the PM to meet us, and we came away feeling he had listened with respect. As I left his office, I turned and said to him: 'You know, Prime Minister, we have support from around 200 Tory MPs for reform, and this is an issue which is increasingly important in the country. You are not going to make it to the 2015 election without promising a referendum on our membership of the EU.'

He looked at me, flashed his smile of assured confidence and replied: 'Andrea, I don't even want to hear the word "referendum" until 8 May 2015,' – the day after the election was due to be held.

Well, he made it two more months. As the history books record, in January 2013, Cameron gave his 'Bloomberg speech' promising an in/out referendum on Britain's membership of the EU. He committed to first entering into a negotiation with the EU to redefine the nature of Britain's relationship with the rest of Europe. The package he came up with would inform the decision-making process for many people, including myself, on which way to vote in the referendum.

The formal talks for the renegotiation began in the summer

of 2015. In the run-up, we reconvened the Fresh Start Project, which I'd had to step away from when I first became a minister. Chris Heaton-Harris did a sterling job of signing up new recruits from the 2015 intake, and our stellar new team, including the future Chancellor Rishi Sunak, drew up what we called a Manifesto for Reform. Our twelve key proposals were fully worked up and easy to implement, including real no-brainers such as stopping the ridiculous carousel of shuffling MEPs between EU offices in Strasbourg and Brussels once a month at significant annual cost, and also taking steps to require the EU's audited accounts to be signed off, which hadn't happened for a decade. When we approached Ed Llewellyn, the PM's chief of staff, to ask for a meeting to present our manifesto, I was impressed at how helpful he proved. Ed was clearly a Europhile, a member of the Prime Minister's inner circle, yet was able to recognise the importance of our work on reform. As well as a couple of hundred MPs, we had begun working with Syed Kamall, Leader of the Conservatives in the European Parliament, and a number of his MEP colleagues.

David Cameron was welcoming, seemingly happy to give us thirty or forty minutes to present our reform proposals. We came away with the impression he was up for it – a good feeling given what was at stake. Because, frankly, what we were presenting the Prime Minister with was something of an ultimatum: to get some serious reform agreed or lose the support of a significant section of MPs. On a personal level, I was determined to wait for the conclusion of his negotiation to see how much of our reform agenda had been secured before deciding whether I would be for Leave or Remain.

I was optimistic he would give our reform proposals his best shot: it was clear he wanted to be ambitious in the negotiation. But I couldn't help a nagging concern creeping in: it never felt there was a point at which David Cameron was prepared to walk away. It actually seemed he was saying to the EU he would support our continued membership regardless, which rather removed the necessity for them to agree to his demand for reform.

In January 2016, Cameron called a meeting of his Ministers of State – now including me – in the Cabinet Room in No. 10, a place we rarely visited. Perhaps as a result, the atmosphere was rather tense. There is a strange thing that always seems to happen in the Prime Minister's aura, whoever he or she is: some people immediately start jumping up and down seeking attention, while others are struck rather dumb. In the case of three dozen ambitious ministers, the jostling was like the start of the Grand National.

Then he began: 'As you know, we are going to have a referendum on the EU. You, as ministers, must vote with your conscience and do what you feel is in the interests of your country and your constituency.'

The penny dropped: he was waiving collective responsibility, the convention by which ministers must always vote with the government or resign. I was just gobsmacked; amazed and delighted in equal measure. At this stage, with the PM still in the middle of the EU negotiation, I had not finally decided which way I would vote. But I knew there was a strong possibility I would end up on the Leave side. Collective responsibility is something I take very seriously, and I had been in agonies thinking I may have to resign from the job I had come to love in order to vote with my conscience. Cameron made clear that he was lifting collective responsibility for nothing but the referendum. Then the questions began, with the Prime Minister bombarded from all sides. As I walked out of No. 10, one question stayed with me: *What happens if you're in a department where you and the Secretary of State disagree?*

Sometime after the meeting, Amber and I were sharing a car back to the department. I knew we needed to have a conversation in the event we found ourselves in opposite camps. 'Amber,' I said. 'I know you'll be with Remain; I'm not decided as yet, but as the only two Commons ministers in DECC, I think we need to agree that whichever way the country votes, there will be no impact on energy policy or energy security.'

To me, the reasons for this were clear: on all the main issues facing the energy sector, including decarbonisation, the EU and UK were as one. The interconnectors – the pipes that provide gas and electricity to and from EU countries and the UK – are privately owned, as is the National Grid, so would be unaffected; angry sabre-rattling by EU leaders would never, in my view, result in them actually seeking to prevent private businesses supplying energy to the UK. Even Northern Ireland, covered by the island of Ireland's energy market, would see at worst a hit to prices but not supply. I thought Amber agreed. We would leave the Energy brief out of it whatever happened.

As the EU negotiation drew to a close in February 2016, I knew my decision would come down to the strength of the reforms Cameron could wring out of the EU. That weekend, I was in my constituency for what we called a Village Action Day: my parliamentary team and I would walk around one of the ninety-two villages and towns in South Northamptonshire, knocking on doors and chatting to people about any local concerns they might have. The heavens opened, so my parliamentary adviser Tommy and I took shelter in a pub. There, with the editorial assistance of Peter Warner, my constituency association president and a master wordsmith, we drew up a detailed letter to my constituents explaining that I would be campaigning for a Leave vote. The question was: would I actually need to send it?

On 20 February, Cameron came back from Brussels and did his best to sell the package of measures he had secured from the EU as a victory. Even at first glance, however, it was clear his agreement in fact amounted to a big fat *non* to reform. To my mind, the failure in the negotiation was Cameron's alone. No, EU leaders had not prioritised reform, but they were never going to. In order to get anything of substance, Cameron needed to be prepared to walk away. Without that, he was fighting with one hand tied behind his back.

With key colleagues in the Fresh Start Project, we swiftly calculated that he had achieved less than 2 per cent of our reform proposals and agreed to issue a statement straight away announcing that the Fresh Start Project membership would come out en masse for Leave.

Disappointingly, a small group of Fresh Start members decided they were going to back Remain anyway, despite the insipid nature of the reform package. So a couple of those close colleagues announced on social media the false claim that the FSP would be backing Remain, deliberately doing so before we had issued our agreed statement. These MPs had been trusted colleagues, which highlights how divisive the campaign had already become. However, my own path was now clear. On 21 February 2016, I hit send on the letter to my constituents announcing that I would be campaigning to leave the EU.

I spoke to Amber again to reiterate our earlier conversation. For me, it was very simple: just as the Prime Minister had lifted collective responsibility but only for the referendum, Amber and I would diverge only on our views of the EU and would not let this difference affect the rest of our political discussions or, indeed, our friendship. I did not appreciate then how vast the gulf between us, and so many other political allies, would become.

A month or so later, I was on a ministerial trip to Brazil when Luke Graystone, my longstanding parliamentary staffer, called. The visit was proving fascinating, an opportunity to learn what the Brazilians were doing in terms of renewable energy, as well as to see their continued work on oil exploration. But it came at an awkward time: back home there was a vote on HS2, and many constituents were annoyed I would not be in Parliament to vote against it. I had not been due to speak to Luke, and I assumed he was contacting me about the HS2 vote. Instead, he told me he was reading on social media about a speech Amber was due to deliver: it seemed she was planning to claim that a vote for Brexit would mean the lights going out across the UK.

I was appalled. By the time I returned home, Amber had delivered her speech. I called her from a packed Heathrow Express to say how disappointed I was by her remarks. For the next few months until the referendum, I found myself in the same uncomfortable position several times, as Amber campaigned on the basis that leaving the EU would imperil our energy security and I tried to avoid the subject.

In the end, I'm sorry to say I also got stuck in. The Fresh Start Project arranged for me to speak on the Energy brief as part of our series of events setting out how Brexit would affect each government department. Taking to the stage, I made perfectly clear my view that there would be zero impact on energy if we left the EU, and that only the island of Ireland's energy supply could be subject to price rises, as the generation comes mostly from the Republic. Later on, our divergence of views was to become rather more personal, and it took a while before we could pick up our friendship once more. Politics is a brutal business, and yet I can't help but acknowledge that it is too important to allow for friendships to distort strongly held differences of views.

Amber wasn't the only figure on the Remain side to disappoint me during this time. David Cameron's experiment in relaxing collective Cabinet responsibility seemed to have unleashed a beast, straining our unity to the extent that one of my clearest memories of the campaign is the outrage I felt at finding myself on the terrace of the House of Commons responding on social media to George Osborne telling elderly people their pensions would be destroyed and so would our NHS if they dared to vote Leave. It was the start of what became known as Project Fear, and I found it appalling. To this day, I still cannot quite believe how ruthless the campaign became.

But the world seemed a little more cheerful when I made my weekly forays across the Thames to the offices of Vote Leave to meet up with my fellow campaigners. They were a great bunch, including senior figures such as Norman Lamont and Nigel Lawson as well as good colleagues whom I knew well by now, like Iain Duncan Smith, Priti Patel, Penny Mordaunt, Michael Gove, Theresa Villiers and Bernard Jenkin. Vote Leave's headquarters was in a modern office block on the Albert Embankment, a bit scruffy but nice and light with lovely views of the Thames. We felt as if we were on a shared endeavour, and our discussions were weighty and knowledgeable – analysing the fundamental problems of the EU and how best to get across to voters the huge benefits of leaving it.

As well as the politicians, there were the usual bright and enthusiastic people you see buzzing around all campaigns, dealing with the media, manning the phones and handling social media. This was when I first came across Dominic Cummings and Lee Cain, who would go on to play leading roles in all our lives a few years later. A week or so into the campaign, IDS asked if I would join the Vote Leave board. I agreed on the proviso that the campaign dropped its high-profile campaign slogan that Britain 'sends £350 million a week' to the EU, which I felt was misleading – £350 million was certainly owed each week, but net of the rebate, £267 million was sent. When I raised the issue with Dominic Cummings, he told me: *That's not my problem, I'm here to win the campaign and we're not changing the wording.* It seemed he had no interest in that technical detail. I told IDS I wouldn't be joining the board.

While the Vote Leave campaign was energetic, it is fair to say it was also at times chaotic, with ever-changing plans. It seemed better to concentrate my efforts on working with the Fresh Start Project, seeking to make the positive case for Brexit and promoting reasons why the UK would be so much stronger out of the EU, as a counterbalance to Vote Leave's Take Back Control. Our group of Fresh Start Conservative MPs set to work drawing up one-page summaries of how Brexit would look in every area of life, from farming to fisheries, immigration, regional policy, the economy and more, launching each at the Vote Leave offices. We also commissioned joint op-eds with Eurosceptic Labour MPs, such as Frank Field, Gisela Stuart and John Mann. The group provided some great intellectual ballast for what we called our Project Hope, to contrast with the Remain side's 'Project Fear'. We held weekly meetings on a Monday, and the collective mood was positive and optimistic about our vision for the future; soon, despite the expert predictions, we were convinced we could win.

As the campaign heated up, I was asked to do an increasing number of media appearances. While I relished making the case for Leave, it coincided with a difficult time for me personally: a close friend in Northamptonshire had lost her husband to a sudden illness and I was trying to support her, and at almost the same time, my mother went into hospital for emergency heart surgery. I remember one surreal Sunday when I went on the *Andrew Marr Show* in the morning, then raced to north London to visit my mother in intensive care. It was horrifying to see my beloved mum, usually so full of life and vigour, with tubes everywhere.

Gradually, as we drew closer to referendum day, I became one of the go-to people at Vote Leave for media appearances. In the final weeks before the referendum, the team began preparing for what would be the two standout events of the campaign: the debates, the first to be held at the ITV studios; the second hosted by the BBC at Wembley. The strength of Boris Johnson's communications skills meant he was an obvious choice for the three-person debate team, while, as a popular Labour MP, Gisela Stuart complemented him perfectly. To begin with, the third slot in the line-up was going to be filled by (Lord) Digby Jones, former head of the CBI. I think it was Michael Gove who suggested that, given I had presented our case in the media quite well, I should replace Digby for the first. By then I had taken part in a couple of other debates in front of an audience, one with *The Sun* and the other with *The Guardian*, so it wouldn't be completely alien to me. But this was live television; I had not done a media event of this magnitude before.

Then began what I can only describe as the extraordinary

experience of debate prep, presided over by Brett O'Donnell, an American coach who had prepped Mitt Romney for his presidential debates against Barack Obama. He was absolutely single-minded about drilling into us the overriding message we needed to nail: *Take Back Control*. We had a number of practice sessions, with advisers including Munira Mirza and Henry Newman taking on the roles of our opponents, Amber Rudd, SNP leader Nicola Sturgeon and the Labour MP Angela Eagle. Our prep team hammed it up hilariously, and to this day whenever I see Henry (who later did a stint as a key adviser to Boris Johnson at No. 10) I can only see Sturgeon's face and hear his wicked depiction of her.

Gisela and I were both focused on getting it right – we would arrive determined and ready to get stuck in. This was something of a contrast to Boris, who would arrive a bit late and distracted for the first few questions. It was clear Boris needed a bit of warm-up time. But it was also obvious that once he got into the zone, he was a great communicator. We had a lot of fun during the debate prep, but it was hard work too. We were at it all day, with people wandering in and out, listening for a moment and throwing in suggestions. Over the course of our prep, we definitely began to appreciate the importance of what we had embarked on – we were aware the quality of the debates really could affect the referendum outcome.

On the night of the ITV debate, we boarded *that bus* with the £350 million slogan on the side (the journeys to and from the debates were the only times I actually went on it) for the short ride to the ITV studio. Each of us had brought a family member along: Gisela, her grown-up son Alastair; Boris, his then wife Marina; and I had my sister Hayley.

Hayley was such a stalwart supporter throughout the referendum. She has four kids, but she dropped everything to look after me. Every time there was a debate or some other big event, she'd come armed with a disgusting mixture of sausage rolls, fruit and nuts, cheese, sweets and green juices. She was always there with a hug, telling me: *You can do this.* I will for ever be grateful for that unconditional love. There is a lovely video taken by Hayley in the green room just after the ITV debate. Boris, Gisela and I are walking into the room as the whole team claps and cheers. Our faces are a picture: we look exhausted and stunned, like rabbits in the headlights. All at once our faces light up as we realise: *We did it!* Then we are all smiles and hugging everyone.

Social media concluded we had just about won the day (highly contested, of course!). There was just one sour note. Closing the debate, Amber said of Boris: 'He's the life and soul of the party, but he's not the man you want driving you home at the end of the night.' It was a pretty mean comment and I have no doubt it hurt. To the Remain team, I'm sure it was considered effective, but I found it spiteful. It is one of the worst aspects of politics – the personal vitriol some show towards those who dare to disagree with them. I was to see plenty of that very soon!

Once the ITV debate was over, I breathed a huge sigh of relief at having got through it and prepared to go back to campaigning as normal. But a few days later came the most appalling news possible: the murder of Jo Cox, a young Labour MP, while she was on her way out of a constituency surgery. I did not know Jo well, but it was a terrible shock to the whole country, and my heart went out to her husband and two young children. At first, it was unclear how badly hurt she was, and I called Ben to tell him I was cancelling all my campaigning that day and waiting – as were so many – to hear if she would be OK. Within an hour or so it was confirmed that Jo had died. Her killer had a history of psychiatric problems and was a far-right sympathiser and white supremacist; as he attacked Jo, he had shouted: 'Britain first.' I felt certain that the campaigns should stop right away, to show respect to her family and friends.

The question was, with voting taking place in a few days' time, should all activity cease for the duration of the referendum? Eventually the two sides came to a mutual understanding that we would resume campaigning, because this is what Jo herself would have wanted. But this would not be business as usual. No one will ever forget what happened to Jo, and I think all the politicians took from her death a determination that the tone of the debate would be as amicable as possible, appreciating that while we may disagree on this one issue of our relationship with the European Union, as Jo herself said, 'We are far more united and have far more in common than that which divides us.'

This shift in approach led to a decision in the Vote Leave camp to have me stay on the team for the next debate, which was to take place at Wembley. I was told that my positive slant on Britain's departure from the EU would offer the right tone, and Boris, Gisela and I had worked well together before. I was proud to be asked but very conscious this was the big one: possibly the main event of the entire referendum campaign, two hours of live television in front of a 5,000-strong studio audience and broadcast on the BBC at prime time.

The bus ride to the studio in Wembley was much longer this time, at least an hour and a half, and there was an amazing atmosphere on board. Boris and Marina, Gisela and both her sons and Hayley and I crowded into the back seats, like kids on the school bus. It felt like being a striker in a football team or a lead actor in a play – the tension was unbelievable. At one point, Boris turned to me and said: 'You know, Andrea, I'm feeling really quite nervous.'

Oh my goodness! 'Boris! If you're nervous, how on earth do you think I feel?'

When we arrived at Wembley, there were more photographers than I had ever seen, all pointing cameras in our faces, and we pushed on through, smiling and waving, all the while thinking: *Uh oh, here we go.* In the green room, the adrenaline was pumping, while the debate coaches repeated: *You're going to be fine, you're going to be great, take back control!* Then the runners came for us; there was no backing out. We were wired up and led onto the stage.

A deafening roar came up from 5,000 people in the audience, and we couldn't help being aware of the millions more watching at home. This was probably the biggest, most contested discussion since the Second World War, and it felt that everyone who cared most about it was with us, screaming their anger or approval. The deafening noise was extraordinary: we literally could not hear ourselves speak except through our headphones. Any one of the six debaters would be halfway through a sentence and half the audience would begin to applaud while the other side roared their disapproval.

The stage was gigantic, nothing like the intimate atmosphere of the ITV debate. Our opponents felt very far away. This time the line-up was Frances O'Grady of the TUC, with whom I would go on to enjoy a positive relationship as Business Secretary; Mayor of London Sadiq Khan, who probably made the least impact of the debaters; and Ruth Davidson MSP, the Scottish Conservative leader. Ruth was a political heroine of mine, and I could well understand her huge following in the Conservative Party. The low point of the debate for me was when she suggested I was lying over the impact of the EU on UK law. I was certain of my facts, and the accusation rankled for some time after. Does it matter? Probably not to many people at the time, and certainly not now, but it bothers me that we want to encourage more people into public service, yet with the stridency of our attacks on those with whom we disagree we don't make it seem very appealing.

We came out of that debate totally convinced we had won, and I was sure at that point we were going to win the referendum too. We had made the best argument, and I was confident that anyone listening who was as yet undecided must surely now vote to leave.

I spent the next few days back in my constituency,

campaigning like my life depended on it. South Northamptonshire would go on to vote to quit the EU by 54 to 46 per cent. My parliamentary aides Luke and Tommy busted a gut for me out campaigning in their own time, staying at my house evenings and weekends. As with every election, the referendum became a family affair. While the campaign team was out knocking on doors, my mother-in-law would cook her fabulous spag bol for twenty, with chocolate brownies for pudding. Afterwards, we would gather in the sitting room to watch the day's events on TV.

When the polls closed on referendum day, my immediate family travelled back to our Westminster flat, with the exception of Harry, who sat his final maths A-level paper on referendum results day. Charlotte, then twelve, was allowed to stay up in her pyjamas and we all sat on our big bed to watch the early results come in. First up was Sunderland, which voted to leave. What had seemed possible, then probable, was now definite: 'We've got this,' I said to the family. 'We're actually going to win!'

Charlotte fell asleep while Ben remained glued to the screen. Meanwhile, Fred and I prepared to head out into the night. I was lined up to do a number of TV appearances, and twenty-year-old Fred had agreed to keep me company. Our first port of call was ITV at midnight, where Fred posed for a photograph with the slightly incongruous duo of Jacob Rees-Mogg and Ed Miliband. Then it was off to the BBC. I had my makeup refreshed and went down to the studio floor. As I sat in the dark, the young woman fixing a mic to my lapel said quietly in my ear: 'Watching you at Wembley is the reason I voted to leave; you're not going to let us down, are you?'

This made a huge impression on me. By then I'd had thousands upon thousands of emails and letters from people saying they were voting Leave because of me. But hearing it directly that night from someone to whom this really mattered, it struck me what a huge issue this was for so many people. I told her: 'No, we're not going to let you down, don't you worry.'

Then it was time to go on air. My timing could not have been more perfect. Minutes later, David Dimbleby looked down the camera lens and said those momentous words: 'The British people have spoken, and the answer is: we're out.'

He then turned to me. 'So, Andrea, you campaigned for Leave; how do you feel?'

What I felt was pure joy – I punched the air. 'Brilliant, just brilliant,' I said.

Fred and I were in great spirits as we headed off for our next round of interviews. Winning the referendum was an amazing team effort and I couldn't have been prouder of the hard work and heart that went into it. That morning, I fell into bed thinking: *This is the most fantastic day* – to be woken with the shattering news of the Prime Minister's resignation.

David Cameron's departure was a disappointment on a number of levels. In walking away when he did, there is no doubt in my mind he let his country down. It was he who set in train the events that were to follow, and he should have stayed around to lead us out. For some Remainers, there's no doubt his resignation was almost revenge: *Serves you right, you sort it out if you're so clever.* I never saw it like that. David Cameron gave us the referendum and promised he would stick with the result come what may. Not to do so was a dereliction of duty at the worst possible time.

This was my takeaway from the referendum and its aftermath: the importance in politics of taking personal responsibility for your own actions. It was a lesson I would feel very strongly as I entered the next phase of my journey and the weight of responsibility fell on my own shoulders.

# CHAPTER SIX

# LEADERSHIP CAMPAIGN

My husband Ben turned fifty soon after the country voted to leave the European Union, right in the middle of the most extraordinary few months of my life. The celebrations served as an incongruous backdrop to the drama playing out in Westminster, a welcome distraction and also a reminder of the constant love and support I enjoyed from family, friends and my loyal staff and colleagues. This juxtaposition meant that the hectic events in my political world were being matched by competing demands in my private life, but it also meant that all my most loved people were unusually close at hand, a real blessing as I entered the gladiatorial arena of a Conservative leadership campaign.

The sense of these two worlds colliding began the day after the referendum, with the shockwaves from David Cameron's stunningly unexpected decision to stand down as Prime Minister still reverberating around Westminster and beyond. With spectacularly bad timing, I had arranged to meet up in Derbyshire with a group of close friends and family to celebrate Ben's landmark birthday. The plan was for us to walk the beautiful

Mam Tor before going for a picnic in a nearby park, then hosting a murder mystery dinner back at the hotel. We had been looking forward to getting together for weeks.

I arrived still reeling from Cameron's announcement and found our group of friends and family entirely mirrored the country in its response to the news. The country had voted 52 to 48 per cent to leave the EU and so, it seemed, had those closest to me. The gathering included dear friends who I hadn't seen for ages, but who had been following the referendum closely. Some were amazed at what had transpired, others were livid and some totally elated. And there I was in the middle of it wondering what on earth would happen next.

The next day we set off for Mam Tor, a four-hour walk with lots of stopping for the older members of the group to rest or peel off on shortcuts. I was in full hostess mode, determined to catch up on all the group's news and make sure none of the grandparents got left behind. But soon calls to my mobile from 175 miles away in London began, all asking similar questions: *What are you going to do? What's going to happen next? Do you want to make a comment? Aren't you ashamed of what you've done? Aren't you delighted about what's happened?*

At the end of our walk and picnic, with my phone still ringing every few minutes, a couple of family members drew me aside and said: 'We are really worried that you might be thinking about putting yourself forward for the leadership. We think the price is too great.'

Overhearing, my old friend Tim Loughton butted in: 'You've got to go for it, you must go for it.'

Back at the hotel, jumping out of a hot bath, two more phone calls came in, one from Penny Mordaunt, a fellow Minister of State, and the other from Michael Gove, the Justice Secretary, both fellow Brexiteers. Michael asked if I would support Boris Johnson; Penny wanted to know if I would stand.

I went down to dinner and tried to focus on Who Dunnit, but the calls kept coming. It was not easy trying to figure out who had killed Miss Scarlett in the dining room with the lead piping with constant interruptions. As well as the calls, emails arrived in first their hundreds and soon their thousands from members of the public, many asking me to stand and some calling me all sorts of names for helping Vote Leave win the referendum.

Well, I did my best to relax and celebrate Ben's big birthday, but I couldn't help the thoughts bubbling up: who should I support for the leadership? And was it possible to think I could go for the top job myself? I knew plenty of people thought I'd done well during the referendum. But I was an energy minister, only my second job in government, not even in the Cabinet. I don't believe in false modesty and I'm a realist. From twenty-five years in business, I was used to sizing up the positives and negatives. When I considered the pros, I assessed that I had the right moral imperative for the job, as well as the determination and passionate belief in the great future offered by our departure from the EU. But the cons were dominated by a real concern: did I have enough experience and inside knowledge of government to be able to hit the ground running? It was an odd experience: I was there having a wonderful catch-up with friends and family – *How are you, so lovely to see you* – all the while doing a cold mental assessment: *Could I really do this?*

I checked in with my immediate family. My mum said do it: 'You would be brilliant. You'll have our backing, you're a quick learner, you can turn your hand to anything, just get on and do it.'

My husband was pretty much the same: 'I'll be there for you; it'll be tough, but we'll do this and it will be amazing.'

My boys, twenty and eighteen, said: 'Go for it, Mum, we're right behind you.'

Cookie was still twelve. Her first reaction was tentative: 'I'll never see you, Mum, I don't want to move house.' Within an hour or two, she had come round to the others' view and was urging me to stand along with the rest. But I was aware how influential her brothers were, and throughout the campaign would remember Cookie's trepidation.

When I got back to London after that wonderful but rather challenging weekend, others' campaigns were already in full swing. I was being bombarded with calls from the newly formed Team Boris, including one from Gove, now acting as Johnson's campaign manager, asking me to go see him. I was happy to. Following the weekend's reflections, I had resolved to back Boris rather than stand myself. I knew he'd been a successful Mayor of London and, given my own lack of experience, it seemed to me that he had what I didn't. I'd seen him work his Boris magic from the referendum stage and knew what a great communicator he was.

At this point, I knew Boris only a little. He had returned

to Parliament at the 2015 election and I'd met him just a few times during his period as mayor, once to discuss creating a sovereign wealth fund by pooling the many different public sector pension pots, and then while campaigning for his second mayoral term. In November 2015, around six months after Boris's return to the Commons, he had invited me to dinner at a Turkish restaurant in Waterloo. I was slightly baffled given we hardly knew each other. He turned up on his bicycle, and over a convivial meal with lots of laughter, he finally got to the point: if David Cameron ever stood down, would I back him to become Prime Minister?

I was a bit taken aback; there was no sign of Cameron going anywhere. 'Well, yes possibly,' I replied, then added, to be mischievous: 'If I don't stand myself.'

'I could see you as a potential Chancellor in a Johnson government,' he went on.

My response had been tongue-in-cheek, but our exchange would prove remarkably prescient.

When I responded to the invitation to Boris's office in Norman Shaw North on the parliamentary estate, I was optimistic about the prospect of working with Boris as leader. Strewn around the room were the remnants of meals, as if a group of people had been in there for days planning and strategising. Michael Gove was there along with Boris. And it was he who began: 'It's been great working with you on the debates – now we want you to join the team that is supporting Boris.'

That was it. I admit I was quite taken aback not to be a more fundamental part of their plans – I had been expecting to be offered a senior role in any new administration helping to deliver Brexit.

Boris told me: *We're not discussing jobs at this stage.*

I pointed out: 'OK, but you will need people with a lot of European Union knowledge around you to deliver on the referendum commitment.'

*Well, I've agreed with Michael that he will be our Deputy Prime Minister, our Chancellor and also the man leading on preparations to leave the EU.*

I looked from one to the other: *You're joking, surely?*

But that really was the plan – the price it appeared that Michael had extracted for supporting Boris. I was bemused. Surely one person could not take on the three huge roles of Deputy Prime Minister, Chancellor and leading us out of the EU? Maybe Deputy PM and Chancellor could be one role, or even DPM and Secretary of State for leaving the EU, but surely not all three?

I told Boris and Michael that in order to join the team I would want to take on either the job of leading EU negotiations or the job of Chancellor while we prepared to leave the EU, focused on protecting the economy and jobs and making the most of the new opportunities.

But Boris confirmed that Michael would be doing it all.

In my view it made no sense and was not in the country's interests. The idea that anyone could do the jobs of Deputy Prime Minister, Chancellor and lead negotiator was incredible; it was far too wide-ranging for one person. I tried to pitch to Boris that he would need a number of senior figures in his government, people he could trust, who fought for Brexit. It was also crucial he had someone with credibility on the economic front in his top team, preferably someone experienced in finance. Since David Cameron had announced his departure, we had already seen the stock market drop, sterling had fallen, and my real worry was that unless there was a credible proposal for the new leadership, we would be in trouble. I was getting quite het up.

Throughout the meeting, Michael was inscrutable, remaining silent as I tried to persuade Boris to rethink. Michael is a very polite and highly effective politician – but he has shown that he goes his own way. Until then, I had been nothing but grateful to him. I believe it was he who had recommended me for the TV debates, giving me such a great opportunity to make a strong case for Leave. So I pitched very hard that a combination of Boris, Michael and me would be a 'dream team', with my financial experience complementing Michael's organisational skills and Boris's flair for communication.

Neither of them would tell me why one man, Michael, needed to do three jobs, let alone how it would be possible. Had Boris told me he didn't want me on his senior team because he had other candidates in mind, or that another Vote Leave colleague would be taking on the EU negotiation, I would have been disappointed but I would have understood. But they kept insisting that it was for Michael to do all three roles.

Our conversation was getting nowhere, and in frustration I left the room. Before I could make it to my office a few floors away, my mobile rang. Would I go back in to see Boris and keep the talks going? The toing and froing dragged on all week. Boris offered a Cabinet role as Secretary of State for Business, but I declined because I didn't just want a job – I wanted to make sure we delivered on the referendum.

At the same time, the emails kept coming, urging me to stand. Penny Mordaunt and Chris Heaton-Harris started to bring longstanding Leave MPs to my office on the lower ministerial corridor – colleagues who were seeking to persuade me to run. The main doubt expressed was that we might not actually deliver the referendum decision under another leader. I did not share the concern of those colleagues worrying about Boris's commitment to leaving the EU, assuming he was as much of a determined Leaver as the rest of us. But having started the week certain I would be backing Boris, the scales were beginning to tip; my priority was delivering Brexit, and now I was concerned that he and Michael were headed in the wrong direction.

Quickly and quietly, I worked out strategy and policy – no small task, but it had to be done urgently. With senior MP colleagues (including the highly knowledgeable Bill Cash), Penny, Chris and I pulled together a step-by-step plan of how and when the UK would leave the EU and also began to think seriously about what I would actually need to prepare if I decided to run. My sisters were great, offering logistical support with family duties, supplying food, even going out to buy me some new clothes for media occasions. Luke and Tommy from my parliamentary office were recruiting other staffers to help, and

Will Wragg, a relatively new MP colleague, came to offer his support. It felt like something important was about to happen.

Finally, the day before nomination papers were due in to Graham Brady, chairman of the 1922 Committee, who would oversee the leadership contest, Boris got in touch again. We had a deal. I would be in his top team, as part of a gang of three made up of him, Michael and me. I was thrilled – but a little voice in my head warned me to be careful.

*How does Michael feel about it?*

*Oh, well, he accepts it.*

Hmmm. I should get this in writing just to be sure. I told Boris that given nominations closed the following day and the suddenness of his decision, I needed something concrete to confirm our agreement. I asked him if he could send a letter over to my office by the end of the day, confirming I would be joining his top three. I also asked if he would tweet along the lines of: *I'm looking forward to announcing my top team with Michael and Andrea.*

Looking back, I wonder how key this was in Michael's decision to back out of his promise to support Boris. I assumed at the time that Boris and Michael had agreed that we three would be a team. But clearly it was not correct to say that Michael was fine with the change of plan.

That evening, Conservative MPs and supporters were holding a summer fundraising event at the Hurlingham Club, and Ben and I had been invited to join the table of some family friends. I was looking forward to it but also feeling rather anxious – by the evening Boris's letter still hadn't arrived. Before the event, there was a reception for Conservative MPs hosted at the Saatchi Gallery. This would be a chance to chat to colleagues, discover what they were thinking about the race and hopefully bump into Boris. As soon as Ben and I walked into the party, I found myself in the company of a group of MP colleagues who were encouraging me to stand and saying they would support me if I did. This was a surprise; the received wisdom was that the contest came down to a straight choice between Boris and Theresa May, the Home Secretary. While I was chatting to colleagues, my husband spotted Boris across the room and went over to greet him.

*Hi Ben. We've got ourselves a plan, haven't we?*

Ben said: 'Yes, I think we have, but Andrea's waiting for a letter.'

'Oh yes, that's right,' said Boris, but he then left the party before I'd had a chance to see or speak to him. Boris told me later that he had the letter in his pocket at the party and forgot to hand it over.

By now, as we were leaving the Saatchi Gallery and preparing to go to the Hurlingham Club, I was feeling jittery. Ben told me about his encounter with Boris, and while it seemed strange to say the least, I had to assume the letter would still arrive. I rang our evening hosts and apologised profusely but told them I couldn't make it to the event. Instead, I returned to my office, where a group gathered: Penny Mordaunt, Chris Heaton-Harris, Will Wragg, Tim Loughton and Luke, all urging me: *Come on, you've got to stand.*

As the evening ticked by, I sent Boris and Gove a text

reminding them that I was waiting for the letter and tweet. No response. By now we had drawn up my nomination form, with Penny as my proposer and Will Wragg as my seconder. We sat there, waiting. And waiting. The minutes passed and I began to think Boris was not going to reply. I was incredulous.

Finally, Luke said: 'It's nearly 10 p.m.; now or never.'

'Fine,' I said. 'Let's do it.'

Luke ran over to Graham Brady's office in Portcullis House, slipped the forms under the door, and that was it. I was in the race.

I texted Boris and Michael again: 'I'm very sorry Boris and Michael, but I was very clear I needed a public statement this evening. I would have been really keen to work with you but am now going to submit my nomination papers. No hard feelings!'

Within five minutes, I got a text back from Boris: 'Sorry Andrea my cock up… We can do tweet now or tomorrow first thing as u prefer.'

I replied: 'Really sorry.' And left it at that.

What conclusion to draw from this extraordinary turn of events? Was it an unfortunate mistake? I'll leave it to others to decide, but it had a profound impact on what was to come.

Making the short walk home to my flat after my nomination papers were submitted, I was feeling stunned by the magnitude of what I had done. I hadn't only thrown my hat into the ring to be Leader of the Conservative Party; I was also now in the running to become the Prime Minister of our country, with a mission to deliver on the referendum. I updated family and close colleagues, and soon my Westminster flat was full of supporters. Ben and the kids were there, as well as Tim Loughton and Will Wragg, all saying variations of: *Game on, this is going to be a huge success.* Even in those first minutes, we were utterly focused: we began to get a campaign ready and the phone rang off the hook with people offering their support and help. It was comforting to hear so many friends and colleagues saying: *You're not alone; we're with you.*

At around 10.45 p.m., Tim looked at my phone, which I had finally managed to put down and which had begun to ring once again. 'It's Gove,' he said, handing it to me.

'Hello, Michael,' I said in a neutral tone. 'Can I help with anything?'

*I'm just rather amazed at the turn of events.*

'You're amazed?!'

He went on to ask: *I just really want to know, if things had been different, if I hadn't been at his side, would you still have wanted to join Boris's team?*

Michael didn't come out and say he was thinking of standing for the leadership himself but instead began asking what I thought of how Boris was performing. This was such an odd conversation. Michael was Boris's right-hand man and presumably the reason I had been snubbed. When I came off the phone, I told the others it sounded as if Gove wished he hadn't gone with Boris. It still never occurred to me that he was planning to betray him.

Early the following morning, I went over to Victoria Gardens to record a quick clip for social media announcing my candidacy. As Luke was filming me on his mobile, a message popped up on his phone from a friend watching the news: Michael Gove had entered the race. I was totally shocked – at first I didn't believe it. But when we got back to the office, I heard his words myself: 'Boris is an amazing and an impressive person. But I have come, reluctantly, to the conclusion that Boris cannot provide the leadership or build the team for the task ahead.'

It all began to make sense – the phone call I had received from Michael the night before and his failure to answer my messages. It seemed he had completely stitched Boris up, not only by ditching him but also in ensuring I wouldn't back him either, by blocking me from being part of the senior team. A couple of weeks later, Boris told me that his phone had been in the care of Nick Boles for most of that evening.

I don't think I quite appreciated initially the damage done to Boris's own campaign by Gove's actions. Instead, in the hours before the nominations closed, I still thought it was most likely he would become the next Prime Minister – and despite the events of the previous twenty-four hours, I thought that would be the country's preference.

Like many, I was reeling from the latest stage in the drama, but I had a leadership campaign to conduct. An early media outing as an official candidate was with Iain Dale on his LBC radio show. It went well; I felt confident about how I had set out my stall. I managed not to talk my opponents down, having promised myself I would stay on good terms with them. It was important to be honourable, and I had made clear to my team that we should play a straight bat. It seems to me that those who put themselves forward for a life in politics all too often become weighed down by the vitriol from the public and the media. So if we indulge in it ourselves, we are dragging politics down even further.

After LBC, it was on to Radio 5 Live. The presenter had just managed to introduce me before she broke off: *We are now going live to Westminster because Boris Johnson has just pulled out of the Conservative leadership contest.*

This was breath-taking, almost farcical. Yesterday Boris had seemed assured of victory. Now, suddenly, he was gone and everything was turned upside down. It was at this point, with Boris out of the race, that I first began to consider that I might actually win. Since the referendum, I had received thousands of emails from supporters; I knew there was good backing for me out in the country. It felt to me that Michael Gove could not now present a realistic challenge. The other two men in the race, Liam Fox, a former Defence Secretary, and Stephen Crabb, the Welsh Secretary, were both strong candidates but seemed not to have enough support. So there was only Theresa May. Now, Theresa was clearly favourite for most Conservative MPs, occupier of one of the major offices of state with years and years of Cabinet experience under her belt. But Theresa wasn't a Brexiteer. And I was clear that this was what it would come down to: Theresa's experience versus my passion for leaving the EU. When Boris came out and endorsed me a few days later, saying, with typical Johnsonian panache, that I had 'the zap, the drive, and the determination' to lead the country, I really felt I was building momentum.

We now entered the first stage of the contest, in which the five candidates battled to win the support of our fellow Conservative MPs, the top two going forward to a run-off decided by the party's membership. In those first few days, I was overwhelmed by the dozens of colleagues wanting to talk to me about their policy priorities for a future administration. To their credit, only a few were seeking the promise of a ministerial job, whereas most were wanting to promote their personal policy ideas, from radical thoughts about new housing to promoting the use of homeopathy. It was difficult to keep to the fifteen-minute time slots that Tim and Chris had allocated for each chat, but fascinating to hear the broad range of ideas from different colleagues.

The only exception was the call I took from David Davis, longstanding MP and a strong Brexiteer, who stood against David Cameron for the leadership back in the Blair years. He asked me to meet him outside Parliament, as he wanted to discuss whether he would support me or Theresa. He got straight down to business: would I appoint him in charge of negotiations to leave the EU? I said it was too early to agree Cabinet roles. He came out for Theresa later that day.

A high point of those extraordinary days was the official launch of my leadership bid at the Cinnamon Club, the old Westminster library turned into an upmarket Indian restaurant frequented by politicians and hacks. The launch was in a stylish private room packed to the rafters with colleagues, journalists, TV cameras and family. Penny organised it at short notice and did an excellent introductory warm-up, and then came my pitch. I set out my vision for the bright future after we left the EU: of a United Kingdom once again a sovereign nation, leading the world in promoting free trade and delivering social justice at home. The sunlit uplands. I explained that I would trigger Article 50 straight away, not wasting any time in getting us out of the EU and delivering on the referendum. But I also made clear I would not use EU citizens' rights as a pawn in the negotiations – their right to stay in the UK would be protected from day one. These latter two commitments are the things I still wonder about today. If these had been enacted, would we have suffered the years of political pain we would go on to endure?

Just the next day the campaign started to get complicated. I came under an amazing onslaught in the media, from claims that I was homophobic, to accusations that I supported fox hunting and that my family was corrupt, and above all, an accusation that I had lied on my CV, which became a pitched battle. These accusations came in so fast, we couldn't keep up, and the pressure was extreme, trying to get to grips with whatever claim was being thrown at me and find the evidence to refute it before it became tomorrow's headline.

Some did give me a fair crack of the whip. Cathy Newman of *Channel 4 News* let me explain my support for same-sex marriage. The BBC's Laura Kuenssberg and Beth Rigby of Sky both allowed me to rebut the claims of lying on my CV and also to set out my political philosophy. Others were less kind. In one interview, Gary Gibbon of Channel 4 asked: 'Does God talk to you?' I found the trashing of my faith, my CV, my intelligence, and even my optimism a hard price to pay – as it was designed to be. To any politician aiming for high office: don't underestimate the pressure. It's not a job to take on lightly.

My sensitivity to this negative media coverage highlighted an important weakness in my armoury: having only been in government for two years, I was not used to the intensity of the spotlight, and not sure-footed enough to get ahead of the attacks. It felt like sticking a finger in a dam, trying to stop the negative coverage and get onto a positive story about leaving the EU and my ambitions for our country.

As we got closer to the first round of voting, I saw more evidence of how my lack of experience was inhibiting my campaign. Iain Duncan Smith arranged for me to meet the senior editorial team of the *Telegraph*, some of the brightest and highest-profile names in journalism. They gave me a two-hour grilling on economics, politics, Brexit, foreign policy, domestic policy and everything else under the sun. Afterwards, IDS told me I didn't put a foot wrong. And I too felt I had done well in front of such a tough media team. I came out of the *Telegraph*'s office on a high, confident they must surely endorse me. Later that afternoon I received a text from the editor saying: *You did great, but we are backing Theresa because she's got so much more experience.* Experience. No matter how quick-witted, smart or passionate I was, I would never be able to beat Theresa on that front.

That night was the first of two hustings before the 1922 Committee of backbench Conservative MPs. And I really messed up. I had spent the day so busy holding meetings with individual colleagues, trying to win them over one by one, that I hadn't taken the time to marshal my thoughts, let alone practise what I was going to say. Big mistake. This was perhaps the toughest electorate on the planet; cynical and many openly hostile. The atmosphere in Committee Room 14 was hot and heavy; sweaty and packed with Remainers out for blood. A lot of them had already made their minds up about my decision to stand for the leadership – no way was I getting their vote! My lack of preparation certainly told. The pitch of my speech was wrong, with a focus on early years, a crucial policy area but not right for this audience. Thrown off by the negative reception, I struggled to get back on the front foot. My colleagues wanted to know if I was equipped to lead them as Prime Minister, the person who would determine the question of whether Brexit would prove a challenge or an opportunity. My speech was too basic to answer that conundrum, and while I redeemed myself to some extent in the question-and-answer session which followed my speech, I knew from the faces of my campaign team that damage had been done. Again, it was a lack of experience, among all of us: neither the team nor I had fully appreciated the vital importance during a campaign of prioritising the candidate's time, particularly to prepare for big public events.

We left the room feeling despondent and went down a set of back stairs, coming out in the library corridor. And there was Amber, with Nick Watt of *Newsnight*.

She laughed in an awkward way: *Oh Andrea, I was just talking about you.*

'Yes, I'm sure you were, Amber.'

*Only tiny little knives.*

'So acupuncture then?' I laughed it off, but I knew what she had been saying: *She's my good friend, but she's very junior, she's got no experience, I can't support her.*

Amber and I have long ago patched up our differences, but at the time it was painful.

And she was not the only colleague to wield the stiletto. A day or so later, I became aware of a message being circulated among Theresa's supporters by Nick Boles, a Gove ally, urging them to vote tactically for Michael in order to stop me getting into the second round.

'I am seriously frightened about the risk of allowing Andrea Leadsom onto the membership ballot,' it read. '...Surely we must all work together to stop AL?'

Boles would later apologise to Michael, who claimed no knowledge of the message. But the episode backfired, and Gove lost some support thanks to the impression it left, compounded by his behaviour towards Boris. I heard that he was pushed hard over it at the second hustings hosted by the 1922 Committee, where I thankfully managed to perform much better than I had in the first outing – I'm a quick learner. And that's another big tip to anyone thinking of going for high office: you need to face up to your mistakes in real time, and don't make them twice.

So, all in all, I was surprised and delighted when the results of the first round of voting were announced and I was placed second, ahead of Gove and in a position which, if I could maintain it, would see me onto the ballot to face the membership. I had superb whipping led by Chris Heaton-Harris, who was almost spot on in his prediction of my vote share. Believing as we did that only a Brexiteer could be elected, I was more convinced than ever that I was on the cusp of becoming Prime Minister. A growing concern, though, was about the gulf between Theresa's vote and my own. In a five-horse race, she had won 50 per cent of the vote, capturing the support of more than twice as many MPs as me, and already some Remainer colleagues were saying they would resign the whip if I won. As the candidate with the fewest votes, Liam Fox was automatically eliminated from the contest, Stephen Crabb withdrew, and so Michael, Theresa and I went on to the final round.

The following evening, exhausted and not a little worried about the anger of so many Remain colleagues, I set out for a round of political summer parties. Will Wragg had loyally agreed to accompany me, as he had done for several days since I became a serious leadership contender. In the taxi to the first party, hosted each year by Margot James MP and Amber for female MPs and journalists, he observed how organised everyone else's campaign felt in comparison to our own hurried affair. It was as if they had been planning this for months, if not years. Theresa's felt particularly professional, headed by Gavin Williamson, later an effective and pretty ruthless Chief Whip. Our campaign, on the other hand, was totally impromptu. As Will put it, the team was hardworking and dedicated, but 'it was as if we were trying to build a jet engine as we were taxiing along the runway'.

I had been looking forward to this party, held at Margot's home. I went along conscious that most of the guests would be Remainers but that they included some of my good friends in politics. As I stepped into Margot's lovely garden terrace in the warm summer evening, the atmosphere felt awkward. While everyone was pleasant on the surface, I felt only just about welcome. It was pretty clear I wouldn't be getting many votes there.

Theresa was a guest too, and at one point someone politely raised a toast to the women who had the courage to put their names forward. Many of those present had already come out for Theresa, and as I left soon after, it was with a stark realisation: politics at that level is just too important for friendship to count. It was awful and yet vital to understand and accept that fact if you want to be Prime Minister. It was clear that while colleagues were too polite in a social setting to display hostility, most of these women were in the Remain/May camp, and I should expect no quarter from them. Likewise, the female journalists I knew well, some of whom had given my campaigns a real boost over the years, were now firmly on the fence – the winner takes all, and personal relationships can't be a part of it. They would wait and see before nailing their colours to mine or Theresa's masts.

From Margot's house I went to the second summer drinks party, this time at the Westminster home of the veteran MP Sir Edward Leigh. The contrast with the women's drinks couldn't have been more stark. Even their homes were chalk and cheese. Sir Edward's was a glorious classical terrace compared to Margot's modern and airy home. The guests were mainly Brexiteers, some enthusiastic younger MPs as well as a number of party grandees who had been campaigning to leave the EU for a long time. There were cheers as I entered, and I was made to feel incredibly welcome – in contrast to what had gone before. These colleagues were not necessarily close friends, but they were now clearly my vital political allies. Many of the longstanding, highly experienced MPs who were also avid campaigners for Leave were now looking to me to deliver for them.

On a pensive walk back to my flat with Ben, my phone rang. The campaign team had lined up what they had billed as a big speech on the economy for the following morning, the day of the final ballot of MPs. I had put notes on the economy together that morning and had been told that a good friend and journalist, Tim Montgomerie, was drafting the keynote address for me to review tonight. Now this was Tim calling.

'So, where are we on the briefing for the speech?' he asked. Oh dear.

I arrived at the flat to find the bare bones of a speech had been emailed over to me, far from the weighty and incisive exposition of my economic philosophy I had been anticipating! By now, it was 10 p.m., and I needed to get stuck into writing the speech myself. It was another key lesson: the buck stops with me. For all that people are generous and rally round, it is vital to remember that when the music stops, you're literally on your own.

The next day, 7 July, was the final, crucial, round of the MPs' vote. I delivered my economic speech in a big room in Millbank and it was fine. Just fine. No more than that. Afterwards, I was whisked away in a car to meet journalists, cast my vote, and then meet up with Ben. We were off to Northampton, where, by sheer coincidence, a certain well-known speaker, one Boris Johnson, had long ago agreed to speak at a big Conservative fundraiser and a parallel charity event we were putting on at the local theatre. It was typical of Boris to be so kind as to stick to the commitment – many others would have justifiably given their apologies after what he had just been through.

Straight after my economic speech, Tim Loughton had agreed with the team to organise a Leadsom for Leader march on Parliament. Watching later on television as colleagues and supporters marched along the street chanting my name, I was laughing but cringing at the same time. The march was designed to shore up support in the face of the hostility of the Gove campaign. My team were aware that Gove's supporters were determined to persuade large numbers of MPs to lend their vote to him to prevent me being in the final two on the ballot, so the march was intended to demonstrate the strong support for my bid. Tim had started the chanting to distract from a journalist who was challenging him quite vociferously about my speech. Some MPs thought the march was fun, but I know others found it pretty undignified.

That march, replayed only much later that day, added to the growing sense that I was not entirely in control of events. The latter stages of the campaign had proved intense: the Boles email, the hostility from the Remain camp, the constant accusations in the media, the speech-drafting confusion; there was only one thing to do and that was to keep calm and carry on.

Ben and I met up on the train to Milton Keynes, and it was there, as we chugged through the outskirts of London, that the call came through: I had gained eighty-four votes, to 199 for Theresa and forty-six for Michael. I was on the final ballot.

I hugged Ben and said: 'This is it. I'm going to be Prime Minister.'

# CHAPTER SEVEN

# AS A MOTHER

Thursday 7 July 2016 started as just another day in the busy life of someone trying to become Prime Minister. It also happened to be Ben's fiftieth birthday. I began by delivering an economic speech and ended with an uproarious fundraiser starring Boris Johnson. It was the day I went through to the final ballot of the Conservative leadership contest with a serious chance of being elected Prime Minister – and it was also the day I began to understand that this was an honour I would have to decline in the best interests of the country. Less than a week after that phone call on the train, Theresa May would enter 10 Downing Street as Prime Minister. It is perhaps no surprise that the events of that period are indelibly etched on my memory.

Those first moments after I received word that I was through to the final round of the leadership contest were pure elation. Ben was as delighted as I was. A cool assessment of the facts – that a Brexiteer would be better placed to steer through Britain's departure from the EU, and that the Conservative membership, then as now heavily weighted towards Leave, would share this view and so choose me – gave me real cause for optimism.

Even then, however, I was realistic about the challenges that lay ahead. Under the terms agreed between Graham Brady as chairman of the 1922 Committee, the outgoing Downing Street team and the Conservative Party, the contest was due to last nine weeks. This seemed to me a catastrophic error.

Ben and I agreed we needed to request a much shorter campaign. The stock market was already dropping and sterling was falling; getting confidence back into the markets as soon as possible was the priority. That meant a new Prime Minister inside No. 10 getting on with the job as soon as possible. Otherwise the economy and jobs would be under threat – we could even end up with the recession that was threatened by Project Fear.

I had another profound concern. Theresa had received 199 votes, almost two-thirds of Conservative MPs, to my eighty-four. I was aware that some Remain-supporting colleagues had already threatened to resign the whip rather than serve under me. There was a real worry that if I was elected by the membership in the face of resistance from the parliamentary party, I could face a vote of no confidence within days of taking office, causing serious turmoil in the country.

As soon as we got in the car to drive to the fundraiser, I called Graham Brady and said to him straight out: 'I'm delighted with the result, feeling completely confident – however, I don't think the country can afford a nine-week campaign.' And I gave him the reasons why I felt such a long contest would be a disaster, focusing on the risk of recession if the markets continued to plunge.

Graham replied: *It's got to be nine weeks – David Cameron and Andrew Feldman insist.*

Feldman was a close ally of Cameron and also party chairman. My understanding was that Cameron had been keen to attend the forthcoming meeting of the G20 in China in September, but this didn't seem a good enough reason to put the economy in jeopardy.

Graham told me he had already put to them that a long leadership campaign might well spark a recession, and that the 1922 Committee preferred a short, snappy contest. I asked him whether this was their idea of saying 'I told you so' to voters. A meaningful silence followed.

My mind drifted back to a conversation David Cameron and I had in the Members' Tea Room after PMQs only a week earlier. Cameron had sat at a table next to me and, as was his habit, leaned back in his chair with his hands stretched behind his head. Smilingly, he said: 'So, Andrea, if you're in the final two, you won't pull out, will you, because Nancy doesn't want to leave No. 10 just yet.'

Nancy, his daughter, was twelve – as was Cookie.

I said: 'My daughter is the same age as Nancy and she's a bit nervous about moving out of her bedroom too…'

Now the timetable for the Camerons' departure from Downing Street had taken on a far greater significance. I asked Graham if he could renegotiate the terms of the contest, with the result moving to the end of July. That would give the new

PM the whole of August to work out a programme for exiting the EU during the autumn. Graham agreed this was a preferable timescale but said it was impossible to change what had been agreed; the date was set in stone. In hindsight, I should have challenged this more vigorously, perhaps gone public with my fears about the damage a long contest could bring about.

What I said instead was: 'Then I'm not sure I should go ahead with this. If I lose, people will rightly ask, "Why on earth did you make us wait nine weeks for our new leader?"'

Then my biggest concern: *The thing is, Graham, I think there's a good chance I might win. And that would be totally against the wishes of a majority of our colleagues, who could make government impossible.*

Graham sympathised with the dilemma but urged me to stick with it. After some back and forth we agreed I would consider it over the weekend and make my decision on the Monday.

Ben and I drove on to Northampton, where Boris was due to arrive at the Royal & Derngate Theatre at any minute. I was fixated on speaking to Boris before the event began. He had come out in support of my candidacy, and I anticipated that with his usual enthusiasm he would turn the evening into a rally in support of me. Given the doubts that had begun to creep in, I had to let him know how I was feeling – and of course the traffic was horrendous. With a few minutes to go before the start of the first charity event, we screeched into the car park and ran to the theatre. Outside were dozens of photographers all shouting: 'Are you going to win, Andrea?'

I smiled sweetly and kept going, thinking how surprised they would be if they knew my inner turmoil.

I managed to grab a few minutes with Boris in the theatre dressing room, quickly explaining my concerns about the nine-week campaign, the impact on the economy and the overwhelming support for Theresa in the party. Boris understood immediately. 'Right, so what do you want me to say then?'

I said I hadn't made a final decision but that it would probably be wise not to be too enthusiastic. Boris quickly got the point – but he also urged me to keep on regardless.

The charity fundraiser went well, and then it was on to the main event upstairs, where a sell-out crowd of around 800 Conservative supporters was waiting eagerly. As I stepped on stage, I could see a sea of faces, everyone chuffed to be in the room with some of the team that had delivered the referendum result, and excited at the prospect that one of their own might be on the cusp of becoming Prime Minister. Boris did a great job of acknowledging my success in getting onto the ballot, without going over the top about my prospects of victory. I have often thought how incredibly kind he was to do that – he must have been devastated by the events of the previous days, and many would have understandably pulled out of this engagement. But Boris ploughed on and as the chairman of the local Conservatives introduced him, he told the audience: 'I rather think you have the most sought-after ticket in the country this evening.'

Looking back, it was a lovely but rather tragic evening – deeply moving because of all the support and good feeling, but all the time my heart was sinking with the knowledge that I would be letting people down if I did not see through the hopes they had for me and for the future of the party. I felt trapped.

I shared my doubts with Chris, who advised me to take some time to think things over. He urged me to relax and keep a low profile over the weekend. I wasn't sure this was a good idea but agreed to take Friday off at least. With the help of Steve Baker, the MP for Wycombe, who had joined my campaign team, Chris and Tim Loughton promised to get the campaign up and running over the weekend, allowing me to hit the ground running on my return to the trail on Monday. In fact, everyone close to me was united in urging me to take a day or so off. Everyone, that is, except my media advisers.

A member of my team had arranged two interviews, describing them as 'soft, friendly chats' for the Saturday papers, introducing my family and my views to the public. One was with the *Telegraph*'s Allison Pearson and the other with Rachel Sylvester of *The Times*. Although Tim and Chris suggested I take the weekend off, the media advice was: 'You shouldn't pull out of these interviews. These are important journalists and they will meet you somewhere local to you.'

Reluctantly, I agreed.

After a fantastic lie-in, I had breakfast with the kids and then dressed in an informal cream linen suit – relaxed but professional. When it became apparent that I would be attending these interviews alone, I didn't particularly think anything of it. I now know this was extraordinarily naive. It should have been unthinkable for a candidate presenting herself as a Prime

Minister-in-waiting to go for an interview unaccompanied. There would be no one to usher through the arrangements, challenge inappropriate questions or even tape the conversation so I would have my own record of what had been said. At the time, astonishing to think of now, I had no idea how problematic this could be. It was another sign of inexperience – and a lesson I would learn the hard way.

So I drove myself to Milton Keynes and met the first interviewer, Rachel Sylvester, and her photographer at the station. No meeting place had been organised, so I suggested a nearby coffee bar because time was short. The place was packed, and while we eventually found a table to ourselves, I was immediately conscious of being watched and overheard. Throughout the conversation, well-wishers kept approaching, which was lovely of them but distracting. Rachel was all smiles; for me it was torture – I could tell people were listening in. I wanted to be anywhere but that coffee shop. But this had been billed as a friendly, get-to-know-you chat, and I felt it would be rude to terminate the interview.

After several years in Cabinet, I would never make that mistake again, but at the time, not only did I go along with it; I also didn't pre-agree the terms of the interview. I expected that, although it was an on-the-record interview, I would be able to make off-the-record remarks by way of explanations of particular views. But, as it turned out, those were never the rules of that game.

So when Rachel asked questions I was uncomfortable with, my response was to explain the reasons I did not wish to pursue this line of questioning, not realising this explanation itself could be included as on-the-record quotes in her article.

We began and it was straightforward enough: *What did you do before politics? What was your childhood like?* I told her my backstory and she seemed fascinated, writing furiously in her notebook and encouraging me to talk at length. We moved on to politics and discussed my interest in the early years. It felt almost an opportunity to set the record straight after my bungled speech to colleagues at the first leadership hustings. I explained how important babies were and that if we could get our policies around supporting new parents right, this could be transformative.

*So do you think mothers should stay at home?*

I was taken aback. 'Of course not. I'm a working mum and had help all the way through.'

*But do you think that for you, being a mother has made a difference to your politics?*

*Yes, of course it has. In particular, my experience of postnatal depression is key to my interest in the early years.*

She then asked about the differences between me and Theresa May, and when I mentioned my economic background, sense of optimism and the confidence that comes from a big family with lots of siblings, in-laws and children, she focused in like a laser on the latter.

'Do you feel like a mum in politics?'

This seemed totally off kilter. It was leading me down a rabbit hole I should have avoided. Instead, with nearby coffee drinkers listening in, I tried to explain my discomfort with this line of questioning, and it led to the biggest mistake of my campaign. It should have been clear to me by then that the multiple questions about being a mum were designed to have me draw a distinction between Theresa and me on the matter of children. In trying to draw a line under that questioning and get to the end of the interview, I stupidly gave her the quote she was looking for.

By now, the interview had gone on for well over the half-hour agreed. I answered a couple more questions then politely said I would have to go. She insisted on continuing with the interview, to the point where I actually had to get up and leave the table. Once outside, the photographer pointed out we hadn't taken any pictures, so I gave them five minutes, doing my best to smile cheerfully while posing in front of the coffee shop and fretting at how late I was to meet Allison Pearson.

By the time I made it back to the station, Allison's train had long since arrived and she was waiting patiently in the ticket hall. The interview with her couldn't have been more different from my conversation with Rachel. We found a quiet corner in a nearby hotel and although Allison asked very similar questions about my life and politics, she also asked about the vision for what my premiership would be: to help people be the best they can be and to make the most of their capabilities; to give people a hand up, to help them to aspire and to give them the freedom to do so. And that meant giving them the best beginning in life through a good early start, a decent education, a strong safety net and opportunities for a secure job and a home of their own.

The *Telegraph* interview was great, and by the time I waved Allison off at the station, I had forgotten all about the previous interview. I spent the rest of the day discussing plans with Chris, Tim and Steve Baker, who was a fantastic addition – extremely organised and efficient and it was reassuring to know he was on my side. But even then, things didn't go smoothly. That afternoon, I reached out to Lynton Crosby, the renowned Australian campaigner who had run Boris's successful mayoral elections and had been due to do so again for this contest. Now Boris was no longer in the race, I wanted to see if he would be willing to support my campaign. The answer came back: he couldn't do that. Then I got in touch with Boris and asked if he would be willing to become more closely involved with my bid. Understandably, he was not up for it, but both responses were blows when I was already looking for reasons to carry on.

*The Times*'s front page dropped on Twitter at about 11 p.m. *What on earth?* There on the front was the most horrendous photograph of me caught in a gust of wind with my hair standing on end. They hadn't used any of the pictures taken that day but had instead gone for one in which I closely resembled the Wicked Witch of the East. It was a sharp realisation of the power images have alongside words.

But the picture was nothing in comparison to the headline, which read: 'Being a mother gives me edge on May – Leadsom'. The words below were just as sickening: 'Tory minister says she will be better leader because childless home secretary lacks "stake in future"'.

It is hard to convey my fury at the time: this was hideously offensive not only to Theresa but also to anyone who has ever struggled with infertility or baby loss, issues that are so dear to me. This portrayal was of course deeply damaging to my campaign, but instead of consulting my team and using cooler heads to determine the best way to limit the damage, I responded immediately. 'How could you?' I tweeted. 'Truly appalling and the exact opposite of what I said. I am disgusted.' This seemed obvious to me, given that my words as quoted in the article were explicitly explaining what I had NOT wanted to say. But I had not spotted the trap, and that's on me.

Thus began a public row over the next few days, as Rachel Sylvester defended her reporting and put out selective clips from our conversation that did indeed support her article. In my own lack of experience, I had not considered it necessary to tape the interview myself, and although I was confident that the full transcript would back up my version of events, *The Times* would consistently refuse to release it.

The damage was done, and the whole episode left me with a strong sense of the power of the press, and how individuals can be portrayed in a way that suits the narrative of the time. I don't fault anyone who takes what they read at face value. Media portrayal of a person or an opinion can definitely be a force for good or ill.

For months I would be outraged at what had happened, but given the passage of time and my greater experience, I can see in hindsight how important is the functioning of the free press – any candidate for Prime Minister of the United Kingdom must be tested on how they respond under pressure and how well they identify and deal with elephant traps. The naivety I showed that day demonstrated I still had much to learn.

I texted Theresa: 'I am totally appalled by the Times headline, this is not at all what I said and I will insist on a full retraction. I'm truly sorry for what they've written – Andrea.'

She responded, graciously and immediately: 'Andrea, thank you for your message. I really appreciate you getting in touch to apologise. Best wishes Theresa.'

Feeling despondent, I said to Ben: 'I can't do this. It's only going to get worse.' Our inexperience was telling. Much as the campaign team was absolutely committed, they had never done a leadership contest either. We were flying in the dark. If I stuck with it and lost in nine weeks' time, any recession caused by uncertainty would be my fault.

But the campaign rumbled on inexorably and so, it seemed, did Ben's birthday celebrations. The next day, Saturday, we had a long-planned barbecue in the garden with some local friends. We considered cancelling and then, as we always did, decided to press on. My good friend and local association president Peter Warner turned up at 10 a.m. and we sat with a sheet of paper writing down the pros and cons of my remaining in the race. Many suggest the *Times* interview was the reason I withdrew from the race, but the truth is it was high on the list of reasons to stick with it, because I would then have a future opportunity to put the record straight.

I also felt strongly that I should not give in to those who were deploying what are sometimes known as the 'dark arts' against me, either because they supported Theresa or because they had their own reasons for wanting to stop me from becoming Prime Minister. That weekend, a Leave-supporting journalist friend called to warn me that a rumour would soon be leaked to the press that I thought Theresa could not become Prime Minister because she has diabetes.

'Well, that's not going to work; no one will believe that given my husband has diabetes too.'

*Don't be so sure*, came the reply.

I sought advice from a number of people, including my mum, who still urged me to carry on. But no one can really put themselves in your shoes at a time like that. It is a lonely decision.

There was one very positive reason for wanting to remain in the contest: the weight of the thousands of people who had contacted me to say: *We've got your back; we want you to win.* I was very conscious that for all my colleagues' reservations, I had fantastic support among party members and in the country at large. The major reason for sticking at it, though, was my sense that having in part been responsible for the referendum result, I should see it through. To walk away would be letting too many people down.

But the cons kept mounting: my inexperience; the lack of support in the parliamentary party; the damage to the economy from a nine-week campaign. We wrote the list and I decided to mull it over some more – then went outside to join the party.

By Sunday night, my mind was made up: I had to pull out.

I kept my counsel and decided to sleep on it one more time before making my decision public – but I couldn't see any other course.

The next morning, I caught the train to London and made my way to Westminster. Now we were in the middle of a full-blown leadership contest, the rules dictated that we could not campaign from offices on the parliamentary estate. So I headed instead to the Cowley Street home of the former MP Sir Neil Thorne and his wife, Lady Sarah. They had generously given us use of the ground floor of their home as our headquarters, and the team was all gathered: Steve Baker, Chris Heaton-Harris, Tim Loughton and Luke Graystone along with Will Wragg, the Corby MP Tom Pursglove, MP for South Derbyshire Heather Wheeler and a gang of brilliant, enthusiastic young campaigners. The room was replete with whiteboards, desks, a phone system, pens and pencils and everything else a political campaign might need. A huge cheer went up as I walked into the room, and it was clear everyone was eager for the campaign to begin. It would be the first and last time I would be inside my own campaign centre.

It was a sickening feeling, knowing I was going to let them down. I went upstairs to thank Neil and Sarah for their generosity in letting us use their home, then called the core team together. 'I'm so sorry,' I said. 'But this is not going to happen. I'm going to withdraw and I'm going to call Theresa May now to let her know.' They were so disappointed and I felt just awful for them. But by now I was completely convinced it was the right thing for the country.

I texted the Home Secretary for the second time in four days: 'Good morning, Theresa, would it be possible to have a quick urgent phone call please?'

She immediately rang back and we had the three- or four-minute conversation which paved her way to become Prime Minister. I told her I was withdrawing from the race and gave her my reasons for doing so. Throughout the entire referendum campaign and leadership contest which followed, my primary concern had been to ensure Brexit was delivered. My fear was that following a nine-week contest, with the recession I believed could ensue, the chance of us leaving the EU would be overtaken and could slip away. However disappointing it was for me personally to give up the prospect of becoming Prime Minister, I had to put what I felt was best for the country first. The conversation was friendly and to the point, and Theresa assured me that her commitment to leaving the EU was genuine. From that moment on, it felt to me as if we were inextricably bound: I had effectively handed her this job, and it was my duty to help her deliver Brexit.

Just before I rang off, I told Theresa I would be announcing my withdrawal in about half an hour and asked her not to tell anyone until I had done so. 'I'm giving you a warning because I know if our situations were reversed, I would want time to get used to the idea that I was about to be Prime Minister.' She readily agreed to keep our conversation secret. I later learned she was so true to her word that she told no one she was about to become PM, not even her husband, Philip.

When I came off the phone, I gathered the whole team

together and broke the news. 'Theresa has promised she will deliver on the referendum and take us out of the EU. And therefore I have to stand aside for her. She's got the most support, the most experience, and she has a game plan, the team and impetus to get going straight away.'

They were very disappointed but absolutely understanding. My colleagues have never openly criticised me for the decision I made that day; in fact, Chris and Heather would later roll up their sleeves and get stuck in again when I ran for the leadership in 2019.

I made my statement on the steps of Cowley Street with the team around me (inadvertently torpedoing an event being held by Angela Eagle to launch her Labour leadership bid, which journalists unceremoniously abandoned). There followed a somewhat unedifying scramble as Ben, Chris, Tim and I made our exit out the back door and into a black cab, only to be tracked down by photographers when we got stuck in traffic! But when we eventually walked back into Parliament, it was as if a weight had lifted. I was so sure I had done the right thing.

Since that day, many people have asked if I regret pulling out of the leadership contest in 2016. It is a question I have returned to again and again, particularly during the tortuous years when Brexit hung in the balance. But no one has a crystal ball in politics – something I would often remind myself. It is impossible to tell what would have transpired had I become Prime Minister. At best, I fear there would have been a recession after a brutal nine-week campaign; at worst, civil unrest over the referendum outcome. That may sound overly dramatic, but I could only take my decision based on the facts as they stood at the time. And so one thing is for sure – even in my dark moments, I have never regretted the decision to step aside.

# CHAPTER EIGHT

# CABINET

I stood in a splendid state room upstairs in Downing Street, waiting to be called in to see Theresa May. By now, I had been invited to No. 10 on a handful of occasions, and I was struck as always by the contrast between the relatively humble frontage of the building and the space and grandeur inside. As befits the place where the Prime Minister of the United Kingdom both lives and works, the surroundings are imposing yet welcoming. On the stairway to the upper floor are hung portraits of all the men and women who have had the honour of serving our country as PM. It was hard not to be conscious that had I taken a different course a few days earlier, it could have been my image up there. I looked around the room, at the elegant furniture and beautiful artwork, thinking how surreal the past few weeks had been. Pulling out my phone, I snapped a quick selfie and texted it to my husband. 'This might have been our home,' I wrote, with a laughing emoji.

But while I was aware how differently events could have played out, there was no bitterness on my part. Far from it – I was both surprised and delighted to find myself in No. 10, given I had no expectation whatsoever of remaining a minister, let alone joining the Cabinet.

The call from the Downing Street switchboard in July 2016 came when I was at a pretty low ebb following my withdrawal from the leadership contest. The premature end to my campaign was a devastating blow to those closest to me, and I was consumed with remorse at the impact on those who had backed me, from supportive members of the public to my family, friends and campaign team. One after another, their faces appeared in my mind's eye: my parliamentary aides Luke and Tommy; my niece and nephew, then eighteen, who had volunteered in that chaotic period in my Commons office; Penny Mordaunt and Theresa Villiers, both ministers who had so much to lose in backing me; Chris Heaton-Harris, Tim Loughton, Will Wragg, Heather Wheeler and Steve Baker, all of whom had worked their socks off. I thought of the young supporters who had turned up to help at Cowley Street, and members of the public who took the trouble to let me know they were behind me. I felt guilty that I'd let down so many people who trusted and believed in me. The magnitude of what I had done in pulling out of the race hit me like a bus. For those first days after the contest I don't think I slept for more than a couple of hours.

I found myself constantly reliving events: what should I have done differently? And while I will probably always regret not pushing back over the nine-week timetable for the contest, I still came to the same conclusion: I had no choice but to withdraw. So I busied myself trying to make it up to people. From the start, I had been determined to fund my campaign myself, and we returned every penny we could and compensated all the young supporters who had taken time off to try to help my campaign. I also wrote personally to all the MPs who had given me their backing, with heartfelt messages of thanks and apology.

But during this period after the contest, above all else I was still Energy Minister. On becoming Prime Minister, Theresa spent her first hours appointing the great offices of state, making Philip Hammond Chancellor, Boris Foreign Secretary and Amber Home Secretary. I was delighted for Boris. He had been so dumped on during the leadership contest and I wished him well. Michael Gove, on the other hand, was excluded – it seemed this PM believed in rewarding honour, which felt the right thing to do.

Amber's appointment was not a surprise, but it had an immediate impact on me. Energy Questions were by chance scheduled for three days after I withdrew, and in Amber's absence I was the only Commons minister left to take them. That meant I went alone to the despatch box to answer dozens of technical and potentially hostile questions from parliamentarians for an hour. Not exactly a walk in the park.

To my enormous relief and gratitude, it seemed that the whips had launched Operation Protect Leadsom, sitting closely around me and making clear their moral support. A large number of backbenchers did the same. Speaker John Bercow was amazingly kind too, and even the opposition held their fire. I felt real warmth from the Chamber that day, a rare and unusual atmosphere.

And here I was, a few hours after Energy Questions, in No. 10, presumably about to receive an invitation to join Theresa's Cabinet. Yet again the game of political snakes and ladders was in full swing – elation turned to devastation and back again in the space of a few days.

I was shown into the Cabinet Room and greeted our new Prime Minister. It was the first time we had spoken since I had called her to concede. I felt quite emotional and would have liked to have given her a hug and said: 'Good luck, I'm really on your side.' But I hesitated, sensing such a display would not be welcome. Theresa was calm and business-like as ever and I did my best to convey how much I wanted her to succeed, assuring her: 'I will help you in any way I can to deliver on the referendum.'

Then she offered me the job: Secretary of State for the Environment, Food and Rural Affairs. I was totally delighted. Of all the Whitehall departments, Defra is the major EU implementation department: up to 80 per cent of everything Defra did at the time – food, farming, fisheries, the environment – was dictated by the EU. I had spent so much time with the Fresh Start Project looking at these areas and what it would mean for the UK should we leave the EU, it felt as if I was made for the brief. It is a big policy department, and with our departure from Europe, Britain had a massive opportunity to do our own thing.

Immediately, I knew what my ambitions would be in each of the key portfolio areas. Farming was a subject I knew well from my constituency. It felt important we kept the farm subsidy element of the Common Agricultural Policy but adapted it to reward increased food production, greening and better environmental stewardship.

Fisheries was another area close to my heart and I was determined to see our fishing communities rebound. I knew taking back control of our coastal waters would mean we could do just that.

I was eager to get stuck into the full range of issues, from the protection of coastal areas and water courses to tackling the illegal wildlife and ivory trades. It seemed the perfect job and I told Theresa I was thrilled to accept.

On top of my responsibilities at Defra, I also now had the privilege of a seat in Cabinet.

Although I had been inside the Cabinet Room a few times by then, nothing will ever compare to walking through the door as a Cabinet minister for the first time and taking my seat at the table. This is a highly ritualised business. Seating is determined by seniority, with the most important office holders such as Chancellor sitting closest to the PM, and places are marked not by name but by title. I sat in front of the nameplate 'Secretary of State for Environment, Food and Rural Affairs', a few seats down from the centre but with a good eyeline to catch the Prime Minister's attention. To my pleasure, I was next to Priti Patel, who had also joined the Cabinet as International Development Secretary, and who became an ally in our Brexit discussions. In fact, I was cheered to see how many Brexiteers were now in senior positions in government. Despite the formality of our meetings, this would largely prove a friendly Cabinet; we swapped private phone numbers and would message each other often.

Theresa's manner in Cabinet was very collegiate. She would introduce a topic briefly, tell you what she thought and then go around the table allowing everyone to have their say. This felt like a strength at the beginning, but within a year the meetings became too long, sometimes heated but actually more often dull. As is the way with these things, some people were mercifully brief, while others were wordy. But it was fascinating to learn everyone's views and begin to anticipate each one's reaction to new challenges.

This was also my first experience of reading the Cabinet minutes which followed on from our discussions. They always reflected what the Prime Minister said at the start and then the Chancellor, before going on to give a flavour of the conversation which followed, without attributing remarks to individuals. At the end, it would say: 'The Cabinet took note.' These weren't votes, they were discussions, and on contentious topics I came to feel that what had been discussed in Cabinet was not always reflected in the minutes, which became a significant source of tension.

Brexit naturally was a frequent agenda item. There were some big characters in the room; David Davis as Secretary of State for Exiting the EU and Boris Johnson as Foreign Secretary were both vociferous in making their views known.

Philip Hammond as Chancellor and Michael Fallon as Defence Secretary were also both dominant characters. As the months passed, I began to feel some of the men were quite overbearing in their attitude towards the PM. This was well demonstrated, in my opinion, when Theresa put forward some ideas to enforce better behaviour from company boards and shareholders in the wake of the British Home Stores scandal, when, under the management of Philip Green, the pensions of tens of thousands of ex-employees were in danger of being lost. As Theresa set out her proposals to stop this happening again, some around her Cabinet table seemed determined to explain why her plans were impossible because 'the world didn't work like that'. Having spent ten years as head of corporate governance for a funds management company, I agreed with Theresa – the world could easily work the way she was proposing, and I found the tone from our colleagues frustrating on her behalf.

Taken together, Theresa's Cabinet ministers formed an interesting group. I was wary of some of the Remainers, who had been so overtly hostile during the referendum campaign. There was a constant sensation of a subtext, of things going on behind the scenes, that people weren't being frank about. After Michael Gove rejoined the Cabinet, I became aware he too was coming to Theresa's defence, evidence of his strong ability to read a room and position himself for the future.

The Chancellor, Philip Hammond, was in my view too negative, particularly when the topic was Brexit. One week, to my delight and astonishment, he agreed to my fervent request to guarantee farm subsidies post-Brexit until the next election, so I sent him a soft toy Tigger as a joke. *See*, the note read, *you can be less Eeyore and more Tigger.*

My new department in Smith Square contained quite the most beautiful Secretary of State's office I had ever seen. The building itself was rundown, and, sadly, on my watch I had to agree a move so that much-needed repair work could be undertaken. But I was able to enjoy a year in the lovely spacious office with its domed ceiling painted Wedgwood blue. There was ornate cornicing and wood-panelled walls, a big mahogany desk and fabulous artwork featuring food and farming, including beautiful landscapes of meadows and wheatfields. There was even a balcony looking out over the Thames. It was stunning, and a privilege to be working there.

Hidden away along the wood panelling was a secret cupboard where the official seals of office were stored. These were handed to me by the Queen when I was sworn in as a Privy Counsellor. Dating back to medieval times, the Privy Council is a group of advisers to the monarch, and these days comprises senior politicians and other dignitaries such as High Court judges, senior clergy and members of the royal family.

The experience of being driven to Buckingham Palace to be sworn in as a Privy Counsellor is unforgettable. My government car drove through the gates and the driver announced: 'I've got the Secretary of State for Environment, Food and Rural Affairs.' We went in and stopped in front of a portico, where a red carpet is laid going into a large hallway. There, the little group of us joining Cabinet were shown into a room to have a rehearsal. This proved a good-humoured affair, as we were each instructed to kneel with one knee on a footstool, one arm by our side and the other lifting a prayerbook. It seemed impossible to contemplate such contortions while in the presence of Her Majesty the Queen – without doubt the most famous woman in the world, and someone who can reduce the grandest of folk to a bundle of nerves.

Boris, there to be sworn in as Foreign Secretary, wondered aloud: 'What if someone were to fall off the footstool?' Not very reassuringly, he was advised that the Queen would almost certainly find it amusing, so not to worry.

Once we had negotiated the first hurdle, we were told we would each then proceed forward to another footstool, this time without the prayer book, where we would take the Queen's left hand in our right hand and brush our lips to it as part of the vow. I hurriedly scrubbed off all traces of lipstick.

Then it was the ceremony itself, presided over by David Lidington, the Leader of the House and Lord President of the Privy Council, who had signed the copy of the Bible I was given to keep. We lined up in alphabetical order, feeling anxious for the person who had to go first and me bemoaning that my name began with an 'L', placing me behind a 'J' – Boris Johnson. *He better not fall off his stool*, I thought.

Of course in the end the ceremony went off smoothly, although I was almost caught out when the Queen handed me the old and valuable seals of office in a small red box which she handled as if they were as light as a feather but which were actually surprisingly heavy. The next challenge was walking backwards to the door and dropping a curtsy, before turning to leave. Then it was back in the ministerial car to Smith Square, where the seals were locked away in the secret cupboard, not to be seen again until I left the department and the next Secretary of State received them from the hands of the Queen.

Soon after I was sworn in, I was invited to Clarence House to meet the Prince of Wales, who takes a strong interest in the issues covered by my department and likes to meet each new Defra Secretary in person. Once there, I was shown into a drawing room, full of antiques but very comfortable and welcoming, with huge puffed-up cushions on the sofas and tea served in beautiful bone china. Not a place for dropping a cup. Prince Charles came in soon after and we had, from my perspective anyway, the most fascinating conversation. He was very relaxed and deeply knowledgeable about the environment and sustainable farming in particular. It was clear this was a conversation he'd had with many Secretaries of State before, and the depth of his knowledge and his years of experience meant he was really worth heeding. After I left, my officials gave me the nod that my audience had lasted quite a long time compared to that of some of my predecessors – which was, I'm told, a sign of a good experience all round.

At Defra, I was also privileged to meet the Duke of Cambridge during a trip to Vietnam for a conference dedicated to preventing the illegal wildlife trade. My interest in this vital issue was greatly strengthened by a visit I made to the specialist police unit dealing with the trade in illegal wildlife, where I saw at first hand the extraordinary lengths to which people will go to smuggle wildlife objects and even live wild animals. While they were doing amazing work with heat sensors and sniffer dogs, a number of officers told me how difficult it was to catch these smugglers without more regulation. Around the same time, the conservation charity Tusk launched a report into the destruction of the global elephant population, and I attended alongside Lord (William) Hague and Prince William. These two encounters were the precursors to the conference in Vietnam, where the issue of ivory sales and other illegal wildlife trading would be the focus, so I was determined to go along myself. It proved to be a highly constructive visit.

As ever, I spent the trip in a haze of jet lag, suffering from the usual problem when flying east of having to prop your eyelids open with matchsticks in the morning and then staying up too late when night falls. We began with a fantastic food and drink exhibition at the embassy, where British and Vietnamese chefs showcased our imported and exported food. When Prince William walked into the packed event, the frisson of excitement was palpable, bringing home very clearly the power of royal patronage.

We met the following day for a one-on-one meeting, where I was struck by the prince's passion for wildlife conservation. As he has often said, he doesn't want his children – and all our children – to grow up in a world where elephants are seen only in zoos. The prince was in a jovial mood, having just taken a stroll to shake off his own jet lag. He was immediately spotted by Vietnamese locals, who followed his entourage down the street, making clear their appreciation for his visit.

Then it was time for the wildlife conference, where the importance of tackling this problem was made abundantly clear. During the day I met with senior politicians from around the world to impress on them the need to pass legislation banning ivory sales and protect endangered wildlife and to discuss some of the work the UK was doing. As ever during a foreign trip, my time was spent in a whirl of multitasking: seeking sign-off from No. 10 to see if I could immediately announce that the next illegal wildlife conference would be back in the UK, talking to domestic and local press, writing op-eds, promoting British food and meeting the second in line to the throne, all while battling jet lag. To my delight, however, we still found time for a visit to a sun bear sanctuary, where I was able to see these beautiful endangered little creatures up close.

My ministerial team proved to be a strong group. George Eustice had already been Farming Minister under my predecessor, Liz Truss, and as a farmer himself was steeped in the sector and was someone I had high regard for. And I was delighted when we were joined by Thérèse Coffey as Minister of State for the Environment, an intelligent and hardworking colleague, and lovely Cornish MP Sheryll Murray. Our Lords minister was Lord (John) Gardiner, whom I didn't know previously but who proved a delightful man. The team gelled from the start, and as Secretary of State I was finally able to deploy my own leadership style, including a weekly ministers-only breakfast meeting where we could focus on policy priorities and urgent issues in private – not rocket science, but it's surprising how few departments regularly get their ministers together.

Defra was huge in terms of personnel, with thousands of civil servants in the core department, plus many more in the Environment Agency, Natural England, Rural Payments Agency and the farming and fisheries bodies. Defra had been labelled by some Brexiteers as 'the Remain department', with its civil servants said to have been devastated by the referendum. When I walked in that first day, I could well imagine some looking askance that they had been landed with one of the arch-Brexiteers. So from the beginning I was determined to demonstrate that I empathised with their feelings but also that there was an optimistic story to tell about Brexit for our key area of government.

We hit the ground running, with an away day at which the senior team, led by the Permanent Secretary, Clare Moriarty, began drawing up our Brexit agenda. I was determined we would lead Whitehall in the extent, depth and ambition of our plans for leaving the EU.

As a Secretary of State, this was the first time I would be recruiting my own special advisers. Guy Robinson, policy adviser to the two previous Defra Secs, was an obvious choice. I had heard that he was deeply knowledgeable about farming and fisheries and a really decent, hardworking bloke. And so he proved to be.

But given how low my confidence was following the leadership election, it was important that the other special adviser, who would be handling the media, was someone who would be totally on my side. I was on the lookout for someone I could trust and who was also a committed Brexiteer. Soon after my appointment, I was delighted to receive a phone call from Lee Cain, who had been head of broadcast at Vote Leave. We had grown to be quite friendly by the end of the referendum campaign, and as he had watched all my media performances, he knew my views and my style. I thought Lee would understand where I'd come from and could help me rebuild. Appointing him appeared a no-brainer.

Working with Guy and Lee was my first proper encounter with special advisers. These spad jobs, as they are known, are now an established feature of our democracy but are in fact a relatively modern creation. The first advisers, tasked with giving personal and political advice to a minister separate from that of the neutral civil service, were appointed by Harold Wilson in the 1960s, but the term 'spad' didn't really take off until the Blair era, when the numbers began to mushroom. Since then, they have taken root to the extent that by the time I joined the Cabinet, it was considered necessary to have at least one media spad and one policy spad.

Until then, I had a vague sense that spads were extra-special civil servants. I certainly did not realise fully the power spads can wield in their minister's name. This can be a great thing if they are bright and personally loyal, but it does mean you have to be extremely careful who you pick. Unlike elected politicians, who often have years if not decades of experience, spads are often young, always unelected, and sometimes with limited life experience outside politics. When they are suddenly given authority over what can be thousands of civil servants, the results can be fraught, particularly in the thankfully rare cases where this power goes to their heads. As many ministers and Prime Ministers have discovered to their cost, the consequences can turn out to be toxic.

Spads can be really good – or really bad. Spads who are there for their minister and who are diligent can be an excellent asset to the team. I am fortunate to have had some great spads who became genuine friends – advisers who understood the extent of their authority and whom I trusted for their advice and knowledge. But when spads become all-powerful, or have their own agenda, it's a recipe for disaster.

In my time in government, I had the chance to observe four of the most (in)famous spads in modern political history at full throttle: Theresa May's duo of Nick 'n' Fi – Nick Timothy and Fiona Hill – and Boris Johnson's deeply controversial chief adviser Dominic Cummings and head of comms Lee Cain. Between them, these four Downing Street spads each wielded more power and influence than is healthy in a democracy. In particular, I came to despise Cummings's bullying ways. And then there was Lee.

Lee was in his mid-thirties when he came to work for me, smartly dressed with shaved head and bright twinkly eyes. He was fun and focused and very professional; quite driven, but, it seemed, in a good way. In those first weeks he spent a lot of time trying to get me to feel better about things, with his constant refrain: 'It's fine, you're doing fine, don't worry about it.' It felt something of a dream team with Lee, Guy and Lucia, who joined the private office as speechwriter, alongside Marc who transferred over from DECC.

From the start, however, things didn't go quite to plan. It was soon clear that Lee was a man in a hurry – good at his job but also very ambitious. My confidence with the media was low through my first months at Defra. After all that had been thrown at me during the leadership contest, now as a Cabinet minister I was a key target for hostile journalists. As my media spad, Lee's primary role was to get me back in front of the press, and his way of achieving this was to encourage me to repeatedly rehearse responses to difficult questions: 'Did you think being a mother would make you a better Prime Minister? Are you ashamed of withdrawing from the leadership?' I would go into defensive or angry mode, and he would say: 'No! You can't say that; you have to rise above it.'

Lee was never unpleasant, but he was persistent. I knew it was an irritation to him, that he thought I should just get over my hesitation with the media and move on. The relationship between us never broke down, but I'm quite sure his patience wore thin. And of course to this day I still reflect on all the hatred and vitriol over 'being a mum'. Every day I hear women (and men) talk about how the joy and responsibility of being a parent affects their lives. Being a mother has shaped my life – it's the best and hardest job I've done, and my children are my joy – but I certainly don't think having kids makes me either a better or a worse politician or leader.

As the months passed, it felt that Lee was keen to curry favour with the Downing Street advisers Nick and Fi. Early on in my new job, Fiona approached me about ongoing correspondence I was having with *The Times* over my request that they release the full transcript of my interview with Rachel Sylvester. While my legal advice was that I had a strong chance of winning a Freedom of Information case, Fiona came to me to ask me to drop it. Now I look back, I wonder whether this was her call rather than an issue of the ministerial code which had been implied – i.e. that a Cabinet minister cannot be involved in this type of legal situation. In any event, Lee went along with it.

Gradually, it was dawning on me that although I was working flat-out in the department, nothing was ever given the green light by No. 10. We did a huge amount of work on areas such as our 25-Year Plans for the Environment and for Food and Farming, on subsidies for farmers, on the banning of ivory sales, on a new deal for UK fishing and on air quality, yet I was never given the go-ahead to launch our schemes. It was always: *Now's not the right time.* I suspect the hold-up was always from No. 10 – I wondered if Nick and Fi didn't want me to be out in the public eye making announcements out of their loyalty to Theresa. So I felt like I was hidden in plain sight as Defra Secretary, making a lot of progress in the department but never in public. Lee would say: 'I've spoken to Nick and Fi and they've said no.' That became the routine.

When Michael Gove took over at Defra after the 2017 election, he soon appeared at the Business and Legislation Committee with various Bills for approval. He had been given the green light by No. 10 for a series of announcements within weeks of taking over! By then, as Leader of the Commons, I was the chair of the committee, and I had to laugh when he said in front of the whole group: 'I'd like to thank Andrea for all her work in Defra because I'm getting to open all her Christmas presents.' Ah well, that's politics for you. I remember being told when I became a Conservative parliamentary candidate: 'If you want to get on in politics, never complain.' How true. By the time Michael took over, Nick and Fi had fallen on their swords after the 2017 election disaster, and with that, announcements on policy and legislation seemed to become much easier.

When party conference season came around in October 2016, I had regained some confidence and was ready to face the limelight again. This was an important moment for me, the first time I would be in front of a gathering of party members since the leadership contest, and I was aware that a number of them had wanted me as their Prime Minister. I didn't know whether there would be anger at me for handing the leadership to Theresa or gratitude that I had done so to avoid a divisive competition. I was determined to deliver a speech which would be light-hearted, punchy and confident. And it was – I loved that speech; it was funny, self-deprecating but also in my opinion highly optimistic about the future.

I began by taking a pop at Labour, which was going through its endless contest to confirm Jeremy Corbyn as leader: 'If Labour want lessons in how to elect a leader, tell them to talk to me,' I said. There was much laughter – phew, a good start – and so it went on.

But the speech – and my returning confidence – were more thanks to Lucia than Lee, who had just become a dad for the first time and so understandably spent little time at conference. Lucia had helped craft that funny speech, and she also gave me moral support through what could have been a challenging first time on the main stage. Lucia proved to be a good example of a great colleague and loyal adviser.

Some months later, when I was moved from Defra to a new role as Leader of the House, I was in no doubt about what I should do. While I was aware most ministers retained their spads when they moved departments, and while I liked Lee and rated him as a talented bloke, I didn't feel that I wanted him to come with me, and anyway I doubted he would be willing. After the reshuffle, Lee didn't contact me, so I thought: *Well, I'll wait a few days to see what happens and then appoint Lucia if I can.* As I would find out later, there was no residual allegiance with Lee down the line.

That party conference of 2016 was notable for one big reason: Theresa used her speech to announce that she was seeking a bespoke arrangement with the EU to determine our future relationship, ruling out the 'Norway' and 'Swiss' versions of Brexit. This came as a surprise to the Cabinet, who had not been informed in advance of her decision. And while it clearly infuriated the Remainers among us (Philip Hammond would later describe Theresa's words as a 'coup'), as a Brexiteer, her words were music to my ears. While Norway has rich oil and fishing resources, and no one can deny Switzerland's strength in financial services and fame for chocolate and cuckoo clocks, neither would claim to have the population or economic diversity of the United Kingdom.

The all-consuming issue of Brexit aside, one of the most urgent matters that crossed my desk as Defra Secretary was a crucial decision on the badger cull. We were now in the third year of an attempt to eradicate bovine TB by keeping the badger population down. After lengthy consultation with the scientists and vets, we did extend the cull. The decision proved exceedingly controversial, yet vital for the many farmers whose livelihoods were threatened by frequent positive tests for TB, often false positives, leading to the destruction of cattle that had sometimes been bred on family farms over generations.

The shadow Secretary of State for the Defra brief was Rachael Maskell MP, who was always punchy in the Chamber while being perfectly friendly outside of it, a characterisation I would give to many of the Labour frontbenchers I came up against over the years. It has always been my experience that relationships between politicians of opposing teams are far more collegiate than the public, or media, appreciates. This is understandable, given the hostilities of heated debate in the Commons, but outside the Chamber our conversations are usually far more constructive and collaborative.

One of the best parts of being Defra Secretary was the opportunity to travel to all parts of the UK and remind myself what an incredible country this is. I met with farmers, fishermen and many food manufacturers, visiting places such as the Yeo Valley Organic Farm in Somerset, Peterhead fishing port in Aberdeenshire, the Tiny Rebel Brewery in Newport and Lakeland Dairies in Newtownards, Co. Down.

It was also a great chance to fly the flag overseas. I attended

SIAL (the *Salon International de l'Alimentation*), the world's biggest food fair, in Paris to promote UK food. I stayed at our beautiful Parisian embassy, where English sparkling wine and UK produce were served at a reception for French and other gourmands. I also travelled to China on a trade mission to deliver £50 million worth of English bovine semen (yes, truly) and to negotiate for the sale of UK chicken feet, as well as to move forward the slow progress towards the approval of UK pork. It was immediately apparent there was a huge demand from the growing middle class there for high-quality, well-grown food and produce from the UK.

In January 2017, I attended the Oxford farming conference, something of a ritual for the Defra Secretary, where the idea is to deliver a speech about forthcoming improvements in food and farming. It proved a tough crowd. The host, *Countryfile* presenter Helen Skelton, asked those present whether they had confidence farming would be better on leaving the EU, and painfully few hands went up. I made a strong case that we could dramatically reduce the red tape farmers had always found frustrating, and build a new financial support system, but came away aware that I had a long way to go to persuade them. I was proud that in my year in charge I was able to get rural farm payments out much faster than in previous years, but it was clear there was much more to do to improve support for food production and environmental goods. To my frustration, however, it would not be me making the arguments in future – not at Defra, in any case.

# CHAPTER NINE

# MISLAYING A MAJORITY

**M**y faith is of profound importance to me, a constant presence in my life that underpins everything else and provides a strong motivation for wanting to help others and do the best I can. But as any Christian will admit, we all fall short every day: your faith doesn't make you a perfect person, but it definitely makes you want to be a better person, and it gives you the belief to keep going. As a politician, my Christianity has been a real source of comfort and support, sustaining me when times get tough and giving me the strength to pick myself up, dust myself off and return to the fray. In short, my faith informs everything I do.

So when I entered the Commons, I had decided to join the Christians in Parliament All-Party Parliamentary Group, which has been something of a safe space, an opportunity to get to know MPs I might have little in common with from a policy perspective. In this group you will find ministers and backbenchers; Conservatives, Labour, Lib Dems, the SNP and members of every other party; Leavers and Remainers; those who have been in Parliament since the dawn of time and recently elected newbies. Over the years I have been to many cross-party gatherings, including hosting suppers at my own flat, where we have put aside political differences and come together as a community of people committed to serving others and God.

The faith life of Parliament is surprisingly extensive, considering how little of it is in the public domain. Prayers are spoken before the Chamber sits for the business of the day, and regular church services are held in St Mary Undercroft, the thirteenth-century blue and gold chapel in the Palace of Westminster. The inside of the chapel is stunning, with a vaulted ceiling with painted gold stars and angels. Visiting the chapel is enjoyed by many who work in Parliament – not just Christians. It gives those who work in the Palace of Westminster a sense that they are playing a part in history, one of a long line of parliamentarians and other key characters in our nation's story. Within the chapel is the cupboard in which the suffragette Emily Wilding Davison hid on the night of the 1911 census in order to record her address as the House of Commons. It was also here, three years after my arrival in Parliament, that the body of Baroness Thatcher lay in state before her funeral, leading me to reflect on how much both women achieved in transforming the lives of those who followed in their footsteps.

A key diary date since becoming an MP is attending Bible study with other Conservative MPs, supported by the Christians in Parliament group, every Tuesday at 8.30 a.m. So on a blustery Tuesday morning in April 2017 I headed off promptly as usual from our Bible group at Portcullis House to get to the weekly meeting of Cabinet in No. 10 at 9.30 a.m.

On this particular day, as we took our seats around the Cabinet table, Theresa May seemed unusually agitated. *Colleagues, I have something to tell you. I have decided to call a general election.*

*Why on earth would you do that?* Like everyone else in Westminster, I was well aware of the speculation around the possibility of an early election to boost our majority, which then stood at twelve. At times it felt as if people were talking of nothing else. And while it was true Theresa was enjoying an extended honeymoon period and the polls were favourable, I had always dismissed the idea. She had just become Prime Minister and we had plenty on our plate already with the countdown to delivering Brexit; talk of an early election seemed a distraction. *Of course she won't,* I thought whenever the subject came up. Except now, it seemed, she would.

Theresa laid out the numbers and it was clear the polling was on our side. Going to the country now seemed certain to give us a decent majority. She assured us her decision was aimed at consolidating Brexit. That January, she had given her Lancaster House speech, in which she had pledged that 'no deal is better than a bad deal', meaning she was prepared to quit the EU without any withdrawal agreement. Two months before Lancaster House, however, a case had been brought in the High Court by a Remain supporter, Gina Miller, that compelled the government to put the terms of Britain's departure from the EU to Parliament. Theresa was clearly worried that with such a small majority, and so many Remain supporters on the government benches, this process would become problematic.

Her fear was confirmed when Dominic Grieve, the former Attorney General, attached an amendment to the Article 50 Bill (which triggered the UK's departure from the EU) requiring a 'meaningful vote' on the terms of the deal at an early enough stage in the process that Theresa could have been required to return to Brussels to renegotiate. The amended Bill passed through the Lords in March with the help of a sizeable rebellion by Conservative peers, including South Northants resident and Europhile former Deputy Prime Minister Lord Heseltine, who was sacked as a government adviser as a result.

With her hands now bound by Parliament, Theresa hoped to reshape the Commons at least, making the case that a bigger Tory majority would ensure an easier passage for future Brexit legislation. I had sympathy for this argument but could not help reflecting that in my own leadership campaign the previous year, I had pledged to trigger Article 50 within days of becoming PM. Had this occurred, maybe there would have been no time for a High Court ruling, no Gina Miller, no meaningful votes and none of the painful parliamentary battles that were to become such a hallmark of Theresa's time in office. But just as there's no crystal ball to look into the future, so there's no time for hindsight in politics. Politicians must make their plans but then continually adjust them to deal with whatever unforeseeable events take place – you just have to try to make the best decision you can with the information available at the time.

Back in the Cabinet Room, therefore, the decision to call an election to smooth the passage of whatever deal we agreed with the EU seemed risky but logical. And while the announcement came as a surprise, I was supportive: Theresa had done her homework and if we needed this election to deliver Brexit – and she was confident she could win – we should back her all the way.

For the next half-hour or so, we remained corralled in the Cabinet Room unable to inform others while Theresa went outside No. 10 to announce her decision to the country. Presumably, this was an attempt to prevent leaks from Cabinet, which had already become a serious problem as discipline among Remainers and Leavers was already breaking down. Less than a year into the job, Theresa was already starting meetings by saying: 'I must remind Cabinet not to leak our confidential discussions.' Who knows who the leakers were? The room was full of spads, civil servants and ministers each week, so any of them could be the culprit. During her time as PM, Theresa launched a few leak inquiries, but with the very serious exception of a national security leak, it proved difficult to get to the bottom of it.

A large TV screen was brought in so we could watch the PM's announcement. On the steps outside Downing Street, Theresa began: 'I have just chaired a meeting of the Cabinet where we agreed the government should call a general election...' And then the broadband dropped out and the screen went dead. The entire room burst out laughing – there was Theresa standing a few yards away addressing the entire nation, except for her Cabinet.

Given the excitement of the unexpected announcement, it should now have been all systems go for the campaign. Unfortunately, as became painfully clear over the next day or so, Theresa's plan for a swift election was impossible under the terms of the Fixed-Term Parliaments Act, which David Cameron and Nick Clegg had dreamt up to sustain the coalition government. This created a serious problem, which should have been foreseen by No. 10 advisers.

While in the past MPs were used to short, sharp, three-week campaigns, this one was to drag out for seven, as Parliament had to formally approve the election for it to take place. It was the first unforeseen disaster of what would prove a car crash of a piece of legislation, stripping the Conservatives of the advantage previous governments enjoyed of the element of surprise. It also meant ministers were bound by the rules to engage in a lengthy 'wash-up' process, to tie up the loose ends of any legislation making its way through Parliament, during which the opposition had the time and space to hit the campaign ground running.

In a further sign that the plan for a snap election had not been sufficiently thought through, no one at Conservative HQ seemed to have taken seriously the rumours that Theresa might go to the country early. Instead, CCHQ was in 'between elections' mode until the eve of the announcement, and it took some time to get the machinery cranked up, key staff hired and campaigning started. This would prove a serious impediment: if you're going to have a general election, you need your campaign resources at full stretch from the start, not downsized in mid-term mode. This was all work which – as quickly became apparent – Labour already had well in train.

During my time in Parliament, social media has come into its own as a campaign tool, particularly at election time. Labour now proved alarmingly adept at using the remainder of our enforced time in Parliament to rev up their online engagement. So the Labour leader Jeremy Corbyn would stand at the despatch box and ask a question of Theresa with no apparent interest at all in her answer, so long as he could get a clip to deliver straight to Facebook or Twitter which would play well with his supporters. Even an innocuous comment would get a *That's not good enough!* type response, duly turned into a clip for the benefit of his following. Those weeks proved deeply frustrating, as the opposition sidelined Parliament in order to reach out to those largely younger, left-leaning voters who got much of their news from social media and certainly weren't tuning in to the Parliament channel – or even the BBC. To make matters worse, Labour took the decision to go negative early on, meaning the tone of the campaign felt ugly from the start. But let's face it, for the Conservatives, the biggest problem with the 2017 election wasn't Labour; it was our own dire campaign.

As always during an election, I spent much of my time out and about across the country as well as in my own constituency, travelling from Edinburgh to Swansea, from St Ives to Cleethorpes, urging voters to support a big Conservative win and get Brexit over the finish line. By the final days of the campaign, knocking on doors across South Northants, including those of some staunch Conservative supporters, most were asking if I thought we could still win. It was clear by then that our potentially big majority was dwindling fast, but I still hoped we would get a majority of thirty or forty. At the very least, I said to myself, we would end up with more seats. How wrong I was. When the result came in and it became clear we were now in a hung parliament, I was devastated.

So what went wrong – and when? Anyone who is planning to stand for office can learn a great deal from the 2017 election campaign. One of its key problems was the lack of clear ownership. Lynton Crosby, the Australian elections guru who had steered Boris Johnson's mayoral successes and also the surprise 2015 success for David Cameron, was supposedly in control. But it seemed that Nick Timothy and Fiona Hill were also in charge. This confusion was problematic from the outset, leading to a lack of campaign discipline and firm direction. On the surface, when it came to the campaign messaging there appeared to be a clear top line: 'strong and stable leadership' to deliver a 'smooth and orderly Brexit'. This messaging was focused entirely around Theresa as a strong leader, to the extent that every single Conservative candidate was described on their Central Office campaign literature as, for example, 'Theresa May's candidate for South Northamptonshire', rather than 'Andrea Leadsom, Conservative candidate for South Northamptonshire'. But if you are going to concentrate entirely on your leader's personality and character, you'd better be totally sure that your leader is willing to pull it off. Theresa is impressive in so many ways, but there is no doubt her personal reserve led her to shrink from this intense spotlight.

Another key problem was that having a razor-sharp focus on the single policy of Brexit also meant that you must not suddenly pivot to another area halfway through the campaign. Yet this is exactly what happened with the manifesto. Nick and Fi spent the weeks running up to the manifesto launch telling Cabinet ministers that there was no room for any detailed policy announcements, in order to maintain the pure focus on Brexit. This was a disappointment to ministers, who always have big ambitions for their departments, but we were all prepared to do it for the sake of the messaging. When this discipline slipped, and Nick Timothy in particular was permitted to give his own pet project an airing, it proved disastrous on two fronts.

First, Nick's central policy, a root-and-branch reform of social care, proved emphatically unpopular. Normally, such a radical proposal would be considered at length, would be subjected to wide consultation, and the public would become aware of it through regular media commentary. So it was a big error to spring this on voters. And second, perhaps more concerning, the departure from the strict focus on Brexit gave an opening for the opposition to move the election on to other ground. This meant that the big story of the day was rarely the EU. Instead, the campaign was first dominated by social care and then by comparisons between Labour's manifesto, with its huge spending pledges, and the somewhat unclear

Conservative policies. Theresa's snap Brexit election was therefore to prove neither snap nor about Brexit.

Written by Ben Gummer, who as Cabinet Office Minister was considered a strong policy guru but then sadly lost his own seat largely as a result of the Tories' general election offering, the Conservative manifesto was inconsistent in its level of detail. In some areas of policy, Ben drew up a high-level 'strategic vision', which was minimalist to the point of being threadbare. In my own Defra section, this led to many policy black holes. For example, I was acutely aware of many voters' concern that the Hunting Act should never be repealed, so I wanted our manifesto to clearly include a commitment to maintaining the legislation. There was also huge support among the electorate for other wildlife issues, particularly the ban on the ivory trade, which I was determined to bring into force. Neither of these totemic issues was resolved in the manifesto, so many voters drew their own conclusions.

A few weeks before the manifesto launch, I was invited to Downing Street at 7.15 a.m. to read the two pages that dealt with Defra. It was the only slot I was given, I had just half an hour to read a paper copy and I was barred from bringing my phone. With the notable exception of positive support for farming, the Defra pages set out little more than a high-level commitment to protecting the environment, supporting all of our sensitive species and banning the illegal wildlife trade.

Within days, I was trolled on social media by the businesswoman turned activist and influencer Deborah Meaden, who urged her hundreds of thousands of followers to stick the boot in over the absence of the ivory ban from the manifesto. I had every sympathy – but I couldn't publicly explain. I would estimate that one missing pledge led to around half a million pieces of hate mail – and probably thousands of lost votes. As it was, Cabinet members got sight of the full version of the manifesto only as we travelled on the bus to the launch in Halifax.

Looking back, I do think the initial focus on Brexit was a wise decision. While it may not have been necessary to strip out all other policy from the manifesto, it was clear there was a huge appetite in the country to see Brexit through as quickly as possible, and if anything, Theresa's 'smooth and orderly Brexit' slogan was too low-key – surely backed up by evidence of the success of the 'get Brexit done' campaign slogan in 2019. At the start of the campaign, the party's polling had suggested that long-held Labour seats such as Bolsover and Great Grimsby in the Labour Red Wall were there for the taking. This proved to be accurate only two years later, when Boris went to the country after two years of wrangling and proved that voters across the country wanted Brexit to be done and dusted.

\* \* \*

It reached a point during the campaign where the focus on Theresa, and the low profile of her ministers in the media, became a story in itself. At the time, I was mid-way through an enjoyable tour of the south-west to support the campaigns of colleagues, many of whom had strong constituency interests in our future plans for fishing. I embarked on this road trip with

Luke, Tommy and Clare Rees, my parliamentary assistant, who were all insured on my car so we could share the driving. We had a great few days. At one point, we started karaoke and decided to take to Twitter for song requests. Just as we were in the middle of a particularly enthusiastic rendition of ABBA's 'Dancing Queen', I clocked a tweet from the *Newsnight* reporter John Sweeney: 'Where's Andrea Leadsom?' Unbeknownst to us, *Newsnight* was on a mission to seek out elusive Cabinet ministers and had sent a crew to Towcester in my constituency. When I failed to appear, the crew filmed themselves wandering up and down Towcester High Street calling: 'Andrea Leadsom, where are you? Where are you, Andrea Leadsom?'

Meanwhile, 200 miles away in Devon, we decided to play along. As we drove past a beautiful woodland nature spot, we pulled over and took a photograph, posting it on Twitter and tagging John. This did not go down well. *Newsnight* now posted a short clip of Sweeney complaining: 'She's mucking about. We want to interview her. We want to ask questions. There's a general election, she's a Cabinet minister.'

For the rest of the day we played cat and mouse, posting our next photograph of the beach at Truro, which sent *Newsnight* scuttling to the town. That night, *Newsnight* showed a film of a reporter running up and down asking if people had seen me, only to be told I had left two hours earlier. Well, my family thought the report was really funny, but there was a serious point. Some people within the party thought it gave the impression that Cabinet ministers were barred from appearing in the media, and that it made our campaign look foolish.

Had polling day come a few weeks earlier, we would surely have secured a majority. As it was, the campaign dragged on long enough for us to self-destruct, and for Labour to gain in strength. It didn't help that Labour was playing the social media game so well. Their tactic was to be on the attack over everything the Conservatives were offering, while refusing to answer the difficult questions about their stance on Brexit. By the end of the campaign, we were no closer to discovering whether or not Her Majesty's Opposition planned to deliver Brexit – an extraordinary position, yet one neither the media nor the electorate seemed concerned with. Instead, Labour focused on making some completely unconscionable promises to young people, implying – and in some local literature even stating – that all student debt would be cancelled.

The issue of honesty came up in a way it never had before with previous Labour leaders. There were serious questions over Jeremy Corbyn's character, given his alleged association with members of terrorist groups and apparent tolerance of antisemitism within the party. Then there was the 'magic money tree', as we dubbed it, with Labour making increasingly extravagant, uncosted promises on everything from nationalising Royal Mail, water and energy to ramping up benefits and introducing massive public sector pay rises. As someone who had always campaigned for sound finances and living within your means, I was seriously alarmed by these reckless promises.

By the time polling day rolled around, my team sallied forth for our now traditional day of megaphoning, before heading to Northampton to lend a hand in nearby marginals.

As night fell and the polls closed, we set out on the short journey to the home of local friends who always host an election night gathering. We announced our presence as lustily as ever, shouting 'Vote Conservative' as we marched up the garden path and into the house. But there were more nerves than there had been two years earlier, or even at my first election in 2010. The atmosphere became ever more tense as we waited for the exit poll, hoping against hope we had made it across the line and would win a majority. We hadn't. As the exit poll came in with its prediction that we would be in a hung parliament, my heart sank and the excitable party atmosphere became one of: *What happens now?*

I watched for another hour or so and then got ready to go to my own count, all the while texting back and forth with neighbouring MPs and fellow Cabinet ministers. The messages were all the same: *If we haven't got a majority, we need to keep Theresa. We can't possibly have another leadership contest; Theresa has to realise she's got our support. We can't let her feel she needs to resign; she's got to stick with it.* For the rest of the night, the messages went back and forth between myself and Chris Heaton-Harris, Julian Smith (who later became Deputy Chief Whip), Michael Gove, Boris Johnson, David Davis, all coming to the same conclusion: that Theresa needed our support. I did not see a single text message suggesting she should go.

This was as much true of David Davis, who has since admitted he was among those who urged Theresa to call what proved to be a highly damaging as well as unnecessary election, as it was of Michael Gove, who I believe argued the opposite.

David was desperately concerned that Theresa would not listen to us and would resign that night, an outcome I was also keen to avoid. Given how fraught the last contest had been, I feared a leadership campaign during a minority government would lead to massive division in the party, economic turmoil and then another election which Labour could win, resulting in Brexit being cancelled. As I sat on those hard plastic chairs in the local leisure centre enduring the long wait for my own result, I was desperately hoping Theresa would have the fortitude to stay in post.

Back at home, I had a call with a very disappointed Prime Minister. 'Please, don't give up,' I urged her. 'The Cabinet is absolutely with you; I will personally do everything I can to support you in delivering Brexit.'

Theresa thanked me for my call but gave little away. I am still not sure whether this reticence is in her character or whether it's because, like so many in politics, she suspects that a frank exchange of views may be used against her.

Some colleagues now turned their wrath on Theresa's spads, Nick and Fi, seeking to blame them for the disastrous campaign. Through the night the calls mounted for them to carry the can for our mislaid majority. I shared the irritation but was on the fence about whether they needed to step aside; after nearly a year in Cabinet I had come to see the value they brought to Theresa. And if there was one thing I now knew about being a senior politician, it was that you need people around that you can completely trust and rely on. This can become a problem if those people let you down, as would prove the case later with Boris Johnson and Dominic Cummings. Nick and Fi's relationship with Theresa was evidence once again of how spads can be totally brilliant or utterly malign. In their case, it almost seemed that they were both at the same time. So it was for Theresa to decide whether or not to hang on to her spads, and I would have backed her had she insisted she couldn't do without them. Ultimately, she determined they would go – and she would stay.

Theresa's decision to remain as Prime Minister after the election debacle came as a relief. I'd had my chance and I'd stood aside for her; now I was determined to help her deliver Brexit. I did not fully appreciate at this stage how difficult the loss of our majority would make this task.

# CHAPTER TEN

# LEADER OF THE HOUSE

No one who witnessed the events of 14 June 2017 as fire engulfed Grenfell Tower in west London will forget what they saw that night. It was immediately apparent from the size and intensity of the blaze that the scale of the disaster would be horrendous. Seventy-two residents lost their lives that night, unable to escape the flames. Dozens more were injured, and many lost their homes and everything they owned.

The general election had taken place less than a week earlier, and the Prime Minister had given me a new job: Leader of the House of Commons. The Commons had not yet returned following the election, but naturally every MP wanted to express their deep sympathy for those affected by the fire, as well as to understand what would be done to provide support. The Speaker gave his permission to use Westminster Hall even though the House was not yet in session following the election, so that Alok Sharma, then Housing Minister, and Nick Hurd, Fire Minister, could provide an update for MPs. For several hours I sat through a harrowing discussion with parliamentarians of all parties. Many were moved to tears as we learned about the horror that Grenfell's residents had faced.

After the debate, I returned to my office feeling I needed to do something. It was suggested I might wish to visit Grenfell. I wasn't sure. Officially, I had no ministerial jurisdiction, but in my new role as Leader of the House, I could pay a visit to pass on the sympathies of Parliament and ask if there was any practical help I could provide. My office sought permission from No. 10 to pay a visit, which I understood was agreed.

Early next morning we set off – Ben, Luke, a private secretary and me. Many of the tenants were resting in a nearby community centre, and I went inside to meet them. It was a humbling experience. These were people who had lost everything; they had run for their lives and now, two days on, they were still in shock. I felt helpless standing among them. All I could say was: 'We're thinking of you, we'll do everything we can, and is there something I can do now?' People were still in shock, trying to piece together what happens now, some simply sorting through bags of donated items trying to find clothes that would fit.

Upstairs, I was introduced to a key member of the local residents' association, who was devastated but also furious at the events of the previous forty-eight hours. I listened as he vented his anger about what had happened. He had been attempting to raise issues around safety at the tower for many years and felt he had never been heard. It was clear that appalling mistakes had been made, and given the trauma he had experienced, I could well understand his hostility towards those in both the local council and the government.

As I left the community centre, a TV crew was waiting with some devastated and furious residents and neighbours. I spoke with them for a while and their anger and fear was terrible, but I took away a number of requests for specific action – it was something of a relief to find some ways to be of practical help. Later, I saw what was in my view the totally unfair coverage of Theresa's visit to Grenfell Tower, where she was criticised for not speaking with residents. She had gone to visit the rescuers – firefighters, police and others – because she rightly wanted to make sure every possible support was being provided in that appalling disaster, as well as to thank those who had risked their own lives to save residents. A year later, survivors came to Parliament to talk about their experiences, and while there are many criticisms to this day of the speed and extent of the help provided, I think Theresa's compassion and support for the survivors was never in doubt.

*   *   *

Grenfell provided a sobering start to my time as Leader of the House, a position I would come to love. As had by now become a pattern, my moye was both unexpected and apparently counter-intuitive. When I was summoned to No. 10

after the election, I had every expectation I would remain at Defra. Not only was I loving the job but the department was performing well. Shortly before the election, I had received good feedback from both the Treasury and the Cabinet Office over our submissions for the Budget and Brexit preparations. David Davis, then Brexit Secretary, told me Defra was seen as something of a model department when it came to the clarity and extent of our work – impressive given the scale of the task, as Defra was historically so closely bound up with the EU.

In hindsight, though, Theresa's decision to move me was a sound one. As a former shadow Leader of the Commons herself, she knew that a hung parliament would make the task of steering Brexit through the House trickier than it had appeared even a month earlier. While I was disappointed to leave Defra, it quickly became clear how integral the new job would be to the whole process of our withdrawal from the European Union.

I was to stay in post for two years, the longest spell in the same job in my entire time in government. It felt as if a lifetime of events was packed into those twenty-four months. Much of my job was now taken up with the tricky, highly technical and politically fraught process of attempting to pass various iterations of Theresa's Brexit deal through the Commons. The complications that came with pressing through the UK's vote to leave the EU in the face of a largely Remain-supporting parliament were clear for all to see. Leaving the EU should have been our core focus and goal, and we should have just got on with it. Yet, as Harold Macmillan said when asked what was most likely to knock his government off course: 'Events, dear boy, events.' And so it was for Theresa.

Her period in office was marked by a number of tragedies and disasters. Even prior to the Grenfell fire, her capacity to remain calm in a crisis was apparent in her steadfast response to horrific terrorist attacks in Manchester and London Bridge during the 2017 election campaign and an attack on Westminster earlier that year.

The earlier incident, in March 2017, had brought the meaning of terror to all those working in Parliament. A terrorist in a car ploughed into pedestrians as they crossed Westminster Bridge, then jumped out and ran through Parliament's Carriage Gates. There, he murdered PC Keith Palmer, before himself being shot and killed by an armed protection officer. The loss of life and the terrible injuries of so many on that day were devastating and will never be forgotten by the families and friends of the victims, nor by those who work in Parliament.

The attack also exposed how vulnerable Parliament itself was to an assault.

On the day of the attack, I had attended a Cabinet meeting in the Commons as Defra Secretary to discuss the prospect of a no-deal Brexit. With such a small majority, every vote was vital, including those of ministers, so Cabinet meetings were usually moved from Downing Street to near the Commons Chamber when a vote was due. When the division bell went, the Prime Minister indicated we should reconvene straight after the vote. I headed out of the room, leaving my phone behind on the assumption that we would be returning after a few minutes.

Following the vote, I left the Chamber by the Speaker's Chair when I noticed the doorkeepers seemed agitated. A police officer was speaking loudly into his radio, saying we needed to lock down. He turned to me and other MPs who were nearby and told us all to return to the Chamber straight away.

We were shepherded back into the Chamber and the doors were locked at either end. And there we stayed for over four hours. A television set was switched on in the Lobby and we closely followed the terrible events that had taken place outside. It seemed the police were working on the assumption that the terrorist had at least one accomplice, who may have been drawn towards the Chamber by the sounds of the division bell and could even now be on the loose inside the Palace. The thousands of people who work in Parliament were all locked into secure areas or advised to stay in their offices. Unbelievably, there was little CCTV in the building, so there was no easy way of checking if an intruder had gained entry.

Those hours passed excruciatingly slowly, as colleagues went from being afraid for themselves and their staff to trying to track down loved ones, to extreme frustration and, finally, navigating challenging issues for those needing their medication. The Reasons Room, a small room next to the Chamber, luckily had a stash of sweets in the cupboard as well as a few dozen

Thank you, Lady T!

The first campaign in South Northamptonshire, 2006

Grand Union Canal in Stoke Bruerne

Running repairs to campaign posters

Visit from the HS2 Minister to inspect the damage

ABOVE Treasury Select Committee in Beijing's Great Hall of the People, 2012

LEFT Budget Day 2015

LEFT Helicopter survival training before visiting an offshore rig

LEFT The Vote Leave campaign team in Brackley

BELOW The great Brexit debates

Launching my leadership bid in 2016

First Cabinet job as Defra Secretary
of State

In the Cabinet Room watching Theresa announce the snap general
election of 2017

2017 – Theresa's new government

Both Houses of Parliament wishing HRH Prince Charles a happy seventieth birthday

The State Opening of Parliament 2017 – part of the Queen's procession as Lord President of the Privy Council

Point of order, Mr Speaker!

Thanking the Leader's Office and legislation staff for their huge effort in preparing for the Brexit that didn't happen…

LEFT With Boris and Gisela, celebrating Brexit on 31 January 2020 at No. 10 – with new blue passport!

BELOW First speech from the back benches

ABOVE LEFT AND RIGHT Launching 'The Best Start for Life – A Vision for the 1,001 Critical Days' with the Prime Minister

An unforgettable day at Buckingham Palace receiving my DBE from the Prince of Wales

Our new King addressing parliamentarians in the stunning setting of Westminster Hall

ABOVE A thank-you party for Team Penny

RIGHT Marking the launch of the *Snakes and Ladders* hardback with Iain Dale

bottles of water. I was kicking myself for leaving my mobile phone downstairs. I hadn't memorised my kids' phone numbers and was worried about Cookie, then thirteen, who took the Tube home from school and would arrive at Westminster Station any minute and walk home to our flat on the other side of the Palace. Not only that, but my younger son Harry was also due to walk across Westminster Bridge to the flat after visiting his grandparents.

I was in a panic and Ben wasn't picking up. Similar stories were playing out all around me as MPs tried to track down their loved ones, and the lack of information was incredibly frustrating. Anne Milton, the Deputy Chief Whip, helped me track down my kids via a circuitous route, but it was a nerve-racking experience that gave me pause for thought. Was political life really worth it if it put my family at risk?

Following the attack, an urgent security review was carried out. The installation of CCTV was one obvious move which could be easily implemented. The other major recommendation was less straightforward.

When I started as Leader, it was already apparent that a robust contingency plan was needed in the event of Parliament's security and ability to function being compromised. The original contingency plan was to have a 'pop-up Parliament' somewhere nearby which would be shared by the Commons and the Lords, and which would be an adequate solution for a few weeks. It was now the view that this contingency was nowhere near good enough: the risk of a disastrous fire or an asbestos leak leaving the Palace uninhabitable for years was made very clear from the regular meetings I now chaired of the parliamentary works team. Following the Westminster terrorist attack, a thorough security review advised that in order to protect everyone who worked on the estate, it would be necessary for the contingency arrangements for elected Members to be located within the secure perimeter of the Palace. This radically moved the goalposts for our contingency planning and exposed the urgent necessity of finally tackling the elephant in the room: that Parliament was no longer fit for purpose.

For decades, successive governments had ducked the truth that the Palace was in no fit state to safely accommodate those who worked there. Over the years, the ancient building had literally begun to fall apart, with chunks of masonry smashing to the ground from the high stonework; it was a miracle no one had been seriously injured as a result. Instead of a full restoration, the response so far had been a series of ongoing patch-ups to the extent there was scaffolding everywhere and parts of the Palace were unusable.

The Palace of Westminster has an open basement running its entire length, with hundreds of chimneys going up through the building. The idea of the architect, Sir Charles Barry, in the mid-nineteenth century, was that open air vents in summer would circulate cooling air, and big steam generators in winter would provide heating. However, in subsequent decades, the basement became the place to put all of Parliament's gubbins

– electrics, wiring, plumbing, sewage – all without a proper map to record what went where, and with plentiful asbestos lagging on the ancient pipes. One of my first visits as Leader was to inspect the basement. I will never forget the sight and smell of a major sewage pipe leak that had taken place only that morning.

Parliament is one of the most famous buildings in the world, at that point playing host to a million visitors a year, and housing 15,000 staff, 650 MPs and 800 peers. The recommendation from several reviews in recent years had been that the right way to restore the Palace was to temporarily move out, to allow the work to press on at speed and with the best value for money for taxpayers. But the cost of even this option, coupled with the politics of MPs being seen to spend money on their own workplace, combined with the desire of many MPs not to vacate the Palace for what could be a decade or more, meant patch and mend had been the only policy to be seriously pursued.

Now, as Leader of the House with a responsibility for the physical safety of both MPs and the building they were housed in, I felt strongly that more decisive action should be taken. When I broached the subject with her, the Prime Minister agreed. Despite the heavy legislative agenda with a clear focus on Brexit, we held a lengthy debate which sought the support of MPs and peers for the creation of a professional delivery authority, based on the model used for the 2012 Olympics, that would take on the responsibility for restoration and renewal, with costs overseen by Parliament. To the enormous relief of many who love the Palace of Westminster, the proposal was agreed. A tentative plan was then drawn up to move the House of Commons to Richmond House, on the parliamentary estate, by 2025, so comprehensive repairs to the Palace could begin.

It is a great regret to me that, despite achieving that consensus, the question of moving MPs to Richmond House has now been reopened for a further consultation and therefore further delay and cost. So our UNESCO World Heritage site remains in grave danger. I do fear that the Palace could end up, like Notre Dame, suffering a serious catastrophe such as a major fire. To those who say taxpayers will be angry with us for 'wasting money by moving', I say that they will be even angrier if Parliament burns down on our watch. When the Palace had to be restored after it burned down in 1834, it took thirty-six years for restoration work to be completed. And let's not forget: as things stand, there is no long-term contingency arrangement for a functioning parliament should that happen here. Preserving Parliament for future generations was a responsibility but also an incredibly worthwhile project to have taken forward.

\* \* \*

Commemorating the centenary of the first women getting the right to vote in 2018 was another great moment. It seems extraordinary that well into the twenty-first century, I was only the 336th woman ever elected to Parliament. In fact, when I arrived in 2010, there were more men elected as MPs in the new parliament than there had ever been women.

The centenary celebrations culminated in the Processions marches across the UK on Sunday 10 June 2018. In London, tens of thousands of people marched from Marble Arch to Parliament Square. I joined female colleagues from across the House, many of whom dressed in the white, purple and green colours associated with the suffragettes and suffragists. Parliament displayed the original Acts of Parliament that gave women the franchise, and all female MPs gathered in Central Lobby for a commemorative photo.

It is striking how hard women have fought over the years to achieve what are now seen as basic human rights. Some gave their lives for the vote, while others were imprisoned even for acts such as putting on plays pointing out the foolishness of denying women the franchise. It is the stark reality that only a century ago a young woman's future was determined by her father until she was passed on to her husband. For all of my colleagues gathered in Parliament Square to mark the centenary, it was a moment to remember how far we had come and how the journey for equality is by no means over.

As a woman in politics today, I am aware I have it far easier than my predecessors, but it inescapably remains the case that female MPs are treated differently from their male colleagues. Women are often called airheads or ugly, or are accused of being successful thanks only to positive discrimination. Social media trolls will threaten rape and even killing your children. At the highest echelons, sexism can also be rife. Women can find themselves sidelined even when they are the most senior person in the room. Politics can often be an uncomfortable environment, but particularly so for women.

Yet despite that note of pessimism, I am confident that things are improving. Over the twelve years I've been an MP, each new parliamentary intake has seen increasing levels of diversity, helping to normalise and inspire more women, including many from ethnic minority backgrounds, to become politically engaged.

But as a woman in Westminster, you still have to stand your ground. This was made clear to me in a comical way soon after I became Leader of the House, as I entered the Chamber for Prime Minister's Questions. Given there are more Cabinet ministers than there are frontbench seats, PMQs is always something of a bunfight. If you want a good spot then you have to get there early, and often squeeze into a very small space. As Commons Leader, however, you have a designated seat next to the Chief Whip and to the right of the Prime Minister. On this particular Wednesday, I walked into the Chamber to find my predecessor as Leader, David Lidington (a friend and good colleague), was sitting in what was now my seat. With only ten seconds to go until PMQs was due to begin, and bearing in mind the convention is that the Leader will always attend PMQs and any other PM statement, I had to plonk myself on the steps next to the front bench, knees pressed firmly together.

As I later left the Chamber, I saw an enraged text from my mother: 'Why were you sitting on the steps? You should not be letting anyone, and especially not a man, take your seat – this is not what I would expect of any daughter of mine!' She was right, as she often (annoyingly) is, and I never let it happen again.

\* \* \*

In the spring of 2018, to my delight, the Prime Minister invited me to lead an inter-ministerial group on early years, recognising the longstanding passion I have for ensuring every baby gets the best start in life. For years, I have held the view that many of society's fundamental problems stem from unhappy experiences in the first 1,001 critical days, the period from conception to the age of two.

I would raise this issue at Cabinet meetings whenever I could – for example if we were talking about looked-after children, or young people's mental health, or how to improve school attainment, or the serious issue of young people's involvement in knife crime.

Colleagues seemed largely receptive, although I know to this day there are a number of MPs who recall, with a bit of eye-rolling, my poorly received speech at the 1922 Committee hustings in 2016, when I was justifiably accused of 'banging on' about babies. Well, I didn't stop, and both Theresa and, as I later discovered, Boris, were persuaded. So many times, I've seen MPs who have pressed a particular cause or campaign for long enough getting their way in the end. It's what keeps most of us motivated to do the job – the chance to make a positive difference to the world or to our community.

That inter-ministerial group included junior ministers across seven Whitehall departments: Education, Health, Local Government, Work and Pensions, Home Office, Treasury and Cabinet Office. The process of chairing the group was fascinating but challenging, not least because dealing with civil servants from so many different departments soon felt like herding cats. Although I have generally found individual civil servants to be helpful and motivated, the process of checking, signing off, escalating and subsequent watering down through 'too many cooks spoiling the broth' does serious damage to the ability of government ministers to get things done, and never more so than when a policy area requires cross-Whitehall collaboration. I sometimes found work which had been delegated to a specific department would be left undone because of personnel changes or competing departmental priorities, and at the actual meetings, ministers would be missing because their private offices had decided something else was more of a priority. Despite these frustrations, between us all we did a lot of research over the following year and came up with some significant policy agreements for the government to take forward. These included a commitment that the government would develop a vision for what a 'great' early years experience would look like for every baby and their family. We also proposed a ramping up of what was then called the troubled families' programme, with more focus on babies and better mental health provision for new parents.

The letter detailing all our recommendations was finally signed off by ministers two days before my resignation as Leader. But an awful lot of water was to flow under the bridge before then.

# CHAPTER ELEVEN

# HUNG PARLIAMENT

*The doors to the great national arena are flung open and the combatants inside prepare for battle, each with their champions roaring their support and baying for the blood of the opposition. In the midst of it all, the emperor stands majestically, poised to deliver his verdict as the spectators' yells become deafening.*

The House of Commons Chamber was often gladiatorial during those long days trying to steer Theresa May's widely condemned Brexit withdrawal deal through a hostile parliament. The tense atmosphere of the Commons during this period was exacerbated by two factors: first, the behaviour of the Speaker, John Bercow, as chair of proceedings, who was as capricious as any Roman emperor; and second, the complications presented by what was now a hung parliament. The last time any party had formed a minority government was in 1974, and while we weren't quite in uncharted territory, the prospect of seeking to govern while lacking executive authority certainly felt challenging. There is a saying that to be able to do politics you have to be able to count; that cliché is writ large in a hung parliament. To form a government, a party needs half plus one of the 650 Commons seats; in theory, excluding the Speaker and their deputies as well as members of Sinn Féin, who do not take their seats, this means 320 MPs. We now had 317. Labour, the SNP, Plaid Cymru, Liberal Democrats, Greens and others together numbered 314. The DUP had won ten seats and, after a protracted and hard-headed negotiation, agreed to enter into a confidence and supply arrangement, meaning they would vote with the Conservatives on legislation relating to Brexit, finance and matters that affected the UK as a whole, such as foreign policy. So now, in these areas at least, we had 327 – a majority. Fine in theory, except sometimes it wasn't – for example when Members were absent due to sickness or family crisis. On occasion we had to ask seriously ill MPs to come in and vote.

This was the mission impossible: getting legislation through a hung parliament on behalf of a minority government. This would be tricky at the best of times, but at the heart of our manifesto was the pledge to leave the European Union, the most divisive issue of our age and one which had split not only political parties but also families and friends across our nation. Without a majority, the scale of the challenge was extraordinarily daunting.

My base for supporting this mission impossible was a beautiful office in the Palace of Westminster – Room 4 in the House of Commons, in the corridor behind the Speaker's Chair. Wood-panelled, it had dark, heavy furniture including a highly polished round table which became the centre of operations for the private office team and me. At one side of the room was an open fireplace laid with sticks and torn-up pieces of the *Financial Times* dating back to the 1950s. I enjoyed showing guests the grand fireplace I could never light. There were also frequent signs of a rodent in residence – whether mouse or rat, I never found out.

Aside from when I was in the Chamber or the constituency, it was here I spent most of my days. The new private office team was both enormously knowledgeable and immensely supportive.

At least once a week, I chaired a meeting of the Parliamentary Business and Legislation Committee (PBL), at which all primary and contentious secondary legislation had to be assessed, amended and signed off for introduction to the Commons or the Lords. In normal times, the PBL had been more of a rubber stamp, but because of the lack of a majority, even the secondary legislation (the practical measures that enable a law to be enforced in daily life) was often sufficiently controversial to come to the PBL, so we could discuss 'handling' – how MPs could be persuaded to support the legislation. It was soon apparent that we would need to pass at least 800 pieces of secondary legislation relating to Brexit alone and would need eight new Bills (primary legislation) to set out our future outside the EU. This in addition to all the other legislation that was 'business as usual'. This would have been impossible to manage if every item had to be debated in the Chamber, so it was clear we needed to use the Delegated Legislation Committee system. But how could we do that with no majority?

That summer of 2017, once the House had gone into recess, I went on a boat on the River Thames for a week-long summer holiday with my family. At one point I jumped off the boat to take a call from Roy Stone, the longstanding adviser to the Chief Whip. The topic of conversation was how we could persuade the House to let us do our job. We spoke for almost two hours, and when I hung up I realised I had been walking and talking for so long the river was nowhere to be seen. It was definitely time for a strong drink when I finally found the boat again. But we now had a plan…

Delegated Legislation Committees (DL Committees) are responsible for line-by-line scrutiny of legislation. This is an underappreciated, critical part of the Commons' work, and when the Chamber is seen with empty benches on the television, it is often because backbench MPs are in DL Committee meetings. The political makeup of DL Committees is determined by representation in the Commons, so the mathematics posed a fundamental problem in a hung parliament. With twenty to forty members of each DL Committee, the numbers would never round up to a majority for the government, meaning the only way we could win a vote would be for every single piece of secondary legislation to be scrutinised on the floor of the House – a totally impractical matter.

As soon as we returned from the summer recess, I proposed a Business of the House motion that there would always be a majority of one or equal numbers on every DL Committee. This was no hospital pass – the opposition could and definitely did 'pray against' plenty of secondary legislation, which meant we would often have to make time for a debate in the Chamber, but at least now we stood a chance of success. There was sufficient goodwill at the start of that Parliament to get this important early agreement over the line; that wouldn't last.

Another innovation we put in place to maintain accord across a fractured House was the formation of a European Statutory Instruments Committee. Made up of a politically balanced group of MPs, this committee would go through each piece of secondary legislation relating to leaving the EU. In the PBL, we devised a traffic light triage system to ensure a smoother passage of legislation: the 'red' measures would go to the full PBL for consideration, 'amber' meant special attention needed to be paid to the concerns of some MPs, and 'green' should mean straightforward approval.

The PBL acted like a kind of Star Chamber for Secretaries of State to present their legislation. In the past, this had sometimes been a fun occasion, as Cabinet ministers proudly showed off popular Bills that were the culmination of months, even years, of work. But now they were brought down to earth with a bump. The members of the PBL were constantly warning ministers to narrow the scope of the legislation, telling them: *We love your Bill, but you can't have it* – because without control of the House, the Bill could be amended to include new laws on completely unrelated issues. We called such legislation 'Christmas trees', with a risk of hostile MPs seeking to add as many 'baubles' as they could.

Our uphill struggle was made far more difficult by Speaker Bercow, who had the authority to grant amendments, which often wildly extended the scope of a Bill or other motion. The Commons clerk might advise that a proposed amendment should be considered out of scope, but the Speaker would invariably make his own decision, disregarding the counsel of his advisers. This was the case with one essential piece of legislation, the Northern Ireland Budget Bill, which the Commons had to pass to ensure public services such as schools and hospitals remained open and funded during a period when the Northern Ireland Assembly was not functioning. A group of MPs introduced an amendment to the Bill on abortion, which was a devolved matter. This was a challenging issue for many. On a personal level, many sympathised with those who wanted women in Northern Ireland to have the same rights to a termination as those everywhere else in the United Kingdom. But out of respect for the core principle of devolution, some of us felt we had to try to block the amendment.

My shadow as Commons Leader was Valerie Vaz, who had been in post a long time and took her job of opposing very seriously – although we could and did cooperate on many cross-party issues. I recall she once described me in the Chamber as looking like a North Korean newsreader in the bright jacket I was wearing. I observed wryly to myself that if I had said that about her, it would no doubt have been front-page news. It was often like that: some great and feisty row – with Val or with Pete Wishart, the SNP spokesman, usually over Brexit, although it could be any element of government policy – and then more friendly conversation on leaving the Chamber.

As Leader, it was important to be collegiate, reaching out

to colleagues of all parties, Brexiteers and Remainers alike. In particular, I tried to support backbench MPs across the House who were trying hard to serve their constituents and raise issues on their behalf.

Private Members' Bills are an important way for MPs to make a difference on behalf of their constituents. They are pieces of legislation which focus on a specific, usually narrow, issue, and more often than not will change lives for the better. During the minority government, we business managers prioritised these pieces of legislation, and it proved a valuable way to create goodwill. So some really important Private Members' Bills became law during this time, including Kevin Hollinrake's Parental Bereavement Act, which gives bereaved parents paid employment leave; Carolyn Harris's Children's Funeral Fund, providing funding to meet the cost of the funeral in the tragic event of the loss of a child; and Chris Bryant's Assaults on Emergency Workers Act, increasing jail time for attacks on police, ambulance crews and other emergency staff.

One measure I am proud of from my time as Leader was the introduction of proxy voting for parental leave, which meant that MPs who were about to welcome a new arrival into their family would in future be able to vote by proxy for the period around the birth. The scheme was to prove helpful during the coronavirus pandemic, when the majority of MPs worked from home and voted by proxy. It was not without controversy, of course, with some colleagues wanting to extend proxy voting to illness and bereavement and others arguing that MPs should never be allowed to vote except in person. The issue was settled once and for all by the sight of Tulip Siddiq, a Labour MP, being brought into the Chamber in a wheelchair to vote, having had to postpone her caesarean section to vote in person. Proxy voting for parental leave was agreed on a trial basis and made permanent in September 2020.

Back in 2017, the heated atmosphere in the Commons Chamber was reflected by the scenes outside Parliament. A multitude of protesters and camera crews now regularly camped outside, making clear their antipathy to the events inside the Palace. Some of the more vocal campaigners discovered the location of my flat and would gather at the communal front door and even follow me around Westminster. While Parliament struggled to find a way forward with Brexit, fervent activists on both sides made clear their displeasure with our progress, interrupting live interviews on College Green with megaphones so that at times it felt to those of us working inside the House as if we were under siege. Politicians on both sides of the debate found themselves under attack, and it seemed that women were a particular target. I regularly had protesters shouting in my face, but so too did Remainers such as Diane Abbott and Anna Soubry. I always did my best, along with the Deputy Speaker at the time, Lindsay Hoyle, to ensure colleagues received police protection in Westminster where necessary.

The situation continued to escalate. If on the odd occasion I took my chance and tried to run the short distance from the Derby Gate exit to Downing Street for Cabinet, I would invariably be spotted by the most vociferous Remain protester, known as Brexit Steve, who would make a point of shouting: 'Andrea Leadsom, aren't you ashamed?'

I was only scared once, when I was Business Secretary and I was unable to get through a protest by car to go home. My media spad, Samantha (Sam), was determined to walk with me, and we tried to avoid the crowd outside Parliament by heading out of Black Rod's entrance at the Lords' end. There turned out to be a throng of people there too, and we were immediately surrounded. Sam and I did our best to talk back to the protesters, but there was no way through. People were screaming and spitting and the atmosphere was deeply unpleasant. The police thankfully 'donutted' us, surrounding us in a protective circle to hustle us out of the area. One officer told me that Diane Abbott and a number of other MPs had been through a similar experience at the other end of the Palace a short time earlier. It was a sign of how high passions were running on both sides, and very unpleasant for those of us on the receiving end.

The constant presence of photographers and television crews camped outside my flat each morning could be almost as challenging as the protesters. That year, my eldest son Fred was living in our flat while he did an apprenticeship. We developed a routine where he would go downstairs to check out the situation before he, Ben and I went downstairs together. Fred or Ben would hold open the door of the government car and I would say a few words to the cameras before driving off. Before entering politics, I had always found the sight of a minister walking past a television camera without answering questions so off-putting that I never wanted to do it myself. Instead, I developed a way to deal with them. When a journalist would shout an awkward question like 'Should Theresa May resign, Mrs Leadsom?' or 'What do you think of Boris Johnson's resignation?' – questions I definitely did not intend to answer – I would smile and say: 'Good morning,' before adding something vaguely related and entirely positive: 'I'm confident that the Prime Minister is committed to getting Brexit done' or 'Jeremy Hunt will be an excellent Foreign Secretary.' I would make my remark something on-topic that probably wasn't interesting enough to broadcast but didn't get me into hot water.

Every Thursday morning I would answer Business Questions in the Chamber. Like a slightly friendlier form of PMQs, these were questions relating to the business of the House – they could be on any subject. I might be asked how many pieces of Brexit legislation had yet to pass through the Commons, or to allocate time to debate the efforts of a charity which had raised thousands for the Royal British Legion, or why the government hadn't published a full list of ministerial responsibilities, or where the government's strategy on road building was, or any number of other things.

Preparations for Business Questions began on a Tuesday, with a run-through at the big round table in my office, where the spads, private office and comms teams brainstormed what might come up. Policy updates from departments across Whitehall would be gathered in a ring binder along with facts on everything from the latest GCSE results to where we were on winter flu, A&E admissions, crime statistics and decarbonisation efforts.

Wednesday evenings now involved a hot bath with a glass of wine and my ring binder, going through it to memorise key facts and stats until the water cooled. At 8.30 a.m. on Thursday, the whole team would regroup in my office with coffee for BQs prep. There were twelve of us around the table, perched wherever they could. My team was joined by my neighbouring MP Michael Ellis, who was now Deputy Leader of the House, one of our whips, Paul Maynard or Mike Freer, and my parliamentary private secretary, Victoria Prentis. Victoria would try to find out what constituency issues colleagues would be raising so that I could give them a proper reply. One person who never succumbed to her charming manner was the lovely late David Amess. He hardly ever missed BQs – one of our most frequent attendees – and always had a punchy matter to raise on behalf of Southend, often finishing up with an exhortation for it to be given city status. While he wouldn't give me a heads-up in advance, he was always appreciative of the opportunity to raise local matters and he would sit close behind me so we could exchange a few words.

The prep sessions consisted of everyone firing questions at me, trying to anticipate what would come up. After two years in the job, I would say we got to about 75 per cent success at predicting the questions. And, like painting the Forth Bridge, when it was over, we had to start all over again for the following week.

Business Questions was hard work, but there was a lot of laughter, and in hindsight I would say being Leader was the best job in Parliament. It was a fascinating period in my career – intellectually stimulating and deeply rewarding. And, above all, it was the great sense of camaraderie I experienced in the Leader's Office that made this a special time. As a team we would go for the occasional dinner together or enjoy a glass of wine at the end of a torrid day. After Business Questions we would always return to the office for a debrief – and if it was someone's birthday, there would often be tea and cake.

The successes during my time as Leader owed a great deal to my special advisers, Marc Pooler and Lucia Hodgson. Both had been with me since my backbench days, and they got on well with each other – which was just as well because they were crammed into a little cubby hole along the Speaker's corridor. In those two years, I really felt the benefit of being around people I trusted and who understood my values and political approach. Marc and Lucia shared my mantra: we will strive to be positive and kind – we won't 'do the dirty' on other people, no matter what happens. This principle was to be tested to the limit.

# CHAPTER TWELVE

# STUPID WOMAN

Speaker Bercow was on the warpath. Chris Grayling, the Transport Secretary, needed to make an important statement to the House. His request to the Speaker's and Leader's Offices had come rather close to the morning deadline, and on a day that was earmarked for an Opposition Day debate, but given the market-sensitive nature of his announcement, there was no other choice. Such an event wasn't unusual or even particularly controversial. But the Speaker didn't see it that way. As Chris prepared to speak, Bercow whipped himself into a frenzy, glaring at me as he criticised 'people traditionally with responsibility for safeguarding the rights of the House' – i.e. me – for the tardiness of the request.

He concluded with a flourish:

If I have to make the point again on future occasions, and to use the powers of the chair to facilitate the rights of this House in other ways, no matter what flak emanates from the Executive, I will do so … as I have always done over the past nine years, and no one and nothing will stop me doing my duty by the House of Commons.

By now I was used to the Speaker's ways and had developed my own ways of dealing with him. When he was on his feet, berating me at top volume for anything from policy to procedure or even just for failing to listen attentively to his latest directive from the chair, I would smile beatifically and then turn my head away from him to ask the whip at my side if he or she had slept well and enjoyed their breakfast. This would infuriate the Speaker, who demanded the full attention of the target of his anger, but as he carried on disrespectfully and aggressively from the chair, I would just continue to 'not hear him', instead asking my colleague if they preferred tea or coffee. Yes, OK, it was a petty response, but, bizarrely, there was not much else I could do. According to the clear rules governing Commons procedure, the Speaker was responsible for behaviour in the Chamber – extraordinarily, including his own. I couldn't make a point of order to complain about his unbelievable anger, nor ask anyone else to step in. So I had to find my own way to deal with him. When his manner was particularly intimidating or aggressive, I would simply ignore him – because that was all I could do.

On the day of this particular statement which so infuriated the Speaker, I did not look at him as he spat out his remarks. When he sat down and allowed Chris Grayling to speak, I took the opportunity to slip out of the Chamber. Soon after I returned to the Leader's Office, I received a note from a doorkeeper asking that I urgently call one of our DUP colleagues.

He told me: *I'm sorry to say that when the Speaker sat down after your altercation in the Chamber, I distinctly saw him mouth 'stupid woman' at you.* He added that one of his constituents who had been watching proceedings had contacted him to tell him they had also seen the Speaker mutter those words.

I thanked him and considered what to do next. I wasn't going to let this go lightly. I returned to the Chamber and stood by the Speaker's Chair: 'Excuse me, Mr Speaker.'

He turned. 'Yes?'

'I understand that following your speech from the chair this morning, as you sat down you mouthed "stupid woman" at me, and this was seen by a Member who has now drawn it to my attention.'

His face contorted with fury as he launched into a stage-whispered rant, saying that he would not be challenged by me, that it was up to him how to manage the Chamber and that he would continue to behave as he wished when in his opinion the government had done something wrong. I asked him how he could justify using the words 'stupid woman', but having said his piece, he turned his head away and started talking to his clerk on the other side of the chair, serving me up a bit of my own medicine. I was dismissed and stood there seething for a moment before leaving the Chamber.

As chair, the Speaker is there to do exactly that: chair the proceedings, ensure backbenchers are listened to and facilitate the government getting its agenda through the House. In a hung parliament, these functions are even more critical to the smooth running of democracy. When you have someone in post who is ruthlessly unbiased and even-handed, who sticks to the rules and listens to advice, then you have a very strong Speaker. If that person also behaves with courtesy, treating all MPs with respect and ensuring that everyone else is also courteous and respectful, then you have a great Speaker. Sadly, during my time as Leader of the Commons, we had neither.

My relationship with John Bercow dated back to before I entered the Commons, when I was selected as the candidate for South Northamptonshire, the neighbouring constituency to his Buckingham seat. Over the years we worked together on HS2, where I often represented his constituents as well as my own. But it wasn't until around 2014 that I began to have concerns, when he attempted to appoint Carol Mills, head of the Department of Parliamentary Services in the Australian Parliament in Canberra, to become the new Commons clerk. Although highly regarded, she obviously didn't have experience of our UK Parliament, and her appointment was seen as controversial among MPs. It seemed such an odd move. The clerk is the utmost authority on House of Commons procedures and standing orders. Why would he want to appoint someone who would know so little about how our Parliament worked? Thankfully, this did not come to pass.

But as time went on, it became obvious that the Speaker's interventions from the chair were growing more verbose. He was increasingly inclined to pick fights with individuals in the open, and even to humiliate them from the chair.

Soon after I became Leader of the House, I was leaving the Chamber when I noticed another MP behind me in the Lobby; it was immediately apparent she was in tears. When I asked why, she muttered something about being on the end of a particularly unpleasant jibe from the Speaker. I sympathised with her, but since the behaviour in the Chamber is a matter for the chair, there was little I could do in public, and as I was to find, raising such issues in private led to extraordinary outbursts from him. During my spell as Leader, I would witness several colleagues upset as a result of put-downs. Others were left angry or humiliated. A number of colleagues, including House staff, spoke to me privately to complain about the way in which they had been treated. This was a serious problem, and not only because no one deserves to be treated like this in their place of work – in this case a workplace which, let's not forget, keeps a permanent record of what is said in the Chamber and broadcasts it to the nation. The tone of the Chamber is also crucial when it comes to the productive and successful passage of government legislation, and in such a fragile atmosphere, the lack of calm, courteous and unbiased chairing was a concern.

The often unpleasant atmosphere increased as a result of the huge frustration around Brexit, and interventions from the chair increasingly invoked anger. Often interventions were belittling, such as former minister Anna Soubry being told from the chair that she 'thinks her views are relevant but we are not interested', and Michael Gove being instructed to 'be a good boy'. It might have seemed funny amid the drama of the

Chamber, but we all saw colleagues humiliated. I vividly remember the Speaker snapping at one MP that he was looking even more peculiar than usual.

There were certain individuals the Speaker would clash with repeatedly. I received a number of complaints from MPs who said that after a spat with the Speaker, they felt they were no longer being called to speak as they would have expected. And the Chamber became an intimidating place to ask a question or to make an intervention; if your sentence was too long or if you were not as succinct as the Speaker considered desirable, you could suddenly find yourself humiliated in front of your colleagues with a taunt which would form part of the parliamentary record for ever. *Take a soothing medicament, man! She needs to calm herself!*

This experience was not reserved for MPs; clerks were also treated to explosive outbursts. I recall waiting outside the Speaker's grand office after being summoned to see him when I heard swearing and shouting through the door. When a female member of staff emerged, she looked shellshocked. I knew my own meeting wasn't going to go well.

Unfortunately, I was to experience many such meetings. The Leader and the Speaker are supposed to have a fortnightly catch-up to talk about matters of the House. To start with, our conversations were relatively cordial, but soon, as the temperature in the Chamber rose, they became more difficult. Spitting with rage and shouting at me from a distance of three feet: *I've been the Speaker here since before you were elected, you don't know what you're talking about, you're wet behind the ears, I'm in charge, I will decide what happens.* It would reach a stage where there was just no point in continuing, and on a couple of occasions I told him: 'I think we've finished this meeting' and walked out. Following one of these episodes, Bercow sent a note to my private office saying that because I was so difficult to deal with, he would in future have an assistant in our meetings in order to protect himself from me. I laughed. From then on, I took my own senior official with me to meetings – but even with witnesses, these meetings were unbelievable.

There is no doubt that I infuriated the Speaker, and I have since reflected on why that was. Here is a man who was kind to me early on and who maintained friendships cross-party for much of his tenure as Speaker. Yet there can be no doubt that his years in the role changed him: it seemed to me he lost his ability to deal with anything other than total compliance or fear – two responses he never got from me. Is it that the trappings of high office, and being surrounded by willing staff, make it increasingly difficult to accept challenge, or even the possibility of being in the wrong? John Bercow introduced some well-regarded reforms in Parliament, particularly around diversity and inclusion, and I think it is a pity his Speakership ended as it did.

\* \* \*

There are a number of bodies on which the Speaker and the Leader are both required to serve. These include the House of Commons Commission, responsible for the finance, administration and governance of the House. The Speaker chairs the commission, in accordance with the governance rules, and the clerk and director general of the Commons attend as non-voting members. Meetings are held once a month and include MP representatives of all the major parties, appointed by the party whips. There are also two non-executive lay members, who advise but do not vote. The commission's dealings are surprisingly opaque – no published minutes (just a summary) and no record of individuals' voting decisions on what can be highly controversial issues. Since the commission comprised only two government representatives, my experience was that the opposition MPs, together with the Speaker, would often vote the same way.

In one of my first meetings as Leader, we discussed a request by the clerk to approve a substantial overspend and overrun on the restoration of Elizabeth Tower and Big Ben. I was concerned at the sums involved and proposed that the parliamentary works team cost out each element so we could make sure taxpayers' money was not being spent unnecessarily. I was outvoted, and wonderful as it is to see the Elizabeth Tower project complete, it was both wildly over budget and hugely delayed.

On a later occasion, the commission met to approve the final details of a pay rise agreed under collective bargaining for House staff including clerks, security guards, chefs and cleaners. The negotiations were almost complete, but the Speaker proposed that there should be a much more significant pay rise for one particular group of lower-paid staff because *they work hard and deserve it*. This would have given a terrible message to all the other staff, as well as undermining the long-established principle of collective bargaining. Thankfully, on this occasion I was not a lone voice and, after a lengthy argument, the proposal was withdrawn.

As time went by, the commission's work became trickier, with meetings frequently cancelled or rearranged at short notice by the Speaker's Office as he wanted to be in the chair. Then, suddenly, the stories of abuses of power that had begun with the #MeToo scandal spread to Westminster. Accusations in the press turned to historical bullying in Parliament and became an almost daily occurrence, with a number of serious such allegations made against the Speaker himself. It was obvious that the Speaker could not be involved in investigating these complaints, nor should he lead the review that was clearly needed. As Leader, I proposed that the two non-executive members of the commission should take over the whole matter of investigating historical complaints. They would come up with their own terms of reference and then oversee an independent investigation into historical bullying of members of House staff by MPs, with no input from any Members of Parliament. Their work ultimately led to the Cox Inquiry into bullying and harassment, chaired by Dame Laura Cox, which concluded that a culture of 'deference and silence' had been used to 'cover up abusive conduct'.

Separately, the Prime Minister had been appalled by the daily allegations of bullying and sexual harassment in Westminster. The Cox Inquiry would probe historical incidents, but both she and I were determined to make sure that in future, any grievances of those working in or visiting the Palace of

Westminster would be dealt with independently, and a new culture of courtesy and respect would be developed. Theresa called a meeting of all the party leaders, in which we agreed to work together on the detailed review that led to the creation of the Independent Complaints and Grievance Scheme (ICGS). The review included members of seven political parties, several peers, members of MPs' staff and representatives from the House staff organisations. It was a highly motivated group, cross-party and diverse, in what would prove one of the most collaborative and collegiate working experiences I've had in politics. It was a tough and lengthy process to get a final report and list of recommendations that not only could everyone on the working group sign up to but, most importantly, would pass through both Houses of Parliament.

It was clear from the early evidence sessions we held to hear from staff past and present that there were major problems in Parliament, but we also discovered that up to 80 per cent of MPs' and peers' staff concerns were workplace disputes stemming from bad management, non-existent induction schemes and lack of training and awareness, plus a lack of any process on offer that could resolve issues. Each MP or peer would be responsible for running their own office, recruiting staff, dealing with expenses, setting workplace targets and giving appraisals. The Independent Parliamentary Standards Authority provides model staff contracts and administers pay and expenses for MPs and their teams but, unlike in most other professional work environments, offers no HR department or mechanism to resolve workplace grievances. So while we were determined to clamp down on the 20 per cent of really serious behaviour, involving bullying and sexual harassment, we were also determined to change the culture, improve training and radically transform the level of support available for staff working in Parliament, including for MPs and peers, who also sometimes struggle to deal with poor behaviour among their staff. The report was approved unanimously and has since been put into practice. And while the headlines around the scheme focused on plans to investigate and punish those guilty of serious bullying and sexual harassment, underpinning it is a new behaviour code designed to ensure that everyone in Parliament is treated with dignity and respect, whoever they are. My hope is that this will have a transformative effect on the culture, while at the same time providing the serious measures needed to ensure that the abuse of power and entitled approach seen among some in the past will not be tolerated or ignored in future.

The issue of bullying and the accusations against the Speaker himself formed part of the backdrop to my time as Leader. By coincidence, the day he mouthed 'stupid woman' at me from the chair, Parliament's Standards Committee met to discuss a complaint against him by David Leakey, a former Black Rod. Because Mr Leakey's complaint was more than seven years old, the committee had to decide whether it should be referred to Kathryn Stone, the Parliamentary Commissioner for Standards, whose role it was to investigate such matters.

As I left the Commons that evening, a Conservative member of the committee came up to tell me: *The Standards Committee has decided the Parliamentary Commissioner should not be allowed to investigate the Speaker over Leakey's complaint. It is completely unacceptable that the Speaker should be the subject of such a review. His position should not be challenged in this way.*

Extraordinary! So here was a serious allegation that was now blocked from being investigated because the Speaker should somehow transcend the rules which applied to everyone else. Eventually, the Cox Report ensured that this and other allegations would be investigated properly, but I think this example highlights how far we still have to go in Parliament to recognise that we are all just people – with all our flaws – trying to do the best we can, and that no one should be put on a pedestal that makes their behaviour untouchable.

While I was still standing by my car amazed at this encounter, the Speaker himself materialised. *Ah, good evening, Leader, you wanted to speak to me earlier.*

I just looked at him in astonishment.

*Yes, I did, and you shouted in my face and then turned your back on me.*

*Yes, well, I'm happy to speak to you now. What is it you wanted to discuss?* Words almost failed me.

*Well, I wanted to discuss the fact that you mouthed 'stupid woman' at me, but actually I now find I have absolutely nothing to say to you.*

And with that I got into my government car, to the great amusement of the driver.

The 'stupid woman' episode had a postscript some months later, during a particularly heated Prime Minister's Questions. I was seated close to the Prime Minister, and as she sat down after an exchange with the Labour leader, Jeremy Corbyn mouthed something that looked very much like the words 'stupid woman'. There was uproar, with him insisting he had said no such thing and everyone with halfway decent eyesight pointing out that no other interpretation was possible. Lip readers even weighed in to debate the matter. When Conservative MPs called on Corbyn to apologise, the Speaker made a lengthy intervention from the chair, saying that Members who uttered unwelcome remarks should apologise for them, but that as he hadn't seen or heard the words in question, the Leader of the Opposition had to be taken at his word.

I turned to the Prime Minister and asked if she would mind if I called a point of order. She immediately agreed.

I stood up. 'Mr Speaker, following your finding that individuals who are found to have made unwelcome remarks should apologise, why it is that when an opposition Member found that you had called me a "stupid woman", you did not apologise in this Chamber?'

The Speaker was momentarily speechless. He stood up with his face turning red and repeated: 'No, no, no, no.' He didn't know what to say. Eventually, he managed: 'I've dealt with that issue separately.'

It is true the Speaker had replied to a letter I wrote complaining about the incident, saying he may have been frustrated in the heat of the moment – but he never gave an apology, then or since.

To me this was just another example of a Parliament that is not fit for the twenty-first century. The fact that 'behaviour in the Chamber is a matter for the chair', including his or her own behaviour; the fact that the House of Commons Commission is chaired by the Speaker, and is opaque in its dealings with millions of taxpayers' money; and the fact that the commission is even now only starting to properly support a professional work environment – all this shows there is a long way to go before we reach the ambition of the ICGS working group that everyone who visits or works in Parliament should be treated with dignity and respect.

# CHAPTER THIRTEEN

# DEPARTURES

Theresa May's second parliamentary term was marked by an extraordinary exodus of ministers from her Cabinet. While this rate of attrition was depressing and demoralising for the government, there was a personal bright side. As Leader of the House, I was also Lord President of the Privy Council. As a result, I had the honour of being in the Queen's presence on many occasions, the first major one being as part of the procession during the State Opening of Parliament, when the Queen comes to the Palace of Westminster to set out the new policy agenda of her government. On that occasion, the toing and froing of trying to establish a majority had meant the date for State Opening being fixed on a day the Queen was due to be at the Ascot races. I was hugely honoured to process ahead of the Queen into the House of Lords and watch her give the speech. I had dressed carefully to be smart but in keeping with the fact that the Queen would not be in robes but rather in day dress. I was wearing a hat with a fairly wide brim, which later one of the papers would claim was in fact a radar dish designed to provide the Queen with racing tips ahead of her afternoon engagements.

A key role of Lord President was the responsibility for attending whenever the Queen appointed new Secretaries of State or swore in new Privy Counsellors. I never tired of watching each new colleague taking their oath: the nervousness of each at the thought that they might trip over a footstool or get the lines wrong; their huge pleasure at being in the presence of the monarch.

The Lord President always has a brief private audience with the Queen before each Privy Council meeting. The Queen's equerry at the time, Nana Kofi Twumasi-Ankrah, known to all as TA, would meet me at the entrance, always dressed in full uniform complete with spurs and a sword. He would walk me to the double doors of the audience room, which would be opened for us by white-gloved staff. Then it was three steps forward, TA bowed, I curtsied, and he would say: 'The Lord President, Your Majesty,' before he took three steps back and the doors closed. It is not permitted to disclose what the Queen discusses with her Privy Counsellors, so I will say only that she was always extraordinarily welcoming and kind, as well as interesting to talk to.

These occasions were such an incredible experience that before my second private audience, I joked to TA: 'If I should die while I'm with the Queen, please tell my family I expired from the immense pride and honour of being in her presence.'

He looked at me totally straight-faced. *Lord President, I'm afraid I cannot allow you to die in the presence of the Queen.* We never put it to the test.

The Privy Council meets wherever the Queen is in residence, which meant that after the New Year reshuffle in 2018 I visited Sandringham with all its festive decorations still in place. It was a surprisingly homely place, with big log fires – and the corgis enjoying the warmth. During my time as Leader, I received two formal invitations to lunch at Windsor Castle with the Queen and the late Duke of Edinburgh. During one lunch I was seated next to Prince Philip. Given his experience overseeing the rebuilding of Windsor Castle following its devastating fire in 1992, (Baroness) Nat Evans and I thought we might discuss with him the restoration of the Palace of Westminster. Always refreshingly blunt, he made it quite clear within a few minutes that he didn't think much of the prospect of parliamentarians getting to grips with such a challenging project. So far, he has been proved entirely correct!

But there was no doubt that the steady rate of Cabinet departures presented a major headache for the Prime Minister and all of us who battled to get Brexit through the Commons. It got to the point where the attrition rate was farcical: during twenty-four turbulent months, sixteen Cabinet ministers handed in their resignations, along with sixty junior ministers, forty-two of those as a direct result of the government's Brexit policies. My office had a challenging task in attempting to ensure the passage of legislation paving the way for our withdrawal through a hung parliament, but the Prime Minister was having to deal with a hung Cabinet, as Leavers and Remainers battled for her ear and a way through the impasse.

I was dragged into the drama surrounding the first departure in November 2017, when Gavin Williamson, the Chief Whip, asked at the end of one of our regular business meetings if the officials could leave the room, as he had what he described as something of a sensitive and very serious nature to discuss. Gavin told me that he understood Sir Michael Fallon was responsible for saying some inappropriate things to me and he wanted to know what it was he said.

Michael was Defence Secretary and we had served together on the Treasury Select Committee back in 2010. Around that Christmas, I had hosted a dinner party for female MPs and we had got talking about some of the flippant things men had said to us over the years. The wine flowed and as we swapped stories of our experiences, I had shared anecdotes of some mildly inappropriate remarks Michael had made during that time on the Treasury Committee. Now, nearly seven years on, Gavin was asking for details.

I told him I thought he must be referring to events that took place in 2010 and explained it was not something I wanted to discuss or needed to complain about. Gavin was not satisfied with that, saying there were some very real concerns and that the Prime Minister would wish to know exactly what was said. I stressed again that this really was no big deal and made clear I did not want this to form a part of any kind of inquiry.

A day or so later, I received a note saying the Prime Minister wanted to see me in her Commons office after PMQs. When I entered, there was Theresa, her deputy chief of staff JoJo Penn, Gavin and myself.

The PM asked me straight out: *What happened with Michael Fallon?*

I told her that I did not consider the matter to be important, but she still wanted to know what had been said. So I told her the story and explained that I had laughed about his remarks with a group of female colleagues and that I had no idea how his words had come to her attention. I even apologised for the fact her time had been taken up by something so inconsequential. It was a very short interview, no more than ten minutes, and then I left.

Less than half an hour after I got back to the Leader's Office, a member of my private office came in. 'I have a call for you, Leader, from Tom Newton Dunn of *The Sun*. Can I put it through?'

I had a bad feeling.

Tom came on the line, telling me he had heard Michael Fallon had behaved inappropriately towards me, and asking me to tell him about it.

I declined to comment, even though my media adviser was subsequently told that without a comment from me, perhaps readers would assume I had deliberately put this accusation into the press myself. When Michael resigned later that evening, *The Sun* ran a story suggesting I had demanded he go, which couldn't have been further from the truth. It later emerged that Michael had been complained about by other women, and for this he apologised. As Leader, I considered protecting the victims of bullying and harassment as one of my most important responsibilities. But I do regret that those trivial incidents involving me were dragged into Michael's case, and it is a poor reflection on the relationship between politicians and the media that when I refused to take part in their story, the result was several TV cameras parked outside my home in Northamptonshire that weekend, clamouring for comment every time I stepped out the door.

So now a new Defence Secretary was about to be appointed, and I did wonder if the role might be offered to Penny Mordaunt. She had done a fantastic job as Armed Forces Minister and was widely considered to be the next minister in line for a Cabinet post. Thinking this could well be her moment, I texted her to wish her luck, and she replied optimistically that she believed now was her chance.

Instead, Gavin Williamson was announced as the new Secretary of State for Defence. This was a total surprise appointment; it was my understanding that Penny had been given more than just a hope she would be the next Defence Secretary. To this day I wonder how my anecdotes about Michael Fallon came to the attention of *The Sun*. We will never know. Ironically, Penny was to replace Gavin at the Ministry of Defence within two years, after he was removed from office over a leak incident.

With Gavin's promotion, in late 2017, Julian Smith now became Chief Whip. We got off to a somewhat rocky start within a few weeks when rumours began that the Prime Minister was planning a reshuffle and the inevitable speculation on the snakes and ladders game resumed – who was going to be promoted? Who was going to be sacked? Stories abound when a reshuffle looms – failures and successes of individual ministers are held out in the press as evidence of their chances of survival. It's a torrid time for every minister desperate to keep their job or get onto the next rung of the ladder, and also a tense period for lots of backbenchers, wondering if this is their chance for promotion. The press speculated that I would be one of those likely to be sacked. As Chief Whip, Julian was integral to the more junior changes in government and, in theory at least, was in the PM's core group considering the Cabinet roles.

The reshuffle began on the morning of 8 January 2018 with the spectacle of ministers walking up Downing Street to learn their fate. And I heard nothing: not a peep, no phone call from No. 10, no whisper from the whips. All day I sat in my office with spads, officials and parliamentary staff wandering in and out, asking: *Any news yet?* Reshuffles are torture at the best of times, and this one was simply excruciating, given the mounting press speculation that I was definitely going to be sacked. By the time the rest of the Cabinet line-up was complete, I was pretty despondent. I was about to begin packing up my office and then, at around 9 p.m., a phone call came in from No. 10.

The Prime Minister came on the line: 'I think you've been doing a good job and I'd like you to stay in post, thank you.'

I ought to have been relieved, delighted even, but all I could think was: *That's it? After all those hours of waiting and all the speculation that I was for the chop?* It's a strange world where the process of reshuffling – based as it is on rumour, speculation and the individual wishes of the PM and her immediate advisers – determines every politician's career. In our world there is little meritocracy, scant reward for long service, and no formal assessment of competencies. In politics it's mostly about being in the right place at the right time, personal loyalties, and the roll of the dice.

The next day, when our paths crossed in the voting lobby, the Chief Whip got both barrels, I'm sorry to say, with dozens of our colleagues watching. I was so furious to have been left, along with my whole team, in total limbo, and not only that, but the negative press – that he could have tempered with just a word of reassurance – had really got to me. The reality is that the stress of political life takes a massive toll, and the whips, notwithstanding their own heavy workload, also have the job of looking after the wellbeing of colleagues.

It would not be the last time we ever had cross words, but Julian went on to become an ally. As with all good pairings of Chief Whip and Leader of the House, we worked well together and were in each other's confidence. He and I regularly discussed the numbers in the Commons, and he would enlist me to try to win over the key backbench Brexiteers in the European Research Group of MPs, a grouping committed to ensuring a clean Brexit. Its leader, Jacob Rees-Mogg, and I would have periodic breakfast meetings to maintain channels of communication, but while the discussions were always courteous and constructive, I have to say I was not successful in persuading him to back the government. As the Parliament progressed, I often found myself at the sharp end of colleagues in the ERG who couldn't understand why I hadn't resigned at the latest affront to Brexit. They took my determination to support the PM's deal as a weakening of my commitment to leaving the EU, whereas in my view, Theresa's withdrawal agreement represented a way to achieve Brexit while keeping the United Kingdom together.

With the Cabinet as divided as Parliament, and the Prime Minister trying hard to achieve consensus by allowing everyone to have their say, our Tuesday morning Cabinet meetings began to drag on. By now, we all knew each other's standpoints, and the arguments became increasingly repetitive. I even once had a joke with the Chief where I slipped out to the ladies' when one of our more long-winded colleagues began speaking and on returning I passed him a note summarising what I thought the minister had said when I was out of the room. He said it was pretty spot on.

In July 2018, with tensions growing over the Prime Minister's Brexit strategy, Cabinet was summoned to Chequers to discuss the withdrawal agreement, the result of her negotiation with the EU to agree the terms of Britain's departure. The evening before, Cabinet members were called into No. 10 to review the text in a private reading room. It was a huge document, around two inches thick, and I sat alongside my colleagues speed-reading and trying to get swiftly to the nub of what had been agreed. I had drawn up a list of key items I needed it to include in order to give the agreement my support and felt I came away with a pretty clear view of what I had read. It wasn't the Brexit I had wanted, but it was still Brexit and therefore, albeit reluctantly, I would support the Prime Minister to deliver it.

As I walked out of Downing Street, a group of pro-Brexit Cabinet allies agreed to meet in Boris Johnson's rooms in the Foreign Office. Boris and I were joined there by others, including Penny, David Davis, International Trade Secretary Liam Fox, Michael Gove and Work and Pensions Secretary Esther McVey. We spent an hour discussing our tactics for the following day and confirming we were on the same page: the withdrawal agreement wasn't what we would have wished for, but it was still Brexit, and we would stick by Theresa as she attempted to get it through the Commons. The impression I had from everyone in the Foreign Office that evening, including Boris and David, was that we certainly didn't love it but we could live with it.

The next day, the Cabinet met at Chequers. This was always a trip down memory lane for me, because my grandmother had lived close by when I was growing up. It had seemed a grand but rather scary place when I was a child. Since then, I had been to Chequers only once before, at the invitation of David Cameron, but this was my first visit as a Cabinet minister. The driveway into Chequers has no grand entrance and signage, just a long winding lane, and it is more like a comfortable if impressive country house than an imposing stately home. We gathered in the main hall to chat over bacon sandwiches and coffee, before moving into a meeting room where seating arrangements had been assigned. There, the Prime Minister laid out her withdrawal agreement. The conversation was business-like but perfectly cordial. Many of us had questions and suggestions, which Theresa did her best to address. I put forward a suggestion that the agreement should include a sunset clause on the Northern Ireland backstop and was assured by the PM that while it was doubtful this could be secured, she would seek to achieve it.

Before our gathering, there had been great media speculation that some Brexiteers might quit the Cabinet in protest at the withdrawal agreement; in response, someone in No. 10 had thought it amusing to brief the press that anyone who stormed out of Chequers would lose their job and ministerial car and would have to walk or take a private taxi home. It might have seemed funny, but there was a hard edge, because there was a very real possibility of Cabinet departures. While the taxi firms of Buckinghamshire were left undisturbed that evening, two days after our Chequers gathering, David Davis resigned. As Brexit Secretary, his anger at being sidelined during the talks which led to the withdrawal agreement was palpable and, I felt, understandable. Steve Baker, my colleague who had worked on my leadership campaign and was serving as Brexit Minister, followed him out of the door. But I was shocked when Boris also quit the next day. In hindsight, these departures could be seen as the moment when the desire of some Brexiteers to see Brexit done became an ambition to destabilise the government to get rid of Theresa and do it themselves. Chequers was that turning point.

The period that followed was difficult for me, as I came under enormous pressure from the Brexiteers to follow David and Boris's lead and resign. With them gone, I was one of a small number from Vote Leave still in the Cabinet, and Steve Baker in particular was forthright in his disappointment at my disinclination to resign. From the time of his own resignation until Britain left the EU, Steve barely spoke to me, a source of deep regret, and indicative of the feelings running so high. Other Brexiteers accused me of disloyalty, of sticking to the job for the pay or the glory. For my part, I was not about to resign: I felt a duty, ever since my decision to drop out of the leadership race back in 2016, to support Theresa to remain Prime Minister so long as she was committed to delivering Brexit – and by my calculation, although not particularly attractive, the withdrawal agreement was Brexit. So I stuck with it.

It wasn't only Brexiteers who made clear their disappointment in me. One Remainer colleague, for whom I had once thrown an engagement party, texted to say she now believed I had only played host to further my ambitions, and she thought that in supporting Brexit I had taken leave of my senses. It was a period of great tension and hostility, when previous friends and good colleagues threw around some pretty spiteful and personal remarks. The whole country was divided; in my own constituency, I had Brexiteers and Remainers accusing me of betrayal, while I battled my own reservations about the process of leaving the EU that we were embarked upon.

My response to what became a regular drumbeat of sackings and resignations was to support the PM as much as I could. We would occasionally speak on a Sunday evening before a big week for the Commons to discuss the mood in the House and try to assess where the focus was shifting. She was always ready to listen, and I felt that we developed a collaborative relationship.

It was around this time that I set up what became known as the Pizza Club, made up of those in Cabinet who were determined to both support Theresa's leadership and achieve Brexit. While most had been Leavers, the group included a number of ministers who had voted Remain but believed strongly in respecting the result of the referendum. At the start, David Davis was still in Cabinet and was one of those I invited to our first meeting. When he walked into the Leader's Office and saw that I had sourced wine, soft drinks and some great Lebanese food, he commented that we should have stuck with pizza.

I had to laugh. After that, the group was known as the Pizza Club in honour of David's blunt assessment – and we did enjoy some pizza a few times after that.

The government limped on, and in November, the withdrawal agreement was approved and published, leading to Dominic Raab's resignation in protest as Brexit Secretary, to be replaced the next day by Steve Barclay.

Those were turbulent times. Normally in the House of Commons, precedence is given on every sitting day to the business set out by the government of the day. The three exceptions to this are Opposition Days (twenty per parliamentary session), Backbench Business Days (twenty-seven per session) and Private Members' Days (normally taken on Fridays). There is limited scope for complex business on those days, yet during the period of the hung parliament, there were a number of highly controversial decisions made by the Speaker that clearly helped backbenchers to thwart Brexit and ultimately led to Theresa May's resignation. Humble Addresses, normally only used for non-political occasions, were brought forward on Opposition Day motions to demand confidential legal and other advice from government; the Speaker permitted emergency debates under Standing Order 24 and allowed backbench MPs to take control of the order paper, enabling them to prevent the government from leaving the EU without a deal. Controversially, the Speaker permitted a business motion (that should have been put 'forthwith' and therefore not debated) to be amended, against advice from his senior clerk. This enabled Remain-supporting MP Dominic Grieve QC to propose (successfully) that if the meaningful vote was not passed during the government's forthcoming debate then the government would only have three days in which to bring forward a fresh plan for Brexit, rather than the three weeks originally envisaged. This combination of the Speaker and Remain-supporting backbenchers left government, and the PM, with no room for manoeuvre.

Unsurprisingly, a group of Conservative MPs responded to the ebbing away of power from No. 10 by calling a vote of no confidence in the Prime Minister. The internal tensions were clear: many Leavers had backed Theresa in the leadership contest and now felt betrayed. The ERG was frustrated and angry. And a number of Remainers, as Philip Hammond, her Chancellor, has since confirmed, felt disappointed we were not signing up to a Norway- or Switzerland-style Brexit, something which would not have allowed the full return of sovereignty to the UK. There was also still anger in the party over the general election: ultimately, every MP relies on their party leader to increase their vote so they can hang on to their seat for as long as possible. Many were now sitting on wafer-thin majorities and as a result were unhappy with the Prime Minister.

Eventually, Theresa won the vote of no confidence by a substantial if not overwhelming majority. Unfortunately, this was as much a sign of fear as a sign of support; many MPs were concerned that if the Prime Minister was removed, a general election would follow which we could lose to Labour. Others in the Leave camp worried she could be replaced with a Remainer who would cancel Brexit. And some just felt sorry for Theresa, for having been put in an almost impossible position when the leading Brexiteers (myself included) had not put themselves forward for the leadership in the aftermath of the referendum. I too supported Theresa in the no confidence vote for all of these reasons and more. I still felt personally responsible for the situation we were in, and I wasn't going to compound that by torpedoing her premiership.

But while Theresa remained Prime Minister, her attempts

to pass the meaningful vote came to nothing and, to my great regret, our departure from the EU had to be delayed. On 29 March 2019, the day Britain was supposed to leave, the House instead voted to extend our membership, with the agreement of the EU itself. It was a terrible day for our democracy, and also a tough day for me and the Leader's Office team, who had worked day and night to make sure all the hundreds of pieces of secondary legislation were in place to ensure a smooth Brexit should the political departure happen as planned. As ever at these times of disaster, food and bubbles are the answer, so I ordered a huge fresh cream cake from the local bakery and stuck a Union Jack and an EU flag on it and we got the whole team together to drink a toast to their success in delivering their bit.

The Prime Minister now turned to the opposition as she sought to find a way through the impasse. This was a major concern, particularly when it became clear that my PBL committee would not be included in the conversations she was having with Jeremy Corbyn and other party leaders. The ad hoc meetings of the Pizza Club escalated – much to the interest of both the press and opposition MPs. At one point, my assistant Tommy was dodging photographers as he took delivery of a pile of pizzas at Carriage Gates and sneaked them up to my office via the back corridor. This led to quite a funny exchange at Business Questions the next day, when Pete Wishart of the SNP said of me: 'It was she who led the pizza putsch – the Cabinet's calzone – where the Brexit mutineers ensured over garlic bread that whatever the Prime Minister cobbles together will be wood-fired.' There were plenty of good times in the knockabout arena of Thursday Business Questions. But as the months passed, Pizza Club discussions were taking place not only in person but by conference call and over WhatsApp and were an almost daily occurrence as ministers became increasingly nervous about Theresa's talks with the opposition. The group now included Michael Gove, Penny Mordaunt, Jeremy Hunt, Sajid Javid, Chief Secretary to the Treasury Liz Truss, Steve Barclay, Health Secretary Matt Hancock, Transport Secretary Chris Grayling, Attorney General Geoffrey Cox and Liam Fox.

On the weekend of 12 May 2019, we held two conference calls to agree a plan of action for what we knew would be a difficult week. We agreed to continue planning for a no-deal exit, and also that there was zero appetite for any attempt to force a leadership contest.

The following week, with Theresa's discussions with the opposition having come to an abrupt end, we gathered at Cabinet as usual. The conversation focused on how we might get the latest version of the withdrawal agreement through the Commons. The PM confirmed that she would give a statement on the agreement after PMQs the following day, setting out the key measures. Following Cabinet, we were invited to read through the agreement to see the changes which had arisen from the Prime Minister's talks with the opposition. A reading room had been set aside for us in the Cabinet Office and I was instructed to hand over my phone while for the next two hours I read the doorstopper of a document. This felt like something of an affront, given that this was legislation I would be presenting at Business Questions two days later; I saw no reason why the agreement should not have been put to the PBL as usual so that parliamentary handling could be properly discussed. I was soon to discover why…

There, buried away, was a clause which effectively stated that if the House voted for a second referendum then the government would bring forward the necessary legislation to facilitate it. This was a real shock, and totally unacceptable. It had certainly not been discussed in Cabinet. Given that our largely Remain parliament would almost certainly vote for a second referendum, this clause basically meant that, in my opinion, it would be certain to happen. And that could mean the end of Brexit, and certainly the end of public faith in the political process. The country had told us what to do and it seemed to me we were now going to ask them again.

My mind raced. *Was my understanding of this new clause in the agreement correct?* This had to be a drafting error – just a simple mistake – and it would surely be corrected if I raised it. But maybe it wasn't an error. *Is the government seriously going to facilitate a second referendum if the House votes for it?*

I phoned Steve Barclay.

*Yes, that is what the clause says.*

It felt as if the world had gone mad. What had been the point of the past two years if we were going to give up now?

I messaged the Pizza Club, suggesting we meet as soon as possible to discuss this extraordinary turn of events: 'Do any colleagues feel there is a way to undo the damage of today?' I wrote.

The answers came back: *Disaster.*

*I think there are options. When shall we meet?*

We considered ducking out of PMQs to meet – until someone rightly pointed out this would look as if we had resigned en masse.

I sent a message to Gavin Barwell, Theresa's chief of staff, who had himself been an MP before losing his seat at the election:

> There is huge disagreement over what was agreed at Cabinet yesterday … The Withdrawal Agreement Bill suggests if a second referendum is supported then a minister 'will make arrangements for a referendum'. This would almost certainly mean extending Article 50 again. I cannot support that. Please can you urgently confirm the Bill will not be presented until Cabinet can agree an approach.
>
> Thanks, Andrea.

I spent the rest of the day and the following morning trying to contact both Barwell and Julian Smith. Neither returned my calls. By now it was Wednesday 22 May, and I was conscious that I had to take Business Questions the following morning. The thought of this was not appealing: I would be required to read out the business of the House and introduce a Withdrawal Agreement Bill which I could not support.

I messaged the Pizza Group again: 'Hello all. I am very concerned referendum two offer now fully undermines our Brexit policy.'

My colleagues replied; almost all were in agreement.

It was now clear that the provision for a second referendum had not in fact been a drafting error and that neither Gavin nor the Chief Whip was going to respond to me. It was also now obvious to me that I could not take Business Questions the next day.

I broke the news to my team first: *I've loved working with you all, but I've come to the end of the road – I'm going to have to resign.*

My private office team had grown used to buzzing in and out of the office, but now they stayed away as Marc, Lucia, Luke, Tommy and I confronted the reality that I could no longer remain in the government. I had always sworn to stick by Theresa so long as she was delivering Brexit – but this wasn't Brexit.

By now it was late afternoon and I was due at Buckingham Palace for Privy Council. I began to write my resignation letter, knowing I would have to phone the Prime Minister as soon as I returned from meeting the Queen. As I drafted the letter, I reflected that I had kept to my one-sided bargain in supporting her to get Brexit done. She had personally promised me when I phoned to tell her I would withdraw from the leadership race that she would deliver on the referendum result, and it was clear to me that she now could not do that.

Privy Council was very poignant. I now knew I would be resigning, though I obviously didn't say anything to the Queen. On the way back to Parliament, I knew I was also saying goodbye to Kevin, my government driver, who had become a good friend. I called Ben and then my mum and sisters; they all agreed I had no choice but to resign.

Once back in the office, I phoned Theresa on her mobile. She answered immediately.

*Well, Theresa, this is the call I never wanted to make. I always wanted to support you to get Brexit done, but I'm afraid the second referendum clause in the Withdrawal Bill is something I cannot support, and therefore I'm so sorry but I'm phoning to offer you my resignation.*

There was a pause, and then the PM asked me what exactly I was concerned about in the Bill.

I pointed out the specific clause and she said: *Let me go away and talk to others about this.*

This seemed astonishing. Surely she must be aware of the impact of the clause and must have decided to include it.

I was tempted, so very tempted, to say: 'Yes, OK, I'll wait while you see if this can be sorted out.' But in reality it was time to go. I had lost confidence.

I told the Prime Minister that I had no choice but to resign. I explained that there was no way I could introduce the Bill in Business Questions the next day, and that I had been loyal to her for as long as I could. I thanked her for the positive relationship we had enjoyed and apologised for leaving her government and for the inevitable problems it would cause.

The PM was matter-of-fact, but it was clear that the house of cards was tumbling. And I felt badly, because it was obvious that my departure would be another blow. Looking back, I do think Theresa probably would have found a way to stop me from quitting if she could, because my departure was in a sense the straw that broke the camel's back. That evening was emotional – I loved the Leader's Office. Knowing as I did that I would be out of government by morning, civil servants and spads gathered together for a last glass of wine and to bid each other farewell.

\* \* \*

Two days later, with the Withdrawal Bill never seeing the light of day, it was the PM's turn to announce her departure.

I think history will be far kinder to Theresa May than her colleagues and many in the press and public were at the time. By the end she was exhausted – as we all were. Exhausted by the rage from MPs, from our constituents, from everyone, Leave and Remain, who thought they were being betrayed. If you were in government during those years, you were stuck in the middle of a divide in which there was no appetite for consensus. It was clear Theresa loved being Prime Minister and took it incredibly seriously. I admired her constant determination to do the job properly in the face of a truly impossible situation in Parliament. She has been accused of confusing stubbornness with strength. I disagree. She did press some votes she wasn't going to win, not because she didn't realise she would lose but because she understood the need to keep the momentum going. At all times she was willing to talk: to her Cabinet, to the ERG, to the DUP, to the Leader of the Opposition, the EU, anyone, if it would help her find a way through. She knew what the mission was, and she was determined to see it to the end. Her failure was never about a lack of commitment.

Ultimately, it took a Brexiteer in Boris Johnson to deliver Brexit. He had that conviction about leaving the European Union that I shared and that Theresa at root did not. Nevertheless, it was her careful, methodical work and patient willingness to negotiate that achieved 75 per cent of the Brexit deal, which meant that when Boris became Prime Minister, he was able to walk in, restructure certain key elements of the deal, and then get Brexit done. Largely because of his sunny view of the future and his very visible commitment to Brexit, Boris then won a huge general election majority that gave him the votes to get the agreement through the Commons.

But that was for the future. Right now, another leadership contest was beginning.

# CHAPTER FOURTEEN

# LEADERSHIP REVISITED

The game was back on. I was determined to deliver Brexit, and there was never any doubt in my mind that if Theresa May stood down, I would enter the contest to replace her. It was a continuation of the decision I made back in 2016 to support Theresa to deliver Brexit, but if she would not or could not fulfil the referendum mandate, I would take up the cause again. This time around, I was well prepared. Recalling Will Wragg's aviation-themed assessment of my first bid for the leadership, this time we would make sure we weren't building a jet engine as we were taxiing along the runway; instead, my campaign would be full throttle from the start. Sadly, second time around and despite taking off well, we didn't have enough passengers on board. If the 2016 bid had been right time, wrong campaign, this time it was right campaign, wrong time. This second attempt at leadership in many ways proved a victim of the first – there are rarely second chances in politics.

The team had begun preparing for a contest that seemed inevitable as far back as September 2017. We formed a group called Forward Look to prepare the ground; it would put in place the kind of planning it was clear during the 2016 contest that other candidates had spent months, even years, working on. Theresa's assured performance in 2016 showed that if you want to be the leader of a political party – and Prime Minister – you cannot wake up one day and say: *Let's do this thing.* You have to be prepared. The Forward Look group was made up of Ben; Peter Warner, my constituency association chairman; my chief of staff, Luke; media spad Lucia; and policy spad Marc. The early support of Chris Heaton-Harris and Steve Baker as whip and campaign manager respectively was critical.

Chris, Steve and I all agreed my last campaign had faltered largely as a result of a lack of preparedness, something we were determined to address this time around. The Forward Look group began to meet weekly and put in hours of work covering everything from drawing up a full set of policies to a media strategy, a campaign schedule and every detail relating to my bid, down to the venue and even the music to be played at the campaign launch. My launch speech was drafted and regularly revised as the Brexit narrative changed. We developed a pretty full manifesto and even a set of opinion pieces in which I would set out my vision to the public. The manifesto included proposals for reform of the social care system, ideas on building jobs and growth in achieving net-zero carbon emissions and – of course – transformative policies for the early years.

At the core of the manifesto was a pledge to deliver Brexit. Key to that, as the country faced another leadership contest, I was determined to learn from what I considered to be the mistakes made by Theresa May's team. As part of the Forward

Look project, I thought carefully about what the management of the No. 10 machinery should look like, knowing it needed to be very different from what had gone before. While having Gavin Barwell, an ex-MP, as chief of staff had been a good idea at the start, he had clearly been overstretched.

In my view, No. 10 had been too aloof from Parliament, which in a minority government it could not afford. My plan involved creating a new role of chief operating officer in No. 10 to bring serious business management into the operation. That COO would have, among other responsibilities, the job of making sure No. 10 staff were properly motivated and supported to do their jobs. It wasn't to be. And it is a great regret that with Boris Johnson's victory this responsibility went instead to Dominic Cummings – not a man famed for his collegiate approach.

As the months passed, Theresa's grip on power became more tenuous, and my Forward Look team stepped up our planning, even though Chris, Steve and I continued to support the PM. Then came Chequers and Steve's departure from the government and his role as Brexit Minister. He wanted me to quit the Cabinet too, and when I didn't, I went from hero to zero in his eyes, even being blanked by him as we passed each other in the corridor. Losing Steve from Forward Look was tough on many levels. Again I was taught the lesson that in politics, your beliefs and priorities will take precedence over friendship and loyalty. It has given me pause for thought many times – can MPs involved in these high-stakes games ever be truly unconditional friends? In my experience, there are a tiny number I would say have been true friends throughout.

One of those is Heather Wheeler, MP for South Derbyshire. Popular with colleagues, she had been a real ally in 2016, and we now had dinner in the Barry Room in the House of Lords, where I set out my plans. To begin with she was amazed I was intending to put myself through another leadership contest, but she was immediately supportive and said that she would back me.

Heather joined the Forward Look team, and she and Chris advised that other leadership contenders were approaching colleagues for support and that I should start doing the same. As a member of Theresa's Cabinet, I didn't feel comfortable professing loyalty to her while openly pursuing my own campaign.

At times this reticence became difficult, as some colleagues were pushing me to let them know my plans in the event of another leadership contest. With other candidates already courting potential supporters, I lost the chance to secure a number of votes. Other than the Forward Look group, there was actually only one other MP I told about my intentions: the Prime Minister. Shortly after she announced in March that she would not lead the country in the next stage of the Brexit negotiations, I told her that when she decided to stand down, I would enter the contest to replace her, but until then she would have my absolute loyalty.

At this stage, I didn't appreciate how advanced some colleagues' whipping operations were. Chris, on the other hand, was very networked into the parliamentary party and could tell which way the wind was blowing. *You need to get out there, start talking to people*, he would say.

So I started reaching out to colleagues only a few weeks before my resignation from the Leader's Office in May 2019 and Theresa's announcement two days later that she was standing down. By the time I officially announced my intention to stand, I was entering what was already a crowded race. It had been known for months that Boris would run, and he was joined by Rory Stewart, Esther McVey, Jeremy Hunt, Matt Hancock, Dominic Raab, Michael Gove, Sajid Javid and Mark Harper. Others talked of standing but in the end didn't have enough early support to get their names on the ballot. As a result of the large number of runners, the 1922 Committee changed the rules for the contest, requiring a minimum of eight nominations for a candidate to stand. In addition, to make it past the first ballot of MPs, candidates would have to obtain 5 per cent of the available votes plus one, their own: this meant securing a minimum of seventeen votes. The scramble for support was intense.

Now in my campaign HQ, Luke compiled a huge spreadsheet to share among the Forward Look team with the names, contact details and known views of each Conservative MP. Now the contest proper had begun, we were finally free to spring into action. Chris, Heather and I divided up the list and set out to talk to everyone. This was a big shock. Unlike in my first out of the blue leadership bid, when I was surprised and overwhelmed by how receptive colleagues were to my candidacy, this time I felt thoroughly ready for what was to come, yet my bid sank almost without trace. The worst of it was that people who for months had been urging me to stand again – *When the time comes, you really must put yourself forward again* and *If only you'd stuck with it last time* – including people I considered I had a good relationship with, were not interested. There was lots of *Sorry, I've already pledged to support Jeremy,* or *Saj is an old friend,* or *I've already committed to Michael Gove,* or, most often by a long way, *I've already committed to Boris; he's the only one who can deliver Brexit.*

Chris had the task of speaking to those who had backed me last time around and was reporting people saying: *She had my support then but never again, because she withdrew and look what's happened.* Frankly, a fair cop from their point of view.

I called a number of former supporters myself and heard first-hand that some were still angry with me for walking away in 2016. There were others who disagreed with me staying in Cabinet through the May years. I recall one bittersweet entry on the spreadsheet saying: 'I love Andrea, but she really blew it. What on earth was she thinking staying in Cabinet? I can't back her now.'

This was of course painful on a personal level. These were MPs I had worked closely with over the years and considered to be allies, friends even. While some heard me out politely, it was clear they would not be backing me this time. And there were quite a number who never returned my calls and texts, including several Cabinet colleagues with whom I thought I had a good relationship.

So my experience is a real lesson for the hardy few who want to go all the way to the top. You have to be totally single-minded about it – you can't let courtesy get in the way – and you have to have both a campaign plan *and* the support of at least twenty colleagues sorted well in advance, ideally under the radar of inquisitive whips. From a core of twenty, a campaign can build momentum. With fewer than that, and faced with new rules introduced with immediate effect by the 1922 Committee, it was impossible to get the campaign off the ground.

My own shortcomings were of course a part of it. Less ruthless than some, but also too reliant on previous allegiance. A good example was my failure to secure the support of Penny Mordaunt, who had sponsored me in 2016. She had since become a popular Defence Secretary and her backing could have proved a turning point in my campaign. I was really keen to get her on board; we had a longstanding agreement – only slightly tongue in cheek – from our days as backbenchers that we would have senior roles in each other's administrations should either of us ever become Prime Minister. On a crucial weekend when the team was making the approach to key potential supporters, my son Fred was running two marathons back-to-back in one day to raise money for a mental health charity. He needed a support team, and the family had agreed to help him. So on the weekend I should have been focused on doing everything I could to win Penny's support I was in the Cotswolds with patchy phone reception and my full attention well away from the drama of Westminster. Penny announced her backing for Jeremy Hunt – a huge blow to my campaign.

In the end, I concluded that the surprising success of the first, unexpected leadership bid caused the downfall of the second, planned attempt. Some MPs had not forgiven my withdrawal in 2016 and others my support for Theresa right to the end. Again, the lesson of politics at the highest level is that it overrides normal friendships and loyalties. Political allegiances count, and backing the winner is the most important currency. But I also learned that there are few second chances, particularly when it comes to a tilt at the top job. So all credit to Boris Johnson for the undoubtedly tough decision he took in 2016 not to stand after all. This time around, he was to be the standout most popular candidate.

And while my second leadership campaign did not exactly go to plan, it wasn't an altogether negative experience either. There was fantastic camaraderie in the Forward Look team, and a highlight was a team-building day where an external consultant analysed our strengths and weaknesses as the group I hoped would enter No. 10 together.

The standout high point of the campaign was the leadership launch, held in the splendid surroundings of the Institute of Mechanical Engineers. Lucia did a great job of getting journalists along, and my family turned out in full to support the team.

Afterwards, we left via the back door to avoid being deafened by Brexit Steve and his protester pals, and made our way back over to the House, where I had a longstanding commitment to speak at the Lobby lunch. This is a fairly formidable affair where politicians are invited to speak after lunch to the entire political Lobby, with the expectation that the speech will be funny. Lucia and my old team in the Leader's Office had put their heads together to come up with some great lines and stories from that extraordinary hung parliament, with great hilarity from the 'B******' to Bercow' prop I flashed at the end.

A drinks party for journalists in my London flat maintained what felt like positive momentum. A sea of faces I had come to know well during fraught Brexit conversations were there: Laura K and Nick Robinson from the BBC, ITV's Robert Peston, Steven Swinford from *The Times*, Gordon Rayner of the *Telegraph* and many others. It was a strong cast and we had a great evening – all off the record, and a real laugh. As the last guest rolled out close to midnight, I consoled myself with the thought that whatever happened next, at least we had enjoyed a cracking good party.

The closing stages of the campaign were a far more difficult experience, chasing votes that just weren't there. In the end, the eleven votes I secured were pretty much out of personal loyalty. It was frustrating that this time around our preparation had been so good – Luke's spreadsheet was so impressive that as we waited outside Committee Room 14 for the results of the first count, Grant Shapps, who was campaign manager for Boris, even asked if he could have a copy to use in the next round.

Of course I felt bad, not just for myself but for the team. Luke was a well-respected chief of staff in Parliament; Lucia and Marc were great spads. And Chris and Heather had effectively put their own credibility on the line for me. Peter Warner too had been working full-time on my behalf. It felt as if everything was in place – except the votes.

By contrast, it was clear Boris was on a different trajectory. It was clear to all that he had the belief to see Brexit through.

Since his departure from the Cabinet after Chequers, he had put in the legwork, making his case to colleagues that only a true Brexiteer could deliver Brexit. A few months before the start of the official campaign, his camp was boosted by the arrival of Gavin Williamson, who had been removed as Defence Secretary and now deployed his formidable skills as a former Chief Whip towards ensuring Boris's numbers were high. Very soon it began to feel as if his victory was inevitable.

We marked the end of my campaign with an excellent team dinner that I booked in the private room of Boulestin, a French restaurant in the West End, followed by Dukes bar, where we drank rather too many toasts to each other. I got home with Ben after midnight, and at around 1 a.m. my son Harry came out of his bedroom and found me sitting very still on the sofa, staring into space.

'Are you all right, Mum?'

'Yes…' I slurred. He found that very funny. It was a long night drinking water and trying to stop the world from spinning.

Once my own campaign was over, I immediately pledged my support for Boris. As far as I was concerned, if it wasn't going to be me delivering Brexit then by my reckoning it had to be Boris. I went to see him at the home of one of his supporters, Andrew Griffith (now himself an MP), just around the corner from Westminster.

Boris was very charming and welcomed me to the fold.

I told him: 'The one thing I would really just love to hear you say is that you'll continue to back my work on the early years inter-ministerial group.'

*Yes, absolutely.*

So with that, I was fully signed up to Team Boris and was soon despatched on his behalf around the country, persuading Conservative associations to back him and tweeting supportive messages when he was taking part in the debates against his final opponent, Jeremy Hunt. And Boris was as good as his word: when I left government the following year, he appointed me to lead the Early Years Healthy Development Review, perhaps the most important achievement of my time in politics.

On 23 July 2019, Boris Johnson was elected Leader of the Conservative Party and became Prime Minister the following day. I was as confident as I could be that he would both deliver Brexit and make a fine Prime Minister.

# CHAPTER FIFTEEN

# BEIS

The inevitable pang of *what might have been* aside, I was genuinely delighted at Boris's victory. I felt not only that he deserved it after everything that had gone before but also that, as a Brexiteer, he was very much the right man for what had become an extraordinarily difficult job. And so it was with a feeling of satisfaction that, on 24 July 2019, I watched on TV as Boris was driven to Buckingham Palace to kiss hands with the Queen and formally become Prime Minister. I wondered if he was still nervous about falling off the footstool.

Now my thoughts turned to what role I might play in the new regime. When I had resigned from Theresa May's government a couple of months earlier, my spads, Lucia and Marc, had automatically lost their jobs as well. This was a matter of huge regret, so I was delighted when Lucia, who had joined Team Boris for the remainder of the leadership contest, was taken with him into No. 10. As Boris began appointing his Cabinet, I got on the phone to Lucia, saying: 'Come on, you must have some intel…?'

Quite properly, she responded: *I can't tell you – but good luck!*
Which only added to the expectations I had of returning to
government.

By now I had been on the back benches for two months.
It had been a strange experience to settle into my old office
in Norman Shaw North, at the far end of the parliamentary
estate, with just Luke and Tommy for company rather than the
battalions of officials and advisers I had become accustomed
to. My Downing Street passes had been cancelled and it felt
rather quiet. Would Boris bring me back into the fold? Or did
I now have too much baggage, from both the 2016 leadership
contest and now having stood against him again in 2019? In
truth, after the rollercoaster nature of the preceding years, I
felt pretty relaxed about my prospects; almost zen. *What will
be will be*, I told myself.

Then the first appointments were announced: Sajid Javid
to the Treasury. Then the phone rang. It was Downing Street,
inviting me to a meeting with the new Prime Minister. I tried
to do the calculations in my head of where in the pecking order
Boris would have reached with his appointments. The other
great offices of state, the Home Office and the Foreign Office,
had both gone, but we were still relatively early in the process,
which implied one of the bigger portfolios. My money was
on either Business (the Department for Business, Energy and
Industrial Strategy, known as BEIS) or Local Government.

The hangover of the preceding two months fell away and
there was a spring in my step as I walked up Downing Street,
smiling in what I hoped was a friendly way at the waiting gaggle

of photographers, before entering No. 10. For the second time in three years, I stood in the waiting room marvelling at the twists and turns of fate.

Then the door opened and the new Prime Minister invited me in. Boris was his usual jolly self, but there was a different aura around him now he had the title of PM and the responsibility that came with it.

*Hello, Andrea, and, sincerely, thanks for all your help with the campaign. It's been great working with you over the years. And now I'd like you to be Business Secretary.*

He went on: *As you know, the Business Department has the Energy brief within it, and I know you've been Energy Minister before and it's something you're interested in. And it's good to have someone in BEIS who has a good financial background as you do.*

I was delighted. It felt like the first time since I had been in government that a Prime Minister had given some consideration to my previous experience and was thinking strategically about where to put me.

As we finished our conversation, there were two important instructions from him: *One: get Brexit done. And two: do not let British Steel go under.*

I agreed, of course, happy that here we had a Prime Minister who shared my total commitment to leaving the EU. As for British Steel, I told him: 'Mission accepted!'

As always after a new appointment, I went from Downing Street to see the Propriety and Ethics team in the Cabinet Office and spent an hour trying to remember every detail of each of my huge family's varied business interests, then it was on to the fun stuff, like mugshots for the department and receiving the passes for my new job.

Then I was introduced to my new government driver, Jason, who took me over to BEIS, a large airy building on Victoria Street. There I was given a warm welcome by my new private office team, led by Alex Chisholm, the Permanent Secretary, who has since become Perm Sec of the Cabinet Office. Always charming, he shook my hand with a beaming smile and said: 'It's a pleasure to welcome you to BEIS – we're delighted to have you.' Alex took me up to the top floor, where the ministerial offices are located. Mine had large windows with superb views of the London Eye and Westminster Abbey. And yet there was something wrong. My predecessor, Greg Clark, is a great colleague, but he clearly had no interest in décor! The room was dominated by a hideous sofa covered in what appeared to be brown plastic, while the big meeting table, a feature of every ministerial office, was shoved against a wall, so that no one seated at it could appreciate the spectacular views out of the window. So my first job as BEIS Secretary was furniture removals with my private office team to turn the room into a welcoming place to work and visit. Having ditched the sofa, we moved a patriotic blue and red one from one of our waiting rooms, which I decked out with Union Jack cushions. I put up photos and brought in some government art that I had taken with me first from Defra and then from the Cabinet Office. We stocked up on packets of biscuits, to make the place more welcoming. That office became very much a home away from home, with long hours and a steady stream of visitors, as I hosted business leaders and stakeholders to pitch our vision of the future for UK plc, as we finally got Brexit done.

The moving-in process gave me a chance to get to know the new private office team, who turned out to be an interesting and eclectic bunch. One played quidditch for England, and another was an expert gardener with loads of design ideas. I found many civil servants at BEIS to be deeply knowledgeable and helpful. I soon got to know the steel policy team, as we worked intensively together from the very beginning to save British Steel. Experience in government had brought home the importance of getting the officials working effectively for my priorities as quickly as possible. The same was true of the ministerial team – getting the team to work together, with shared priorities and common purpose, was vital. In that early period of the Johnson government, the BEIS team consisted of Kwasi Kwarteng, Nadhim Zahawi, Kelly Tolhurst, Chris Skidmore and (Lord) Ian Duncan, with strong PPSs in Craig Tracey and David Duguid.

With such a broad policy range in the department – from heavy industry to nuclear to cutting-edge science to small business, workers' rights and climate change – it was sometimes difficult for a team with such disparate portfolios to share common goals. To help the process, I set up a weekly meeting in my Commons office for the ministerial team and Alex Chisholm, which after a short while proved to be a friendly, energising time.

The first weekend in the job, I was going camping with my sister and our kids at an annual Christian event. She and I have done this every year since the children were tiny. This time I cut the visit short, arriving on the Friday and arranging for Jason to pick me up from the campsite in Peterborough on the Monday. After a scramble to find a shower and somewhere to plug my hairdryer in, I was ready to set off for our first big trip, to British Steel's base in Scunthorpe. This was a truly extraordinary place, with its vast heaps of waste and huge array of derelict buildings alongside its working sites. A good deal of security is needed to keep people away from the parts of the site that are out of use and now unsafe, with tumbled-down old furnaces here and there. I could not have been more impressed, on the other hand, by the highly motivated workforce and their trade union, whose staff proved genuinely constructive and a pleasure to work with. We developed a good relationship: the union leaders were willing to be flexible and negotiate on aspects of the workers' contracts, such as outdated pay and leave arrangements, in return for job security and a decent workplace. It was a privilege to meet all the different groups at Scunthorpe, and I felt a buzz as I left and prepared to get to grips with this crucial part of my new brief.

Two months before my arrival at BEIS, British Steel had gone into compulsory liquidation, putting 5,000 jobs at immediate risk along with an estimated 20,000 in the local supply chain. Theresa May and Greg Clark had agreed to keep the plant operating while a buyer was sought. It soon became apparent that the deal BEIS had been negotiating with Ataer Holding, a subsidiary of Oyak, the Turkish military pension fund, was not going to happen. So I spent much of those first months at

BEIS working flat-out but very much under the radar to secure another buyer. We made contact with the Jingye Group, a big family-owned steel company based in the Chinese province of Hebei. Alex Chisholm had been to see them shortly before my arrival and reported back good things about the firm's corporate and social responsibility and workplace conditions, with schools on-site, homes built for employees and good health facilities for the workforce. The chairman, Li Ganpo, was a real steel man, as was his son, Li Huiming, who was now running the company as chief executive. And they were seriously interested.

So the first four weeks of my time as BEIS Secretary were devoted to trying to make the deal. By now, it was mid-August, and I was in two minds over whether I should go ahead with a much-needed summer holiday. Following the events of the previous few years – Brexit, the leadership contest, the hectic pace of life as Leader of the Commons, my resignation and another tilt at the leadership – I was pretty tired and in need of some quality time with the family. On the other hand, as Business Secretary, saving British Steel was my top priority. A few months earlier, Ben had booked a villa on a Greek island, which was both remote and set up with an excellent WiFi connection, on the grounds that it would be the perfect hideaway, providing both privacy and connectivity.

With just days to go before the trip, still undecided about whether or not to go, we agreed in principle the sale of British Steel over dinner with the chairman, the CEO, Alex and Eddie Lister, Boris's highly regarded chief of staff, who had thrown his all into helping pin down the Jingye sale. Everyone was thrilled. It would take many months of effort to finally close the deal, but we all had a good feeling about this – British Steel would be saved.

And that holiday proved the perfect combination of work, rest and family time. We set up a daily three-hour call where I dialled into the teleconference room at BEIS for a series of thirty-minute meetings to make sure I stayed on top of the fast-moving preparations for Brexit. So some time before Covid-19 changed all our working habits, I had an early taste of home working.

In some ways, I was disappointed on returning to the Energy beat after four years away to discover how little had changed since I had moved on. There were some positives: the decision to take coal off the system by 2025 was happening much faster than envisaged and there had been a big reduction in the cost of offshore wind, while the solar industry was still growing. But there were clearly still big problems with the other two legs of the 'energy trilemma' – keeping the lights on and the cost of energy bills down. It was clear to me that we could be far more ambitious when it came to decarbonisation, including in building new nuclear capacity.

On the business side of the brief, British Steel aside, most of my time was devoted to preparing for Brexit. As Business Secretary, I attended the daily meeting of the XO Committee. Chaired by Michael Gove as Cabinet Office Minister, these meetings could last for several hours and were designed to interrogate every aspect of Brexit, from the Northern Ireland border to fishing, HGVs, passports, customs forms, the mail, pets travelling abroad and everything else in between. XO was held in the Cobra meeting room, where a giant interactive whiteboard allowed action points to be recorded and addressed in real time.

In many ways, Michael was the ideal person to take on the task of chairing the XO, given his strength as a detail person. He was good at cutting to the chase and arriving at clear, actionable points at each meeting. He definitely ran a tight ship. On some days, Boris's chief adviser Dominic Cummings would turn up to the XO, usually late and always scruffy, and would provide sometimes helpful, but often critical, comments to the assembled ministers. No filters, and no regard for the efforts of the assembled politicians. Dominic had previously worked as a spad to Michael, and they remained close – when they were together at XO, it often became the Michael and Dom show, with ministers struggling to get a word in edgeways as they bantered back and forth.

I did not take to Dominic Cummings. From his arrival in No. 10, rather than devoting himself to his powerful role in a methodical and collegiate way, he had particular whims, it seemed to me – specific policy issues on which he had strong views. A number of these issues fell under my remit: corporate governance, executive pay, science funding, space technology. And he would go directly to the responsible civil service teams, instructing them to do what he wanted.

His views on ministers and on the civil service are on the record – according to Dom, most are pretty useless. He could have led profoundly positive reform from his powerful position as the PM's chief adviser. But in my experience, his approach was to bully, not to lead. And I can't stand bullying. I would ask my officials not to respond to aggressive demands, assuring them: 'I'll speak to him.' And that set us up for a number of confrontations. In private, I thought of Dom as a bit like the Eye of Sauron from *Lord of the Rings*: if his gaze fell on your particular policy area, it was in trouble. The way to deal with it was to slip around the side when he wasn't looking...

The Eye fell on my BEIS portfolio several times, which inevitably led to clashes. The first conflict came over his longstanding and highly publicised desire to create a British version of ARPA, the US Advanced Research Projects Agency, which he intended would provide billions of pounds towards enabling scientific discovery, with no checks and balances at all. The UK already funded established research institutes to the tune of £9 billion of taxpayers' money each year at the time, with, admittedly, too many checks and balances in place. This nevertheless accounted for many brilliant UK success stories such as in life sciences (which later developed the coronavirus vaccine at miraculous speed) and some of the amazing cutting-edge technology for which Britain is known.

What Dom wanted was a new fund, completely separate, to facilitate new and brilliant thinking akin to the US putting a man on the moon. It was a great idea, and BEIS officials began work on it straight away. My successor but one, Kwasi Kwarteng, was able to launch ARIA, the Advanced Research and Invention Agency, to great excitement a year later. So far so good, but the problem was that Dom was intent on instructing officials to set this new fund up without any checks and balances – for remit, for value for money, even for timescales. So I was asked by officials to get involved.

The dilemma was that Dom's vision was admirable, and I could see that 'no strings' would be a superb way to free brilliant scientists and inventors to create new ideas the world has never even contemplated. But value for taxpayers' money is at the heart of all government expenditure; it would be naive to think that handing out billions with a minimal audit trail would be a reasonable thing to do. It became a sore point.

Another flashpoint was state aid. It was ironic, because Dominic and I were both passionate Brexiteers. On my arrival at BEIS, I inherited a plan which would have more or less replicated the EU's state aid scheme in the UK. My intention was to adopt a British version of state aid rules, which would combine maximum flexibility for ministers with protecting them from the demands of failing businesses. Dominic's view, however, was that we should not have any state aid rules: we had left the EU, and putting in place any rules at all would be to undermine our Brexit freedoms. It was a fundamental difference of opinion, and when decision day came around, Boris ultimately sided with me and Saj, his Chancellor, who also felt state aid rules were needed to protect taxpayers from unreasonable demands. Dominic was not at all pleased.

It was now that my former spad Lee Cain also came back into my life. Lee and Dominic had remained close since their Vote Leave days, and when Boris entered No. 10, he brought Lee with him. Initially, I was delighted for Lee, wishing him every success despite our difficult relationship at Defra and my reservations about Dom, who was clearly a close colleague. But it soon became apparent that being in No. 10, his dream job, gave Lee a powerful stick to wield, and he wasted no time in wielding it.

In September 2019, the board of the defence firm Cobham sought approval to be bought by a US private equity firm. There was significant public concern, given that as well as being a much-loved UK brand and a very successful business, Cobham dealt with some sensitive military provision. While both sides were keen to go ahead, I was concerned enough to refer the matter to the Competition and Markets Authority, now chaired by my old colleague from the Treasury Committee Andrew Tyrie.

By November, the inquiry was complete, and the authority informed us there was no reason not to allow the takeover. Likewise, advice had been sought and given by the Defence Department, and I had also set a number of tight conditions around the takeover. The formal announcement that the go-ahead had been given was highly market sensitive, and I planned to deliver it at 5 p.m. on a Friday after the markets had closed. We were now in purdah ahead of the general election, but the announcement still needed to be made. I had informed Downing Street of my plan earlier that week, and my team had been told to go ahead, but then, at ten minutes to five, my mobile buzzed – Lee Cain.

In no uncertain terms he told me: *You have to pull the announcement.*

I told him this was impossible: a couple of defence journalists had already been briefed to expect an announcement – it was standard practice to alert a small group of press just prior – and the risk was that in delaying the announcement it could have an impact on the share price.

Lee's response was furious – he ordered me to stop the announcement, and then hung up.

I was astonished – we managed to hold off the announcement until early Monday morning, to allow the No. 10 comms team to get their ducks in a row, while not breaching any market rules. Pretty much from then on, my relations with these two powerful advisers were poor. As someone in the know told me afterwards, Lee Cain and Dominic Cummings both told Boris: *You have to get rid of Leadsom.*

In politics, events, challenges and crises are a daily feature, and BEIS was often on the front line of the response. Shortly before the Cobham deal reared its head, the close-to 200-year-old travel firm Thomas Cook teetered on the edge of collapse. The weekend of 23 September 2019, I was called into an emergency meeting chaired by Transport Secretary Grant Shapps (whose department led on government relationships with travel firms), where it soon became apparent that Thomas Cook could not be saved. The bailout they were asking for came with a £200 million price tag, and it was clear from speaking to Rishi Sunak, then Chief Secretary to the Treasury, that this would be a drop in the ocean, keeping the firm solvent for only about four days, and that given how over-extended Thomas Cook had become, far more would be needed in the months and years ahead. There seemed little point throwing good money – taxpayers' money – after bad. But it was a devastating blow for both customers and staff. The immediate priority for Grant was getting holidaymakers home safely, and after that the hard work began to do what we could to save jobs. While we sought a buyer for some residual parts of the business, I worked with the Department for Work and Pensions on the jobs side, trying as far as we could to cushion what would be a very hard landing for thousands of Thomas Cook employees.

The pace of work continued through the autumn. In October there was a Queen's Speech, which provided BEIS with plenty to be getting on with, including driving the publication of the long-awaited Energy White Paper. And I finalised the changes I wanted in the department's own strategy and objectives: putting 'leading the world in tackling global climate change' at the heart of all we do; tackling our 'Grand Challenges', such as developing UK space technology; and making the UK the best place in the world to work and to grow a business.

While I was focused on my department, Parliament continued to be the locus of political drama, as the battle to secure Brexit reached its denouement. Cabinet was now an utterly different place under Boris's leadership compared to what it had been in Theresa's day. In appointing his Cabinet, Boris had jettisoned her approach of seeking a balance between Leavers and Remainers – we were all Brexiteers now (even those who had voted Remain back in the day) and fully behind him as he battled Parliament. Our meetings were also shorter, as Boris did not give everyone present an opportunity to present their case, as Theresa had done. Instead, he would set out his view and ask if anyone had any thoughts. One or two might comment and then the conversation moved on, so that the meetings were both much more brief and more constructive. We were at last all on the side of getting Brexit done.

I soon came to feel that Boris could prove to be a very good Prime Minister. He was accessible, helpful and happy to get involved, such as during the tricky, fast-paced negotiations over British Steel. With some exceptions, namely Dominic Cummings and Lee Cain, I was also more comfortable with this iteration of No. 10, finding Eddie Lister and Munira Mirza of the Policy Unit really constructive and helpful to work with.

But the problems of a hung parliament did not cease with the arrival of a new Prime Minister. As we moved into the autumn, Boris took the high-stakes gamble of proroguing Parliament. His move came as a surprise to many but was symptomatic of the frustration of trying to get Brexit done with such determined opposition. We on the side of Leave felt we clearly had the moral high ground as we were trying to deliver the will of the people. When Boris, in another bold move, decided to expel rebel Conservative MPs from the party whip, there was an outcry. While I had not been expecting such a punchy decision, I was supportive of a hard-line approach. It felt important to hammer home the clear message that our new PM would stop at nothing to deliver on the decision of the referendum. Yet despite all his manoeuvres, and particularly after the High Court ruled the prorogation illegal, it soon became apparent that a general election was the only way to resolve the impasse.

In November, Boris called an election for 12 December 2019, the first Christmas poll for nearly 100 years.

My final clash with Dominic Cummings came during the election campaign, as Chris Skidmore, Science Minister, prepared to attend a meeting of the European Space Agency. Despite its name, the ESA does not come under the purview of the EU and is, rather, an intergovernmental body, including such countries as Canada. The UK's longstanding involvement has always been a source of pride, allowing us to share in triumphs including the creation of the European Space Station and the Mars probe. The ESA commands investment from many countries around the world, and every few years a fresh funding round is held. In December 2019, the UK had just signed up to continue its funding provision. To my astonishment, a few days before his departure on paternity leave, Chris was phoned by No. 10 and told not only that he was to pull out of the meeting but that Britain would no longer be contributing to the ESA. Furthermore, he was asked to try to call off the meeting altogether until after our general election. Totally bizarre.

I got on to Eddie Lister and tried to explain: we committed to funding the ESA back in the summer; this is a multinational organisation and this meeting has been in the diary for a long time; asking for this multinational gathering to be cancelled is like saying: 'Cancel the G7.' It doesn't work like that. I never got to the bottom of what was going on, but looking back I wonder if Dominic had assumed the ESA was an EU body, putting it squarely on his list of meetings to eliminate.

Ultimately, I had to get on the phone to the PM himself and warn him that Chris had been told European leaders would begin calling Boris directly if he was determined to withdraw UK funding. Boris immediately understood the point and not only approved Chris to go to the meeting but demanded we make a big noise in the media about how successful our future involvement in the ESA was going to be. This we happily did. A strong piece of evidence that a Prime Minister can be let down by his inner circle of advisers when they haven't done their homework.

As we moved into election campaign mode, I was fully aware that I had upset the powerful duo of Dominic Cummings and Lee Cain and I probably should have realised that my days in government must now be numbered. But, blissfully unaware, I set off with great enthusiasm to campaign in an election I was sure would see us across the line to delivering Brexit. This meant, as usual, travelling around the country to support colleagues, which I love doing. It always involves a lot of eating of fish and chips in seaside towns, and jelly babies and singing on long road trips. Once again, my team and I did a tour of the south-west, getting down to St Ives to campaign with good friend Derek Thomas. Another trip took us northwards to the Red Wall seats and beyond – we campaigned with my long-time Bible study friend Martin Vickers in Cleethorpes (and had some fantastic Grimsby fish and chips), and I was the sole member of the Cabinet who got to Blyth Valley to support our great local candidate, Ian Levy. Ian's unexpected capture of Blyth Valley would be the standout moment of election night.

As Business Secretary, a lot of photo opportunities were taken at local businesses and I seemed to spend much of the campaign in a high-vis jacket; all good fun. This time around, I felt fully invested in the manifesto, having worked with whip-smart Munira Mirza, a key author, to include many of my departmental priorities on employment, decarbonisation and science, as well as a section committing the government to take forward the early years agenda with the inclusion of family hubs as a way to support new families.

When the results came in, in the early hours of election night, there was a strong showing for me in South Northants, with my majority increasing by 5,000 votes to 27,761, a 62 per cent share. By now, gloriously, it was clear the Red Wall had fallen, to be replaced by a new Blue Wall in the Midlands and the north, and Ian Levy was just one of 107 new Conservative colleagues. This was a huge night for those of us first elected nearly ten years earlier in 2010, who after a decade in Parliament had only experienced working in coalition, with a wafer-thin majority or in a hung parliament. Suddenly, we had what every MP dreams of: a good strong working majority of eighty.

Almost immediately the results were in, the press began to speculate that the victory would mean Boris would have a reset of his Cabinet. And, annoyingly, my name was one of those in the frame for being moved on. This speculation at every reshuffle always got me down, and I'm sure there were other colleagues feeling the same frustration. This time around, I also knew there were at least two men in No. 10 who were almost certainly against me. So when I was asked by Boris to stay on at BEIS after the election, it was a relief as well as what felt like a vote of confidence. Returning to the department, I was given a wonderful reception – it was great to be back with the certainty that we could now finalise our advice to businesses on Brexit, get on with long-awaited legislation and really lean into the net-zero transition.

Success on many fronts was in reach. But after just a few weeks, there were fresh reshuffle rumours and, yup, once again my name was in the headlines.

## CHAPTER SIXTEEN

# MARCHING ORDERS

F ive men were positioned around the room as I entered the Prime Minister's Commons office on 13 February 2020. Any illusion that this might be good news had been dispelled by the appointment in the Commons – the traditional forum for sackings. Walking up Downing Street is reserved for the lucky ones destined for survival or promotion.

Fresh from his election victory of two months earlier, the Prime Minister should have been in an ebullient mood; instead, he looked almost sheepish, his well-known aversion to confrontation written all over him. Beside Boris sat Mark Spencer, the Chief Whip, a lovely bloke and someone I considered a friend. We had recently co-hosted a drinks party, and he seemed understandably uncomfortable to be greeting me in these circumstances. Across the room sat Eddie Lister, the Downing Street chief of staff I had come to respect so well. His face too told a story; his neutral expression somehow highlighted the inevitability of what was to come. Gentleman number four was a stranger to me, presumably a No. 10 official whom no one thought to introduce. And then there was

Lee Cain, sitting behind me, out of my line of sight, staring straight ahead. I got the desperate urge to laugh; I resisted. No Dominic Cummings, I noticed.

The whole set-up felt staged. We all knew why we were there: I was being sacked from my job and there was no choice, as for so many others in this situation before me, but to take this crushing blow on the chin.

It still feels extraordinary to this day to have been sent to the back benches at what I would describe as a time of fast and positive progress in so many areas. In fact, until a few days before the reshuffle, I was determined to ignore what I thought was yet again just 'media fluff' about my impending doom. Just two months earlier, following the general election, I had been asked by the Prime Minister to remain in post. Having survived yet another round of premature reports of my political demise in December, I felt comfortable in my position in Cabinet. The conversation in which Boris had invited me to stay on had given me fresh impetus and empowerment to crack on with the job. I had secured stronger commitments in the BEIS arena in what was Boris's second Queen's Speech in three months, when, a few days after the election, we set out our agenda for what would now be a majority government.

Over Christmas, I wrote a pitch to No. 10 setting out how the UK could lead the world on tackling global climate change, by making the forthcoming COP26 – the UN Climate Change Conference, which was due to be held in Glasgow later in the year – a resounding success. This led to a meeting with Eddie Lister in which we had a constructive conversation on how we could turn the drive to tackle global climate change into part of the levelling-up agenda by building our green economy. This would generate thousands of jobs and create growth right across the UK, maximising the interest held by so many young people in jobs in green sectors. My focus was to shift the narrative from climate change to green growth, green jobs and the green economy. It was my strong belief that in the post-Brexit world, the UK's green economy could be bigger than financial services, traditionally the jewel in our crown. Eddie seemed to listen with enthusiasm, and I left our meeting with the firm impression that No. 10 would support the vision.

Just after the New Year, proposals for the green economy were discussed in Cabinet. Boris seemed on board with the plan – there were already as many as 350,000 green-collar jobs, and in my view that could reach 2 million by 2030. I thought we should begin right away, with a programme of decarbonisation in the north of England, revitalising the oil and gas basin in Scotland and building more offshore wind farms. I came away from the meeting confident that the Prime Minister and Cabinet would back what was an exciting programme of work.

At the same time, the 'events, dear boy' did not stop. In January 2020, I received a call from the Department for Transport to say the airline Flybe was in danger of going bust. My immediate view was: *We are not going to let this one go*. Having seen the fallout from Thomas Cook, when we were invited to step in only after it was too late to save it, I was determined to prevent another collapse. Over the weekend – crises always do seem to break at the weekend – I managed to persuade the airline's owners, the US private equity firm Cyrus Capital, the Stobart Group and Virgin Atlantic, not to put the firm into administration but to keep it alive while we looked into ways we could help. With the assistance of Sarah Munby, who is now Permanent Secretary of BEIS, we explored all our options and I felt we did have a route to save the airline, if we could persuade the owners to keep funding it.

Right up to the day I left BEIS, Flybe was hanging on in there; leaving when I did was definitely unfinished business. Back in January, however, I had no sense that I would not see through the Flybe crisis, or any of the many other projects underway. I was optimistic about the future and, as I went off to the Downing Street party to celebrate Brexit on 31 January 2020, I felt only relief that the destructive emotions that had followed the referendum seemed to be behind us, and we could now get on with the task of governing, not as Remain and Leave, but as a unified government with a shared endeavour going forward.

The Brexit drinks at No. 10 were preceded by a regional Cabinet in Newcastle, where I was delighted to meet John and Irene Hays, the couple whose Sunderland-based family business, Hays Travel, had taken over many of Thomas Cook's retail outlets, saving thousands of jobs. I also had an interesting conversation during the north-east trip with a local contract manufacturer whose company made all sorts of things, from toothpicks to iPhone cases to hairdryers. He told me how, when he first heard Leave had won the referendum, he was greatly concerned, a fear which seemed confirmed when his order book from customers on the Continent fell sharply as we approached the day of Britain's departure. Then, he told me, he had 'picked up the Yellow Pages and started ringing UK companies to drum up orders'. And his order book for the first quarter was twice what it had been the previous year. It was a lovely encounter, and confirmation that Brexit would be a success for those with the aptitude and attitude to make it so.

When we got back off the train from Newcastle, I met Ben for a quick supper before the two of us headed over to No. 10 for the party. As we walked up Whitehall, there were people everywhere with flags and whistles, screaming with delight and generally turning Brexit Day into a great big party. We could hear the roars in Trafalgar Square, where leading Brexiteers were giving speeches. Someone spotted me and shouted out: 'There's Andrea Leadsom!' And soon I was surrounded by a happy crowd wanting to pat me on the back and shake my hand.

The walk along Whitehall and the joy of so many who were marking the moment of Britain's departure from the EU will go down as a real highlight. That night was a hugely optimistic and joyous occasion for many, and I hoped that now the country could come back together and enjoy the Brexit dividend I was confident would be achieved.

There was a festive air in No. 10 as Ben and I walked into the party. The famous old building was lit up with red and blue lights, while in the grand rooms upstairs waiters circulated holding trays of Kent sparkling wine and canapés with traditional English fare: mini Yorkshire puddings with beef; Welsh lamb on skewers; tiny ploughman's bites of cheddar and pickle. For me, the gathering was much more than an office party: this was the actual moment of Brexit, the culmination of a grand project. Outside, a clock illuminated on the front of No. 10 counted down the minutes to the actual moment of departure at 11 p.m. (midnight Brussels time), while inside Cabinet ministers mingled with friends and colleagues from Vote Leave. I chatted to former Labour MP Gisela Stuart, with whom I had become close during the debates ahead of the 2016 EU referendum, and got a photo with Boris, Gisela and a new blue British passport. Looking around me, I was surprised to see so many young officials and Downing Street staff – and relatively few politicians by comparison. Most of the Cabinet were there, but I was conscious that the 'big celebration' was actually up the road in Parliament Square, where thousands were gathered to show their delight at Brexit finally being delivered, and to celebrate the occasion with singing and fireworks.

I walked across the expanse of the Pillared Room to chat to Lee Cain, and as I approached he returned my smile and greeting, but it didn't reach his eyes and he seemed aloof. *What's up with him?* I wondered. A tiny bit of 'after all we've been through…' went through my mind, but hey-ho, he had moved onwards and upwards. We did an obligatory 'got Brexit done' selfie and I moved on to speak to someone else.

Two weeks later, Lee was a silent figure sitting stony-faced behind me as I was sacked. And just nine months after that, it was Lee's turn to walk the plank, after a particularly nasty round of briefings within No. 10.

The little vignette with Lee at the Downing Street party was in many ways trivial, but his attitude led me to reflect on the role of special advisers and our political system more broadly. When I first met him, Lee's claim to fame was dressing in a chicken suit to taunt David Cameron while working at the *Daily Mirror*; he had come across to me as a charming, twinkly-eyed, fun-loving professional. But the years he spent as a spad and in No. 10 had changed him – the power and responsibility he now had meant he certainly didn't need to pass the time of day with an old colleague.

Dominic Cummings also gave me cause for reflection that evening. In recent months he had demonstrated his ruthless focus on those policy areas that he wanted to personally drive forward. He had become a feared figure in Whitehall, open in his apparent contempt for elected Members of Parliament as well as for many in the civil service.

As the countdown to 11 p.m. began, Boris jumped onto a box and banged a small drum, then said a few cheerful, grateful words to all the staff, MPs, peers and Brexit supporters in the room. Nicely done. Then he handed the microphone to Dom, inviting him as the *real Brexit hero* to take the stage. The room waited to hear Dom's response. Total silence for what felt like a whole minute. Then Dom muttered a few inaudible words, handed back the microphone, jumped off the box and buried his head in his hands. Overwhelmed with happiness? Stage fright? Who knows. There was an awkward silence then nervous applause and a few cheers. The contrast with Boris – who was cheerful, witty and charming – could not have been greater.

That evening left me with the sense that elections, brutal as they are, do give MPs and even the Prime Minister a profound sense of duty and the need to look out for the greater good, as well as a voice to articulate that imperative. Not necessarily so with spads.

Depressingly for me, within days of the party the whispers began again: there was going to be another reshuffle and my name was one for the chop. The week before the reshuffle, I did an interview, in conjunction with Denise Wilson, head of the Hampton-Alexander Review, on the subject of a government-backed audit of the FTSE 100, assessing levels of female directors on company boards. This involved Denise producing a report and then publicising it in the mainstream and social media.

That weekend, I was enjoying a rare lie-in when Ben came in with coffee and the papers and said: 'You're not going to like this…'

The front page of the *Telegraph* carried a bizarre story characterising my promotion of the Hampton-Alexander Review as some kind of warning to Boris not to carry out a rumoured 'cull' of female Cabinet ministers. This was so far from the reality of what had been produced as to be absurd. It was hard not to suspect the fingerprints of No. 10 staff on this surreal spin to the report.

'That's ridiculous,' I said to Ben. 'I honestly don't think Boris will sack me. It's just the media creating a story out of nothing.'

Looking back, I can view what happened next with a degree of equanimity. Politics is the giant game of snakes and ladders, and it was my turn to tumble back down to the bottom of the board. Fairly or unfairly, I had been judged and found wanting.

I was later told by someone close to No. 10 that I was the number one target of Lee and Dominic, who were determined that I must go. Ironically, only a few months after my departure, it was Dom's and then Lee's turn to slide down that snake, and both left No. 10 under something of a cloud. This turn of events somehow did not surprise me, since in the public eye they had become by now the political equivalent of Darth Vader and his stormtrooper.

On the night before the reshuffle, I wasn't so nervous as to pack up my BEIS office, but I did say an extra heartfelt goodbye to the team as I departed for the day. It was awkward for all of us. The officials wished me good luck, but they had obviously read the press too and were aware they might not be seeing me in the role of BEIS Secretary again. It was a humiliating experience.

Even after six years in government, and having been marked for sacking ahead of almost every reshuffle, I could never get used to the embarrassment of knowing that my family, friends and colleagues were reading this stuff in the press day after day. That evening, I went for a drink with my sisters, but lovely as it was to be with them, there wasn't much they could say.

The next day, Marc and Sam Magnus-Stoll, who had joined me at BEIS as my media spad following Lucia's departure, came over to my flat very early to await the news – good or bad. With Ben included, the four of us sat in the living room, chatting nervously and speculating about what fate had in store for us. Sam is great fun, chatty and extremely loyal, and she did her best to keep our spirits high.

'No way, you're not going to get sacked,' she was saying. 'Why would you? You're doing a great job; the civil servants love you. There's no reason why the Prime Minister would get rid of you.'

Marc, a very considered character, was less optimistic about my prospects. He had been the first person I recruited when I became an MP in 2010 and had been with me throughout, from my parliamentary office to becoming a civil servant at Energy, then on to Defra, the Leader's Office and finally to BEIS as my policy spad. I could tell from his demeanour that he was concerned; even more than Sam and I, he was tapped into No. 10 and had seen the brutality of the atmosphere there. Cummings had been unnecessarily abrupt with him at recent spad meetings, and it was clear the BEIS team was under some threat.

After about an hour, I received a call from No. 10 asking me to go to the Prime Minister's office in the House of Commons.

Was there any chance this was to confirm my current job? 'No,' said Marc. 'Keeping the job or being promoted is always at No. 10. If it's in Parliament, it means you're being sacked. Sorry.'

I knew Marc was right. Jason pulled up outside in the government car for what was a pretty sad final journey over to the House. As we drove, I fielded text messages from the BEIS team, who had by now heard I was being summoned to Parliament rather than Downing Street and knew exactly what that meant. Jason drove around to Speaker's Courtyard and we said our goodbyes. Jason too was under no illusions as to what was about to happen.

Marc and Sam had accompanied me over to the House and when we spotted a gaggle of journalists in the corridor, they told me to continue on without them while they intercepted the pack. As I looked back, I felt a pang of guilt, knowing that as I was about to lose my job, theirs would go too, through no fault of their own. I thought as well how tough it was that I would be unable to say goodbye to my team at BEIS and that my office would be packed up and sent round to me in cardboard boxes. The whole process is undeniably awful.

I made my way up the back stairs to the Speaker's corridor and along to the Prime Minister's office. As I ascended, I passed Julian Smith coming down the other way.

'How did it go?' I asked, already knowing what must have transpired.

*Well, I've been sacked. Good luck.*

I knew that same fate awaited me on the other side of the door, yet there was nothing I could do to avoid it. Shoulders back and in I went.

After being greeted by the welcome party of five men, I listened as Boris came straight to the point: *You've been in government for a long time, and you've had a really good innings, and now I would like you to take a step back for a while.*

'So you're sacking me?'

*Well, I just think, you know, I need to give other people the opportunity. And you've had a very good stint, six years in government.*

I said: 'Yes, but Boris, only seven months in your government.'

He assured me this was not the end of my ministerial career: *You'll be back. But I would just like you to take a step back for a while.*

It was clear that nothing I could say would save me. I wasn't going to have a tantrum or be anything other than calm about what was happening. It wasn't necessary to prolong Boris's own discomfort. In a flash of empathy, I could see the situation entirely from his perspective. Just as we never really know why we are given a job, sometimes there is no specific reason someone is deprived of a job either. Prime Ministers are in a difficult position: clearly, they can create enemies by sacking people, but they can also store up trouble for themselves by failing to bring colleagues forward. To fail to appreciate that would be to misunderstand the game.

So there it was: I was no longer a Cabinet minister and I was resolved to go quietly. But there was one thing I did want to secure as the price of my departing with good grace.

'What about my work with the early years? Can I take that forward from the back benches?'

As someone who had just lost her job, I was far from speaking from a position of strength. But since becoming Prime Minister, and even before that, when we were both in Theresa May's Cabinet, Boris had always been very supportive of my work on children and babies.

*Yes*, came the reply. *Yes, you can definitely do that.*

# CHAPTER SEVENTEEN

# PANDEMIC

So much would change so quickly after I walked out of Boris Johnson's Commons office that bleak day in February 2020 that at times it was hard to catch my breath. Even as I met up with Ben and my spads, Marc and Sam, for a fabulous lunch and several bottles of champagne at the Goring Hotel straight after to thank them for their amazing, loyal support, and to commiserate that they had also lost their jobs that day, we had no inkling that a deadly pandemic had already begun its inexorable progress around the world and was poised to breach the United Kingdom's shores – if it had not done so already.

As a Cabinet minister for four years prior to the advent of Covid-19, I can say with certainty that pandemic planning was never discussed at any Cabinet meeting I attended – not on Theresa May's watch nor following Boris's arrival. Yet now, to paraphrase Sir Edward Grey's famous words, the lamps were going out all over Europe – and the world. And as I write, in the spring of 2022, they are yet to fully come back on. Just over a month after my departure from government, the Prime

Minister issued a stay-at-home order and lockdown began. Since then, no one in this country or around the world has been untouched by coronavirus. For Members of Parliament like myself, the most basic requirement of our brief, to serve our constituents, became the most overwhelming and urgent issue. Within a few short weeks, my world as well as that of everyone around me was utterly transformed.

I was too busy to spend much time feeling sorry for myself about the loss of my BEIS job, and just as well. I've since spoken to other colleagues who have been sacked; it has been described as 'like a bereavement', 'a total humiliation', 'devastating'. For those who have been in high office for some years, leaving government does feel like being put out to grass without having completed the race. Try as you might to look at the big picture – the need to make way for the next generation of up-and-coming politicians – it is a horribly public and painful experience.

So when the pandemic hit, my world shrank completely. As a minister for six years, I had got used to the fact that long hours of each day were dominated by my departmental brief, with time on Fridays, weekends and recesses devoted to the constituency. Now, however, it was all hands on deck in South Northamptonshire, and my whole parliamentary team pivoted to focus on the constituency. Like millions of employees across the country, the team found ourselves in a virtual world of endless Zoom and Teams meetings and WhatsApp groups.

And as with millions of families across the country, when full lockdown was announced, my children all moved home. This was an unexpected development. Freddie had just turned twenty-four and was living and working in London, Harry was nearly twenty-two and at university, and Cookie was sixteen and at boarding school. I had not expected to have all three back at home for long periods again and it was great. The age gap between the two boys and their sister, which seemed huge as they were growing up, shrank now they were just about adults, and living together meant days of working in different spots around the house, meet-ups for tea breaks and 'egg walks' to buy local eggs with an honesty box, as well as loads of family banter. We took turns grocery shopping and cooking and had some excellent theme nights – from putting on ski jackets and drinking mulled wine under the stars on a cold winter's night to a great virtual beach party and quiz with neighbours. When restrictions allowed, my whole team did a socially distanced sponsored walk on behalf of the Dementia Society.

Having that strong team around me was vital during lock-down. Many of them have been with me for a long time – Luke, Sarah Jackson and Maggie Clubley. Just before lock-down, Tommy Gilchrist left for a promotion after five years on the team and was replaced by Laura Dunn, who took on the role of communications as well as managing my campaigns in South Northants – challenging HS2, delivering a relief road, a bypass and a community hospital to name but a few. During lockdown, Laura organised the filming of short videos with medical, food and financial advice for constituents during lockdown, and Luke put up a dedicated coronavirus section on my website to keep people informed as soon as any advice changed.

It is hard to convey the scale of the crisis at the community level. The local cries for help as well as offers of assistance began immediately. We were receiving at least 500 emails a day, many focusing on basic needs: older people unable to secure a shopping delivery and so left without food; people separated from loved ones in care homes and terrified for their safety; the vulnerable who could not access medication. These were issues replicated in every constituency in the land, and with responses to urgent questions asked of central and local government inevitably taking several hours if not days, MPs and their teams had to muddle through as best they could. Luke was asking fellow staffers and I was contacting other MPs. How could we assist an HGV driver who needed to extend his licence? Where could we get medication for a clinically vulnerable child? What about a second homeowner whose boiler had blown up? What support could we give to a constituent whose mother had died overseas? It had always been my practice until then to answer emails with paper letters which I signed myself, either for posting or for emailing as an attachment, but it was immediately apparent this would take too long.

My entire team was working flat-out every day trying to answer each email and resolve every problem as quickly as we possibly could. We held a daily team call to share information; it did feel in those early months that departments were too slow to respond to what were very pressing concerns. Easy to criticise, I know.

As weeks turned to months, it became obvious that the assumption that lockdown would be a brief but brutal experience was too rosy, and that in fact we were in it for the long haul. We kept replying to hundreds of emails and phone calls every day and kept up a stream of video and social media advice about the pandemic, while also highlighting local businesses that were offering home deliveries and community groups supporting those self-isolating. It felt relentless.

As the only officially designated key worker on the team, I was the one person allowed to help constituents out with deliveries of food or medicine; it made me smile to see people's surprise as they realised their MP was delivering their groceries. We were working non-stop, most days until ten or eleven at night, just to keep up with the deluge of requests for assistance.

Then, in the summer of 2020, as the virus abated somewhat and restrictions were slightly lifted accordingly, I finally began the project of my dreams.

# CHAPTER EIGHTEEN

# BACK TO BABIES

**B**oris Johnson is definitely keen on art. That was the thought that breezed through my mind as I watched the Prime Minister sitting at a tiny table with a group of three-year-olds in a nursery in west London while he enthusiastically set about drawing a banana. Beside him, a little boy was crayoning a slice of melon with about as much skill, but it was easy to see how much Boris was enjoying chatting to this little person with all the candour that very small children possess. It was March 2021, just over a year since my unceremonious sacking from the Cabinet, and I was back at the Prime Minister's side once again. Except this time, rather than being told I was surplus to requirements, I was launching, alongside the Prime Minister, 'The Best Start for Life – A Vision for the 1,001 Critical Days'.

This extraordinary turn of events stemmed from my appointment nine months earlier as the government's early years healthy development adviser, tasked with drawing up a review of government support for the first 1,001 days of life, from conception to the age of two. This work, which is still very much underway, has been the greatest privilege of my career.

And yet the appointment to what has been my dream job, one I feel my entire political life to date has prepared me for, began in the most unprepossessing of circumstances. In my final moments in Boris's office, as he delivered the *coup de grâce* to my Cabinet job, I had squeezed out of him a commitment that I could continue from the back benches the early years work I had begun in government. I had no way of knowing whether Boris would actually see this promise through, or whether he had clutched at the request as a way to get me out of the room as painlessly as possible. After a couple of weeks had passed, I decided that I was not going to leave anything to chance.

I went to the Chief Whip's office and challenged Mark Spencer: 'You were sitting next to the Prime Minister, you heard him promise I could do something on the early years. Did he actually mean it?'

*Yes – and he is determined to follow through on it.*

Another ten days or so passed and still I had heard nothing. By long-established custom, following my departure from Cabinet, I was permitted to give a personal statement to the Commons; this was due to take place one Wednesday after Prime Minister's Questions.

I approached the Chief Whip again: 'Look, just to warn you, I've written two versions of my personal statement. One is light-hearted. The other points out: "I was promised I could take forward my early years agenda. Several weeks on, why has nothing happened?"'

Mark – a friend and decent colleague – said he would do his best to help.

I later discovered from someone who was there that, while briefing Boris on the day's business at the 8 a.m. No. 10 meeting, Mark had informed him I was due to make my personal statement after PMQs that day. Boris said he was looking forward to it, only for the Chief Whip to say something to the tune of: *You may not like what she has to say. She's saying she isn't getting anywhere with the promise she could be your early years adviser.*

At which the Prime Minister apparently leapt to his feet, declaiming to those present that he had made me a promise and it must be made to happen.

Sure enough, later that morning I received a phone call from Matt Hancock, the Health Secretary, saying: 'It's fantastic you're going to be doing this early years development review. How can I help?'

With that sorted, I was delighted to give a light-hearted personal statement instead of the rebuke I had been fully prepared to give. Photos on the day show Boris grinning broadly as I pointed out that the Prime Minister had a very personal interest in the best start for life – his little boy Wilfred was born a few weeks later.

My appointment as the government's early years healthy development adviser was made official in July 2020, meaning I could be fully absorbed in a policy arena which has been my great passion in politics. For the next eight months, I led a review of early years policy, culminating in the publication at the end of March 2021 of a vision to give every baby the best start for life. To Boris's great credit, I was supported by a team of six full-time civil servants who proved brilliant at their jobs, coping magnificently with the limitations imposed by lockdown. Both Luke and Laura also joined the review team, contributing their own knowledge they had built up while working with me. When travel was impossible, the team organised virtual visits so we could find out what was going well and badly in children's centres and carry out deep dives into issues from health visiting to psychotherapy, and from couples counselling to breastfeeding support. Above all, we talked to parents – of all shapes and sizes and from every background. And after the review reported, we went on to put into place an implementation plan for transforming the support for babies and their parents and carers through those critical 1,001 days.

I came at the Early Years Review with the confidence born of years in government which meant I had well-established relationships with many Cabinet colleagues, understood how the civil service operates, knew my way around ministerial departments and also how to get the Prime Minister's ear.

My motivation for going into politics, like every MP, was always to make a positive difference in the world, coupled with my own determination to make life easier for other parents than I had found it. It almost felt as if everything I had done since becoming an MP had led me to this point, a place where I could really change things for the better in an area where I had some specific expertise.

The review was like a baby itself – a great joy, but very demanding! We worked flat-out during the research phase. Luke, Laura and I spent hours live-editing the final report, trying to keep the core of our proposals from being watered down by civil servants in other Whitehall departments. The most challenging aspect of our review was that its policies fell under the purview of so many different government departments. Family hubs and children's centres are led by the Department for Education; midwifery, health visiting and mental health support policies belong to the Department for Health and Social Care. The delivery of early years is determined by the Department for Levelling Up, but prevention policies like smoking cessation and domestic violence reduction fall under the remit of the Home Office and the Department for Work and Pensions, the latter also identifying the neediest families through their responsibility for child benefit and other welfare provision. And then you've got the Cabinet Office, which has responsibility for banging heads together across Whitehall. And at the end of all that, there's the Treasury, which has to approve anything that involves budgetary spending. Quite a challenge of coordination.

Key to the review's success was the decision by our civil service team leader that, unusually for an independent report, our review should be put to a full government write-round. The write-round process ensures that collective responsibility can be upheld. Every government minister receives a letter explaining every major new policy that is proposed. Each letter, written by the minister responsible, sets out the policy idea in some detail and invites comments. Ministers can submit a 'nil return', i.e. agree with no comment; they can write back enthusiastically in support; they can write back to try to block the policy; or they can write to agree it subject to certain conditions. Serious disagreements go to the Cabinet and Prime Minister to rule on.

In our case, I was delighted when, as lead Secretary of State, Matt Hancock agreed the write-round could go ahead, and I rang a number of ministerial colleagues to try to oil the wheels. The results were positive, with Dominic Raab as Foreign Secretary and Priti Patel as Home Secretary writing in support, and Kemi Badenoch and Steve Barclay, both at the Treasury, also helpful.

Of all the friends of the review in Cabinet, I was particularly grateful to Matt, who proved so supportive of the early years project. His well-known enthusiasm for technology proved an asset, as he pressed the NHS's digital arm to sign up to creating a digital version of the Red Book, to be rolled out for every new birth in England from April 2023. This would replace the paper Red Book containing the records of babies' birth and early development. Jo Churchill, then the Health Minister, was another real ally; she was determined to get the early years workforce into a place where they could deliver on our vision. Working with the two of them at the Department for Health was a pleasure. From the Prime Minister himself to Munira Mirza, director of the No. 10 Policy Unit, the ambition and determination to transform early years provision was clear. On several occasions I had to appeal to the PM on WhatsApp, or urgently meet with Munira, to unblock emerging problems. There's no doubt in my mind that the review would not have happened if I didn't have those close contacts from years work-ing with each of these colleagues.

On a broader point, I am hopeful that the Early Years Review, and in particular how it was embedded into govern-ment policy, will pave the way for other backbench colleagues to champion policy change going forward. My experience provides something of a road map – if you stick with some-thing you believe in, and create the necessary network, you can achieve a great deal, even from the back benches.

A few days before the report's publication, I met with the Prime Minister in Downing Street. I knew I wouldn't get this opportunity often, so I gave him a two-minute elevator pitch on early brain development and why this work could change our whole society for the better.

I put it to him that humans are unique in the animal king-dom in the extent of their underdevelopment at birth. What other animal can't fend for itself at all until it is at least a year old? Yet when humans are born the physical underdevelopment is just a part of it – the brain is also only partially formed, and it is our earliest experiences that shape our lifelong emotional and physical health.

I also mentioned to the Prime Minister that the peak period for language development is eight to fourteen months, so if you want your child to grow up trilingual, speak to them in three different languages during that time. They may not formally learn languages again until they're teenagers, but that early pro-gramming will enable them to have a leg up in language skills.

The Prime Minister's eyes lit up at that point and he told me that in the Downing Street flat with Wilf, then ten months old, he would ask him: 'Where's Dilyn?' and Wilf would look around for the dog, because he already knows exactly who Dilyn is.

In short, we had a great conversation and the Prime Minister agreed to launch the review with me at a nursery he had been wanting to visit for some time.

And that is how, a few days later, I found myself with Boris explaining to Beth Rigby of Sky News, in the presence of a room full of small children and their mums and dads, why the best start for life is the way to change our society for the better. Beth had always taken an interest in my early years work, so it was great that it was she who was the pool reporter that day. The report launch highlighted to me that there are those in the Lobby and broadcast media who really will get behind a policy. As well as Beth, Laura Kuenssberg of the BBC, Steve Swinford of *The Times*, the *Sunday Telegraph*'s Ed Malnick, Nick Watt of *Newsnight*, Macer Hall of the *Express* and Chris Hope of the *Telegraph* would all ask me from time to time: 'How are the babies going?' Allies among the men and women of the press were a big boost on the day and it is great to be able to recognise their contribution over a long period of time.

Many colleagues from across the House have championed early years reform with huge enthusiasm over the years, none more so than my colleagues Tim Loughton and Ed Timpson. Frank (now Lord) Field, retired Labour MP, has been a huge ally, as was Dame Tessa Jowell (sadly deceased), who kicked off the Sure Start programme for Labour almost twenty-five years ago. The few who still roll their eyes and mutter about 'Leadsom banging on about babies again' have pretty much been drowned out by the voices of colleagues from successive new intakes who are passionate about transforming services for the early years. Those who joined the Conservative ranks in 2019 have been particularly supportive, including Siobhan Baillie, Miriam Cates, David Simmonds, Nickie Aiken and Cherilyn Mackrory to name just a few.

So with the vision launched in March 2021, we dived into the implementation phase, beefing up the Start for Life Unit to 25-strong, and planning the roll-out of six key action areas across England. The one big fly in the ointment was that the vision, now agreed government policy, did not have any funding attached to it. Critical was to develop at great speed a submission for the next Spending Review, with the first draft due in July, for announcements to take place in October 2021.

From the cost of family hub transformation to the creation of a digital Red Book, and from the cost of establishing a parent–infant mental health support service to upgrading breastfeeding support across England, everything we had planned carried a price tag. And it wasn't just the new services themselves but also the costs of measuring improvement, reviewing the early years workforce and pulling together Start for Life offers that took our time and effort. And all of the detailed Treasury form-filling was taking place with a team which, at that stage, had still never met in person, with all our meetings conducted over Teams.

Finally, the day came in summer recess when the Spending Review draft submission was due. I was with my family in Crete in that same villa with the superfast broadband so that meetings could continue each day. I asked to review the final draft before it was submitted, but this was declined on the grounds that I wasn't a minister. This was a rare low point in the project for me – in fact the only time I considered resigning.

After much toing and froing, I was given twenty-four hours in which to come up with my own 'chairman's bids' that would be submitted alongside the formal proposal.

Staying with us in Crete were my parents-in-law, our three kids and several of their friends. 'Right,' I told them. 'By the end of today we've got to come up with a Spending Review submission of half a billion pounds that the Treasury can buy into. Can we divide up the different action areas and can you all work out what the reasonable cost is likely to be and then check each other's answers?' Not the traditional family pool-side activity!

I felt a credible spending allocation must be at least half a billion pounds, to demonstrate how serious our plans were – but we also needed to recognise the challenge the Treasury would have in considering any bid given the state of the economy after Covid.

The work in Crete was thorough and the calculation ultimately came in at £567 million. As good as their word, the Start for Life Unit officials carefully checked all the numbers and then submitted the chairman's bids alongside their own figures.

When Parliament came back in September, I was eventually allowed to have sight of the full submission. Working from the newly disclosed information, I compiled a one-page list of all the priority bids and sent it to Munira Mirza as well as to Claire Coutinho, MP for East Surrey and Rishi Sunak's PPS, asking to see the Chancellor.

Claire was a great help, and very soon I found myself in Rishi's office in the House of Commons, where I took him through the figures. At the end of our meeting, he told me it was a clear case for funding and although it was going to be a very tough settlement, he would do what he could. Having been the Local Government Minister at the time of the review into early years that I carried out for Theresa May, he also assured me he was personally totally behind the report.

As the days rolled on, with no news from the Treasury, I became increasingly gloomy about the chances of any of our bids succeeding, let alone getting close to the half a billion figure we had put in for. We even held discussions in the Start for Life Unit about what we could do if we got literally no new funding at all. The reality was beyond all hopes and expectations.

It was just a few days later, when I was on the way home from my old university, that Rishi called and I was back up that ladder to the top of the board – not as visible to the outside world as climbing the greasy pole of ministerial office, but to me this was the culmination of more than twenty years of campaigning, and a real chance to make the world a better place.

So on the day of the Autumn Budget and Spending Review, I took my seat in the Chamber with great expectations.

And with a smile, the Chancellor said:

> All governments should aspire to provide greater life chances for future generations, but few governments can match our ambition. So let me now turn to what this Budget does to support children. The evidence is compelling that the first 1,001 days of a child's life are the most important. My right hon. Friend the Member for South Northamptonshire has recognised this with her inspirational report. We are responding today with £300 million for a Start for Life offer for families; high-quality parenting programmes; tailored services to help with perinatal mental health; and, I am pleased to tell my hon. Friend the Member for Congleton [Fiona Bruce], funding to create a network of family hubs around the country too … We are confirming £150 million to support training and development for the entire early years workforce. To help up to 300,000 more families facing multiple needs, we are investing an extra £200 million in the Supporting Families programme…

Anyone who says you are too small and insignificant to make a difference has never lain awake in a dark room with a mosquito buzzing around. Persistence pays off, and I think this commitment to babies is just the beginning.

\*     \*     \*

For me personally, there was a wonderful postscript in the summer of 2021 when Luke came into my office and said: 'You might want to see this.' 'This' turned out to be an email from the Cabinet Office saying that I was being recommended for an honour for services to politics – Dame Commander of the Order of the British Empire.

That evening was the first since the ban on eating in restaurants under pandemic restrictions had been lifted, and several weeks earlier I had made a reservation at the Goring Hotel – the very place Ben and I took Sam and Marc to thank them for their hard work after I was sacked from the Cabinet. And, in a lovely twist of fate, the people Ben and I had invited to join us for dinner were Chris Heaton-Harris and Heather Wheeler, who had been such good friends through the years.

The honour was not yet official, but Chris and Heather and my family kept it to themselves for the next few weeks. I was particularly proud to see the citation reflecting the importance of the early years work.

As the title of this book reflects, political careers are tumultuous, with amazing highs and stomach-churning plunges. But, as with a real game of snakes and ladders, it seems that to appreciate the peaks it is necessary to experience the troughs, that only after tumbling down a snake do you find your way to the next ladder that could take you back up the board.

Thank you to all who have followed this story. If at times I have left the impression that being a politician is a terrible job, then I want to assure you that this is far from the case. To serve and represent others is the highest calling anyone can have, and I would not alter a day of my journey. The trials can be great, but so are the rewards. I have seen some incredible things and met some amazing people. And most of all I have had the opportunity to make a positive difference.

We all know a week is a long time in politics. Who knows where the next roll of the dice will lead?

# AFTERWORD

It was already sweltering hot at 5.30 a.m. when I awoke on what was supposed to be my big day – the *Snakes and Ladders* book launch in July 2022. After two years of planning and writing, it was finally here. My office was full of boxes of books, we had a fabulous party arranged in a stunning Westminster townhouse, and friends, family, parliamentary colleagues and journalists were travelling from near and far to celebrate with me. I only wish I'd had the chance to enjoy it...

Launch day excitement, however, was not the reason for my early rise. Following a tumultuous few months, I was running Penny Mordaunt's campaign to succeed Boris Johnson as Prime Minister. We were in the midst of an unbelievable summer heatwave, and Penny had moved into my flat so that we could keep on top of the contest but also so she could get a good night's sleep and avoid the constant media attention. Harry had given up his bedroom to go and stay with his girl-friend – he was OK with it so long as Penny became PM...

It is difficult to distil the series of events that led Boris from his landslide election victory in 2019 to his 'them's the breaks' speech on the steps of Downing Street, but I found myself, as ever, somewhere in the middle of the furore. Sue Gray – of Cabinet Office 'Propriety and Ethics' fame – had finished her report into No. 10 lockdown breaches and concluded there were numerous failings of leadership. In responding to constituent enquiries, I had agreed with Sue's findings and within minutes of my first email reply being sent, my response was passed to the *Daily Mirror*, resulting in a flurry of headlines saying I had called for Boris to resign.

I have to confess I had thought he might survive even then, and if anyone could it probably would have been him. Putin's invasion of Ukraine in February 2022 had caught the world unprepared, and it was Boris who took a leading role, providing immediate UK support to Ukraine and persuading our allies to do likewise. Volodymyr Zelensky even appeared by video link in the House of Commons Chamber to thank the UK, not just for the military effort but also for the Homes for Ukraine initiative that gave refuge to over 115,000 Ukrainians who moved into the homes of UK citizens. Many MPs hosted a family in their own homes, as did Ben and I, delighted to help Ukrainians in every way possible to defeat the Russian aggression.

The combination of Boris's leadership over the Russian invasion and the enthusiasm for his communication skills among parliamentarians, as well as an instinctive loyalty to the leader of the party, had kept most of us in check. Even so, media speculation about what was referred to as 'Partygate', and the number of letters of no confidence being sent to the 1922 Committee, increasingly drowned out all else.

Perhaps even then Boris might have managed to cling on, but the suspension of Conservative MP Chris Pincher following allegations of inappropriate behaviour prompted questions about whether the Prime Minister was aware of previous complaints before appointing Pincher as Deputy Chief Whip. When Downing Street's initial account of events was proved to be untrue, Rishi Sunak abruptly resigned as Chancellor just minutes after Sajid Javid resigned as Health Secretary. What followed was like a tumbling pack of cards as dozens of ministers resigned, and although Boris tried to appoint replacements – giving a first taste of ministerial office to many 2019 intake MPs – within days he had to conclude that 'the herd' had moved on and his position was untenable.

During those painful months, when Partygate was sucking all the energy out of the government, you can imagine some of the conversations going on around Westminster:

*We must keep Boris at all costs.*

*Why haven't you sent in your letter yet?*

And then the elephant in the room: *Who could replace him?*

It was one of those conversations that had led to Penny reaching out to me in late spring, first asking if I was considering a third tilt at the top job. To be honest, I had talked about it with Ben but concluded there was no way – I had my chance in 2016 and had learned the hard way in 2019 that second chances are unlikely. Third chances are essentially unimaginable.

So I told her no, and she then asked if I would back her. I had always thought Penny would be a superb candidate for Prime Minister – I believe she is still the one Labour fears most. As a naturally loyal person and a member of the government, however, Penny was in the unenviable position of juggling the conflict between 'business as usual' and planning a leadership campaign – a strain many politicians will be familiar with. While I was keen to run her campaign, and had some pretty relevant recent experience, we didn't really get into the swing of it until Boris's shock resignation on 7 July. However, Penny did have a strong early advantage in her fantastic team of whips, led by Craig Tracey.

The speed at which the leadership contest accelerated and took over our every waking moment was, as always, astonishing, with intense media scrutiny, demands for policy proposals, interviews and above all, calls and meetings with MPs who were considering backing Penny. Within three days we had created a policy team to write about Penny's priorities, a comms team to manage media requests coming in by the hundreds, an operations team to manage everything from Penny's diary to her transport to studios and then a groundwork team to manage the huge interest and support from party members across the country. So there we were in 30°+ heat, in the febrile atmosphere of an election campaign with an incredible number of candidates, and all the angst, plotting, black ops and backroom deals of a political bestseller.

In spite of one or two teething problems, a triumph of the campaign was the launch in the Cinnamon Club, where a lot of people really 'saw' Penny for the first time. She has a compelling backstory of hard work and loyalty and her candidacy was an easy sell to colleagues looking for someone who would demonstrate empathy and calm, with a real injection of humility and humour. In fact, if you've never heard Penny give the 'humble address' response to the Queen's Speech in June 2014, you should look it up. To this date it's one of the funniest speeches I've heard in Parliament.

The core campaign team – about twenty colleagues and a few volunteers and staffers – barely paused for breath in the two weeks that constituted the parliamentary phase of the contest. The key to victory was to keep momentum in each round of voting to get to the 120 votes that would ensure Penny's place on the final ballot of party members.

Each round of votes knocked out the candidate with the lowest number, and it was gruelling for all of them. No matter how many times you experience these campaigns, it's a brutal process, and those eliminated earlier included Kemi Badenoch, who had injected some much-needed energy into the hustings, and Suella Braverman, who was clearly a hit with the membership from lots of the feedback we had. Tom Tugendhat, meanwhile, seemed to share many of the same would-be supporters as Penny. It was certainly a wide field and it was difficult at the time to step back and appreciate how many excellent candidates we had.

By the final round – down to Liz Truss, Rishi Sunak and Penny – we had been in a strong second place all the way through each round, so we were understandably optimistic.

Who knows what happened in that final day or so? By the time we got to the final, there were a lot of proxy votes around, so it was increasingly unpredictable and as ever there were promises and cajolements behind the scenes that meant there was some switching going on. Even so, when we gathered with the now forty-strong core team of Penny supporters in a big meeting room in Portcullis House, there was real shock and dismay, and even tears, when the result came through and Penny was third. Who would do it, eh?

As disappointing as it was to have come within eight votes of second place, Penny took it on the chin and gave a rallying few words thanking and encouraging everyone to stick with our belief in teamworking and wished us all luck. And that was it once again. All that effort comes to nothing, all that momentum stopped in its tracks. Rolled the dice and lost.

\*　　\*　　\*

Conservative MPs gathered in the Queen Elizabeth II Conference Centre to welcome our fourth Prime Minister in twelve years as Liz Truss took to the stage, clearly delighted with her victory and raring to get on with tackling the issues that were piling up in her in-tray – not the least of which included Putin's invasion of Ukraine, the subsequent energy crisis and the cost-of-living crisis resulting from both that and the coronavirus pandemic.

For a few days there was the usual flurry of anticipation about who would get government jobs. Penny was appointed

Leader of the Commons – a role I had loved for two years under Theresa May's premiership – to much press speculation that this was beneath her as it wasn't one of the 'four great offices of state'. For Penny's campaign team there was nothing. Pretty much the same for Rishi's team. Normally an incoming PM will take a magnanimous view of those who came close to winning, appointing a team that reflects the level of support for other candidates, but that was not the case this time. I wonder if that played a part only two months later when Liz needed some friends and drew a blank.

Raring to go though the new Prime Minister was, fate had other plans. Just a couple of days later, sitting in my usual spot in the Chamber behind the PM, who had just unveiled plans to protect consumers from soaring energy bills, I noticed a sudden tension on both front benches. Sir Keir Starmer got up and left the Chamber and I could see a note being passed to the PM. My stomach lurched; for some time it had seemed that Queen Elizabeth was unwell, and I wondered if the news we'd all been dreading might be about to break.

The death of the Queen shook the whole world. As President Macron of France put it, 'To you, she was your Queen. To us, she was THE Queen.' People poured in from around the globe, making their own pilgrimages to Buckingham Palace, leaving flowers and gifts by the thousands, which eventually spread across Green Park – now home to a whole colony of Paddington Bears (and marmalade sandwiches) and a glorious floral tribute in gratitude for a lifetime of dedicated service.

There followed a number of unforgettable experiences, from

the Queen's lying in state in Westminster Hall to the extra-ordinary spectacle of the state funeral. It's one of those times when everyone will remember where they were and what they saw. For me, I had the privilege of being present at the arrival of Her Majesty's coffin at Westminster Hall. As a previous Lord President of the Privy Council, I also had the great honour of attending the Accession Council and saw Penny, as the new holder of that office, lead the proclamation of King Charles III. Penny had come over for a quick meal with Ben and me the evening before and it was clear how awed she was at the great responsibility ahead, but her flawless delivery was a source of pride for many who backed her for PM.

Only a month after the official mourning period, after a disastrous 'mini-Budget' and a miserable party conference, we were – unbelievably, surreally, ridiculously – plunged into yet another leadership campaign even shorter and more brutal than the last. Even more extraordinarily, Boris seemed deter-mined that this was his time to stage a comeback, and while Penny was an instant frontrunner, the resulting Boris and Rishi 'revenge' story sucked the energy and oxygen out of every other campaign.

Nevertheless, Craig and I were utterly determined to get there this time, and we were SO close. With 100 nominations required, a threshold designed to limit voting among MPs to a maximum of one round, we reached ninety-four committed supporters. When Boris pulled out at the eleventh hour, the whole mood of MPs changed for those final few hours of the campaign. It became clear that for many it was no longer about who got the job but rather a contest between those who wanted to give the membership their say by having two candidates and those who – for various reasons – just wanted it to be over immediately with an appointment, even if that meant getting someone who wasn't necessarily their first choice. We were in spitting distance of the 100 nominations needed, but a few of Penny's supporters started to waver, and with ten minutes to go until the deadline for nominations, Craig and I had to walk across to Graham Brady's office and once again concede defeat. Brutal.

Back in the summer, when joking with guests at my book launch about the *Snakes and Ladders* title and how a roll of the dice can see you surging all the way up to the top of the board or plummeting to the bottom, I could never have known just how far the analogy would be tested in the next few months.

This time, there was a bit of a happy ending to the chaotic series of events. Several of Penny's key supporters finally got the recognition they deserved, and Penny was reconfirmed in post as Leader of the House of Commons.

As for me, I was invited to keep my post as the government's early years adviser until the end of this parliament. I believe it's only Ben Wallace, Secretary of State for Defence, and Fiona Bruce, the PM's special envoy for freedom of religion or belief, who have held their roles, as I have, through three traumatic years and three Prime Ministers. Babies, peace and faith – I'll take that!

# BREXIT LEGISLATION TIMELINE

**7 DECEMBER 2016**

The House of Commons vote on respecting the outcome of the referendum is passed by a large majority.

**2 FEBRUARY 2017**

The government sets out its strategy for exiting the EU in the White Paper 'The United Kingdom's exit from, and new partnership with, the European Union'.

**16 MARCH 2017**

The European Union (Notification of Withdrawal) Bill receives royal assent after completing all its stages in Parliament, satisfying the Supreme Court ruling that ministers 'require the authority of primary legislation' and giving the government the legal power to notify the European Council of the UK's intention to leave the EU.

**29 MARCH 2017**

Theresa May writes to European Council President Donald Tusk to notify him of the UK's intention to leave the EU.

**30 MARCH 2017**

The government publishes the 'Great Repeal Bill' White Paper.

**18 APRIL 2017**

The Prime Minister calls a general election to be held on 8 June 2017.

**8 JUNE 2017**

The general election results in a hung parliament, with the Conservatives winning the most seats.

**13 JULY 2017**

The government introduces the European Union (Withdrawal) Bill.

**7, 11 SEPTEMBER 2017**

The European Union (Withdrawal) Bill has its second reading.

**22 SEPTEMBER 2017**

In a speech in Florence, the Prime Minister sets out the UK's position on how to move Brexit talks forward, offering a transition period after the UK formally leaves the EU in March 2019.

**9 OCTOBER 2017**

The government publishes two White Papers, 'Preparing for our future UK trade policy' and the 'Customs Bill: legislating for the UK's future customs, VAT and excise regimes'.

**1 NOVEMBER 2017**

Sir Michael Fallon resigns as Secretary of State for Defence following allegations of inappropriate behaviour.

**8 NOVEMBER 2017**

Priti Patel resigns as Secretary of State for International Development over a conflict of interest following meetings with the Israeli government.

**13 NOVEMBER 2017**

The government announces a Bill to enshrine the withdrawal agreement between the UK and the EU in domestic law, the Withdrawal Agreement and Implementation Bill.

**14 NOVEMBER 2017**

The European Union (Withdrawal) Bill begins its committee stage.

**20 DECEMBER 2017**

Damian Green resigns as First Secretary of State over an issue of honesty.

**8 JANUARY 2018**

James Brokenshire resigns as Secretary of State for Northern Ireland due to an upcoming operation to treat lung cancer.

Justine Greening resigns as Secretary of State for Education after refusing to accept a new position at the Department for Work and Pensions.

**16 JANUARY 2018**

The European Union (Withdrawal) Bill has its first day in report stage.

**17 JANUARY 2018**

The European Union (Withdrawal) Bill has its second day in report stage and also the third reading.

**18 JANUARY 2018**

The European Union (Withdrawal) Bill has its first reading in the House of Lords.

**30–31 JANUARY 2018**

The European Union (Withdrawal) Bill has its second reading in the House of Lords.

**21 FEBRUARY 2018**

The European Union (Withdrawal) Bill begins its committee stage sittings in the House of Lords.

**28 FEBRUARY 2018**

The European Commission publishes the draft withdrawal agreement between the European Union and the United Kingdom.

**19 MARCH 2018**

An amended draft withdrawal agreement is published to include agreed legal text for the implementation period, citizens' rights and a financial settlement.

**29 APRIL 2018**

Amber Rudd resigns as Home Secretary following a hearing by the Home Affairs Select Committee on the Windrush scandal.

**16 MAY 2018**

The European Union (Withdrawal) Bill completes its House of Lords stages.

**26 JUNE 2018**

The European Union (Withdrawal) Bill receives royal assent, becoming the European Union (Withdrawal) Act.

**6 JULY 2018**

The Cabinet meets at Chequers to agree a collective position for future Brexit negotiations with the EU, to be published as a White Paper the following week.

**8 JULY 2018**

David Davis resigns as Secretary of State for Exiting the European Union in opposition to the Chequers agreement.

**9 JULY 2018**

Boris Johnson resigns as Foreign Secretary in opposition to the Chequers agreement.

**15 NOVEMBER 2018**

Dominic Raab and Esther McVey resign as Secretary of State for Exiting the European Union and Secretary of State for Work and Pensions respectively in opposition to the draft withdrawal agreement.

**4 DECEMBER 2018**

MPs hold the first of a planned five days of debates on the withdrawal agreement and the UK–EU future relationship.

**12 DECEMBER 2018**

Conservative MPs trigger a vote of no confidence in Theresa May as Conservative leader, which she wins by 200 to 117.

**8 JANUARY 2019**

A successful amendment to the Finance (No. 3) Bill limits the government's financial powers in the event of a no-deal Brexit.

## 9 JANUARY 2019

Ahead of a planned five days of Brexit debates, the Speaker John Bercow allows an amendment to the business motion by Dominic Grieve, passed by 308 votes to 297. The amendment means that if the government loses the 'meaningful vote' on 15 January 2019 then the Prime Minister will have to present a new plan within three days.

## 15 JANUARY 2019

On the fifth day of Brexit debates, the meaningful vote takes place, resulting in a defeat for the government, losing by 432 votes to 202. Theresa May uses a point of order to set out how the government intends to proceed, and in his response the Leader of the Opposition tables a motion of no confidence in the government.

## 16 JANUARY 2019

MPs debate a motion of no confidence in the government, which the Prime Minister wins by 325 votes to 306.

## 29 JANUARY 2019

MPs debate the Prime Minister's 'Plan B' deal, with the Speaker John Bercow selecting seven amendments for debate, all of which are moved. Two amendments are approved, indicating that a majority of MPs are a) against exiting the EU without a deal, and b) against the Northern Ireland backstop in its current form.

Following the series of votes on the amendments, the amended motion is passed.

**14 FEBRUARY 2019**

Several amendments are made to a government motion seeking the continued support of the House in negotiating the UK's exit from the EU, in accordance with the approach that won a majority of MPs on 29 January 2019.

Three amendments are selected:

- The official opposition amendment – aiming to set a deadline for another meaningful vote – is defeated by 322 votes to 306.
- The SNP amendment – requiring that the government immediately begin negotiations for an extension to Article 50 – is defeated by 315 to 93.
- Anna Soubry's amendment – requiring that the government publish its most recent no-deal briefing documents – is withdrawn after the government offers to release no-deal information.

The unamended motion sees the government defeated by 303 votes to 258.

**26 FEBRUARY 2019**

In a statement to the House of Commons, Theresa May promises MPs a vote on delaying the UK's departure from the EU or ruling out a no-deal Brexit if she loses the second meaningful vote the following month.

**27 FEBRUARY 2019**

In a House of Commons debate on the UK's withdrawal from the EU, the Speaker John Bercow selects five amendments to the government's motion. MPs divide three times during the debate and a fourth amendment passes without a division:

- The opposition amendment – laying out support for Labour's alternative Brexit plan – is defeated by 323 votes to 240.
- The SNP amendment – stating that the UK should not leave the EU without a deal 'under any circumstances' – is defeated by 324 votes to 288.
- Alberto Costa's amendment – guaranteeing the citizens' rights part of the withdrawal agreement be implemented even if there is no deal – is approved without division.
- Yvette Cooper's amendment – noting the Prime Minister's statement that she will return to the House of Commons the following month for a series of votes on her deal, the prospect of leaving without a deal, and extending Article 50 – is passed by 502 votes to 20.

**6 MARCH 2019**

During a debate on the Trade Bill in the House of Lords, the government is defeated by 207 to 141 over an amendment that would oblige the UK to seek to remain in a customs union with the EU post-Brexit.

**12 MARCH 2019**

Following a debate on the European Union (Withdrawal) Act, the second meaningful vote takes place, which the government loses 391 to 242. Theresa May confirms she will open the debate the next day on whether to take no-deal off the negotiating table, with Andrea Leadsom making a short business statement to that effect.

**13 MARCH 2019**

In the second day of debate on the UK's withdrawal from the EU, the Speaker John Bercow selects two amendments to the government's motion, both of which go to a division:

- Dame Caroline Spelman's non-binding amendment (moved by Yvette Cooper) – ruling out a no-deal Brexit at any time – is passed by 312 votes to 308.
- Damian Green's amendment (known as the 'Malthouse Compromise') – setting out the process for a managed no-deal Brexit – is defeated by 374 votes to 164.

The day's final vote sees MPs voting on the government's amended no-deal Brexit motion: 'That this House rejects the United Kingdom leaving the European Union without a withdrawal agreement and a framework for the future relationship'. The motion is passed by 321 votes to 278. The Prime Minister confirms that the government will bring forward a motion the next day on whether the House supports seeking to agree an extension to Article 50 with the EU, confirmed by Andrea Leadsom in a short business statement.

**14 MARCH 2019**

In a further day of debate on the UK's withdrawal from the EU, the Speaker John Bercow selects five amendments to the government's motion, four of which go to a division:

- Dr Sarah Wollaston's amendment – requesting an extension of Article 50 in order for a second referendum to take place – is rejected by 334 votes to 85.
- Lucy Powell's amendment (itself an amendment to Hilary Benn's amendment) – specifying that any extension to the Brexit process should end by 30 June 2019 – is defeated by three votes: 314 to 311.
- Hilary Benn's amendment – allowing MPs to take control of the parliamentary business on 20 March, potentially to hold indicative (non-binding) votes – is narrowly rejected, by 314 votes to 312.
- Jeremy Corbyn's opposition amendment – rejecting both the Prime Minister's deal and a no-deal Brexit, while also seeking an extension of Article 50 to allow time to find a different approach – is defeated by 318 votes to 302.
- Chris Bryant's amendment – saying the government cannot bring the same deal to MPs for a third meaningful vote – is not moved.

The day ends with MPs voting on the government's amended motion, seeking permission from the EU to delay Brexit beyond 29 March 2019, which was passed by 413 votes to 202.

**18 MARCH 2019**

In a statement to the House of Commons, the Speaker John Bercow says that a further meaningful vote will be ruled out of order if the motion was 'the same or substantially the same' as that of 12 March 2019.

**21 MARCH 2019**

The European Council agrees to an extension of Article 50 to 22 May 2019 provided the withdrawal agreement is approved by the House of Commons the following week, and an extension until 12 April 2019 if the withdrawal agreement is not agreed.

**25 MARCH 2019**

In a debate on the UK's withdrawal from the EU, the Speaker John Bercow selects three amendments to the government's motion:

- The opposition amendment – calling on the government 'to provide sufficient parliamentary time this week for this House to find a majority for a different approach' – is not moved.
- Oliver Letwin's amendment – calling for Commons business on 27 March to be set aside for a series of indicative votes – is passed by 329 votes to 302.
- Margaret Beckett's amendment – saying that if a no-deal Brexit is ever a week away, MPs must either approve a no-deal Brexit or the Prime Minister be asked to seek another, longer extension – is narrowly defeated by 314 votes to 311.

The main motion, as amended, is passed by 327 votes to 300.

**27 MARCH 2019**

MPs debate a Business of the House motion – moved by back-bencher Oliver Letwin – providing for indicative votes to be held, which passes by 331 to 287. The Speaker John Bercow selects eight motions to be voted on:

- John Baron's 'no-deal' motion – proposing leaving the EU without a deal on 12 April – is defeated by 400 votes to 160.
- Nick Boles's 'Common Market 2.0' motion – allowing continued participation in the single market and a 'comprehensive customs arrangement' with the EU post-Brexit (until the agreement of a wider trade deal guaranteeing frictionless movement of goods and an open border in Ireland) – is defeated by 283 votes to 189.
- George Eustice's 'EFTA and EEA' motion – proposing remaining within the European Economic Area and re-joining the European Free Trade Association but remaining outside a customs union with the EU – is defeated by 377 votes to 64.
- Ken Clarke's 'customs union' motion – requiring a commitment to negotiate a 'permanent and comprehensive UK-wide customs union with the EU' in any Brexit deal – is defeated by 271 votes to 265.
- Jeremy Corbyn's 'Labour's alternative plan' motion – proposing a close economic relationship with the EU – is defeated by 307 votes to 237.

- Joanna Cherry's 'revocation to avoid no-deal' motion – requiring the government to stage a vote on a no-deal Brexit two sitting days before the scheduled date of departure should the government not have passed its withdrawal agreement; if MPs then refused to authorise no-deal, the Prime Minister would be required to halt Brexit by revoking Article 50 – is defeated by 293 votes to 184.
- Margaret Beckett's 'confirmatory public vote' motion – requiring a public vote to confirm any Brexit deal passed by Parliament before its ratification – is defeated by 295 votes to 268.
- Marcus Fysh's 'contingent preferential arrangements' motion – calling for the government to seek to agree preferential trade arrangements with the EU if the UK is unable to implement a withdrawal agreement – is defeated by 422 votes to 139.

**28 MARCH 2019**

Andrea Leadsom announces the House will sit on 29 March to debate the government's Brexit deal.

**29 MARCH 2019**

Following a day's debate, the government loses the third meaningful vote by 344 votes to 286.

**1 APRIL 2019**

A business motion by Oliver Letwin providing for further indicative votes passes by 322 votes to 277, with the Speaker John Bercow selecting four motions:

- Ken Clarke's 'customs union' motion – requiring any Brexit plan to include a commitment to negotiate a 'permanent and comprehensive UK-wide customs union with the EU' – is narrowly defeated by 276 votes to 273.
- Nick Boles's 'Common Market 2.0' motion – proposing UK membership of EFTA and the EEA and allowing continued participation in the single market and a 'comprehensive customs arrangement' with the EU post-Brexit, including a 'UK say' on future EU trade deals – is defeated by 282 votes to 261.
- Peter Kyle's 'confirmatory public vote' motion – requiring a public vote to confirm any Brexit deal passed by Parliament before its ratification – is defeated by 292 votes to 280.
- Joanna Cherry's 'parliamentary supremacy' motion – seeking an extension to the Brexit process or, should this not be possible, providing for Parliament to choose between either no-deal Brexit or revoking Article 50 – is defeated by 292 votes to 191.

**2 APRIL 2019**

Yvette Cooper's European Union (Withdrawal) (No. 5) Bill – seeking to further extend Article 50 – has its first reading in the House of Commons.

**3 APRIL 2019**

MPs debate a business motion by Oliver Letwin to allow MPs to pass the Commons stages of Yvette Cooper's Bill by 10 p.m. and provide time for further debate when it returns from the House of Lords. Hilary Benn's amendment to allow further indicative votes to take place results in a tie, with 310 on each side. The Speaker John Bercow casts his vote to side with the noes, resulting in 311 votes against and 310 in favour. The business motion – setting out the arrangements for the afternoon's debate on the Cooper Bill – is then passed by a majority of one: 312 votes to 311.

Yvette Cooper's European Union (Withdrawal) (No. 5) Bill passes its second reading debate by 315 votes to 310 and goes to committee of the whole House.

- George Eustice's amendment – preventing the government from being forced to hold a vote if the European Council proposes an extension date that is different from that requested by Parliament – is defeated by 313 votes to 304.
- The government's amendment – ensuring the Bill does not limit the power of the Brexit Secretary in seeking an Article 50 extension – suffers a heavy defeat, with 400 votes against the amendment and 220 in favour.
- Amendment 1 – limiting any extension to 22 May 2019 – is defeated by 488 votes to 123.

The Bill passes its third reading by just one vote: 313 to 312.

**4 APRIL 2019**

The European Union (Withdrawal) (No. 5) Bill passes its first and second readings in the House of Lords.

## 8 APRIL 2019

The European Union (Withdrawal) (No. 5) Bill passes its committee stage and third reading in the House of Lords and returns to the House of Commons, where it is passed by MPs and later receives royal assent.

## 9 APRIL 2019

As a consequence of Yvette Cooper's Bill, MPs debate the motion on the Prime Minister's plan to request an Article 50 extension until 30 June 2019, with the government winning the vote by 420 votes to 110.

## 10 APRIL 2019

An extension to 31 October 2019 is agreed by the UK and EU27, with the possibility of leaving earlier if the withdrawal agreement is ratified by both parties before this date.

## 1 MAY 2019

Gavin Williamson is dismissed as Secretary of State for Defence after an investigation into a breach of the Official Secrets Act.

## 22 MAY 2019

Theresa May gives a statement to the House of Commons on a new proposed Brexit deal.

Andrea Leadsom resigns as Leader of the House of Commons in opposition to a proposed Withdrawal Agreement Bill which would allow for a second referendum and which she would otherwise have to introduce in her Business Statement the following day.

**24 MAY 2019**

Theresa May announces that she will resign as Leader of the Conservative Party on 7 June 2019, triggering a leadership election in the party, and staying on as Prime Minister until a new leader is chosen.

**12 JUNE 2019**

In a cross-party attempt to pass legislation to block a no-deal Brexit, MPs debate a motion which is defeated by 309 to 298 votes.

**24 JULY 2019**

Having won the Conservative Party leadership race, Boris Johnson formally becomes Prime Minister.

Philip Hammond, David Gauke, Rory Stewart and David Lidington resign from their Cabinet roles in protest at Boris Johnson's willingness to leave the EU without a deal.

**25 JULY 2019**

Boris Johnson gives a statement to the House of Commons committing to the 31 October 2019 date for leaving the EU with or without a deal.

**3 SEPTEMBER 2019**

Oliver Letwin is granted an emergency debate which he uses to bring forward a motion to take control of Commons business. MPs later back a motion to allow a debate on Hilary Benn's European Union (Withdrawal) (No. 6) Bill. The legislation would set a deadline of 19 October 2019 for the Prime Minister to get MPs to pass a withdrawal agreement, pass a motion agreeing to a no-deal Brexit or write to the EU requesting an extension of Article 50 to 31 January 2020. The vote passes by 328 votes to 301 and results in twenty-one Conservative MPs losing the whip.

In response, Boris Johnson announces that the government will table a motion triggering a general election should the European Union (Withdrawal) (No. 6) Bill be passed by the Commons.

**4 SEPTEMBER 2019**

The European Union (Withdrawal) (No. 6) Bill passes its second reading and committee stages. Following this, a government motion to hold an early general election fails to pass the required 434 votes despite a majority voting in favour.

**5 SEPTEMBER 2019**

The European Union (Withdrawal) (No. 6) Bill passes its second reading in the House of Lords.

**6 SEPTEMBER 2019**

The European Union (Withdrawal) (No. 6) Bill returns to the Commons after passing all its Lords stages.

**7 SEPTEMBER 2019**

Amber Rudd resigns as Secretary of State for Work and Pensions due to disagreement with the government's approach to securing a deal.

**9 SEPTEMBER 2019**

Upon completing its parliamentary stages, the Bill becomes law: the European Union (Withdrawal) (No. 2) Act 2019. At the end of the day, Parliament is prorogued.

**11 SEPTEMBER 2019**

The Court of Session in Scotland rules that the prorogation of Parliament was unlawful.

**17 SEPTEMBER 2019**

The Supreme Court begins a three-day hearing into the prorogation of Parliament in a case brought by Gina Miller.

**24 SEPTEMBER 2019**

The Supreme Court rules that the prorogation of Parliament was unlawful.

**17 OCTOBER 2019**

MPs agree that Parliament should sit on Saturday 19 October to debate a proposed Brexit deal.

**19 OCTOBER 2019**

In a rare Saturday sitting, Parliament fails to agree a way forward, resulting in Boris Johnson writing to the EU to request an extension as set out in the European Union (Withdrawal) (No. 2) Act 2019.

**21 OCTOBER 2019**

The government attempts to table a motion to agree a way forward, but the Speaker John Bercow rules that it is the same in substance as the motion from 19 October 2019 and therefore can not be brought forward again in the same session. The government introduces the European Union (Withdrawal Agreement) Bill, setting out a three-day timetable for its passage.

**22 OCTOBER 2019**

The European Union (Withdrawal Agreement) Bill passes its second reading by 329 votes to 299. However, the programme motion to set out the timetable for the passage of the Bill is rejected by 322 votes to 308, effectively pausing the legislation.

**28 OCTOBER 2019**

The UK and the EU27 agree to an extension to 31 January 2020.

**30 OCTOBER 2019**

Ministers approve the European Union (Withdrawal) Act 2018 (Exit Day) (Amendment) (No. 3) Regulations 2019 to reflect the new 31 January 2020 exit date.

The government introduces the Early Parliamentary General Election Bill, setting a date of 12 December 2019 for an early general election, which completes its Commons stages.

**6 NOVEMBER 2019**

Alun Cairns resigns as Secretary of State for Wales following claims that he was aware his former aide had interfered with a criminal trial.

**12 DECEMBER 2019**

In the general election, the Conservative Party wins an overall majority with 365 seats to Labour's 202.

**20 DECEMBER 2019**

The European Union (Withdrawal Agreement) Bill passes its second reading in the Commons by 358 votes to 234.

**7 JANUARY 2020**

The European Union (Withdrawal Agreement) Bill has its first day in committee stage in the Commons.

**8 JANUARY 2020**

The European Union (Withdrawal Agreement) Bill has its second day in committee stage in the Commons.

**9 JANUARY 2020**

The European Union (Withdrawal Agreement) Bill passes its third reading in the Commons and moves to the House of Lords.

**13 JANUARY 2020**

The European Union (Withdrawal Agreement) Bill passes its second reading in the House of Lords.

**14 JANUARY 2020**

The European Union (Withdrawal Agreement) Bill has its first day in committee stage in the Lords.

**15 JANUARY 2020**

The European Union (Withdrawal Agreement) Bill has its second day in committee stage in the Lords.

**16 JANUARY 2020**

The European Union (Withdrawal Agreement) Bill has its third day in committee stage in the Lords.

**20 JANUARY 2020**

The European Union (Withdrawal Agreement) Bill has its first day in report stage in the Lords. In the Commons, a Lords amendment providing for EU nationals living in the UK to be given documentation confirming their right to be in the UK passes by 269 votes to 229.

**21 JANUARY 2020**

The European Union (Withdrawal Agreement) Bill has its second day in report stage in the Lords and passes its third reading before being returned to the Commons with amendments.

**22 JANUARY 2020**

Lords amendments to the European Union (Withdrawal Agreement) Bill are debated in the Commons, with MPs voting to remove each amendment. The Lords then debate and accept the changes proposed by the Commons.

**23 JANUARY 2020**

The European Union (Withdrawal Agreement) Bill receives royal assent and becomes the European Union (Withdrawal Agreement) Act 2020, meaning that legislation is now in place to implement the withdrawal agreement negotiated by the UK and the EU.

**31 JANUARY 2020**

With Boris Johnson's withdrawal agreement ratified by the EU, the UK leaves the European Union at 11 p.m., entering a transition period in place until 31 December 2020.

# ABOUT THE AUTHOR

Author photo © UK Parliament/Jessica Taylor

The Rt Hon. Dame Andrea Leadsom DBE has been the Conservative MP for South Northamptonshire since 2010, prior to which she worked in the banking and finance industry for twenty-five years. Alongside her business and political career, Andrea has been founder, chairman and trustee of a number of early years charities since 1998.

Between 2014 and 2020, Andrea served in government as Economic Secretary to the Treasury, Minister of State at the Department of Energy and Climate Change, Secretary of State for Environment, Food and Rural Affairs, Leader of the House of Commons and Secretary of State for Business, Energy and Industrial Strategy.

She is currently serving as the government's early years healthy development adviser, chairing the cross-Whitehall Start for Life Unit to implement policies around the 1,001 critical days.

# INDEX